EDUCATION AS A POLITICAL ISSUE

In memory of
Shona Alexis Macrae
1977 - 1991

Education as a Political Issue

JANET McKENZIE

Avebury

Aldershot · Brookfield USA · Hong Kong · Singapore · Sydney

Published by
Avebury
Ashgate Publishing Limited
Gower House
Croft Road
Aldershot
Hants GU11 3HR
England

Ashgate Publishing Company
Old Post Road
Brookfield
Vermont 05036
USA

A CIP catalogue record for this book is available from the British Library.

ISBN 1 85628 445 X

Printed and Bound in Great Britain by
Athenaeum Press Ltd, Newcastle upon Tyne.

Contents

Tables

ix

x

Foreword

Under the distinctive leadership of Margaret Thatcher, the 1980s in Britain was a period of considerable political, economic and social change. One key area of social expenditure that has been transformed by Thatcherism is education. Janet McKenzie's book provides an in depth quantitative and qualitative analysis of education as a political issue. On the basis of both national and local data sets, it systematically covers attitudes and political behaviour in relation to education. It is arguably one of the most detailed accounts of the politics of education during the Thatcher era.

On a personal level, I would like to take this opportunity to note that Janet McKenzie was a model ESRC funded doctoral student. This fine piece of sociological research was completed on time under difficult circumstances. Throughout her studies she demonstrated considerable ability, commitment and enthusiasm, all of which are in evidence in this splendid monograph. I wish her well in her future career as a researcher and teacher.

Stephen Edgell
Reader in Sociology
University of Salford

Acknowledgements

In completing this research, I received help from many individuals and institutions. I am indebted to the staff of Hatfield Polytechnic for accepting me on my first degree course without the usual qualifications. The research for this book was financed by the Economic and Social Research Council, Award No. A00428624318. I was particularly fortunate in having Stephen Edgell as supervisor for my Ph.D.. His guidance was invaluable. He was meticulous in his approach to my research and obviously devoted a great amount of time and energy to the many reports I submitted to him. Throughout this research I also benefitted from the help and advice provided by Vic Duke. He not only helped me to deal with many computing problems, but also read drafts of my work and provided valuable comments. Staff and students at Liverpool Institute of Higher Education and the Open University have also provided moral and practical support. I would particularly like to thank Graham White and the staff in the Sociology Department of Liverpool Institute of Higher Education for their understanding and support during the last few weeks of writing-up my thesis and the up-dating of my work to create this new version. Special thanks are due to John Davidson for his unique blend of computer expertise, wit and patience in helping me to prepare the final copy. On a personal level, and not least, I would like to thank my parents, Doris and Cliff Nicholls for their inspiration, Roddie for his invaluable good humour and my daughters Nicole and Marie Chambers for their constant support.

Thanks are also due to the following for permission to quote from their publications:

The British Educational Research Journal for P. Broadfoot (1988) reprinted from the BERJ, Vol. 14, No. 1, pages 4, 5, 7.

The British Sociological Association and the author for P. Saunders (1989) reprinted from Network, No. 44, page 3.

Cambridge University Press for G. Parry, G. Moyser and N. Day (1992) Political Participation and Democracy in Britain, pages 16, 138, 242, 250, 262, 432.

The Chartered Institute of Public Finance and Accountancy for CIPFA, Statistical Information Service (1985/6 Actuals) SIS Ref 52.87.

The Claridge Press for the Hillgate Group, (1986) Whose Schools? A Radical Manifesto, pages 4, 5 and 7.

Comparative Education for P. Broadfoot (1985) from Comparative Education, Vol 21, No 3, page 273.

The Conservative Political Centre for Conservative Research Department (1985), Education, Politics Today, No 14, pages 282 and 286, and the Conservative Party Manifesto (1987), page 18.

The Critical Quarterly for R. Lynn, reprinted from C.B. Cox and A.E. Dyson, (1970) Black Paper Two: The Crisis in Education, page 32.

Gower for numerous references to the British Social Attitudes surveys and reports.

Guardian News Service Ltd. for articles by I. Crewe, F.F. Riley, M. Walker, quotes from I. Macdonald, Manchester City Council, M. Thatcher, various dates.

Harper Collins Publications for S. Edgell and V. Duke (1991) A Measure of Thacherism.

International Thomson Publishing Services Ltd. for S. Ball (1990) Politics and Policy Making in Education, page 38; S. Bourque and J. Grossholtz, pages 107, 111, 118, 207, J. Siltanen and M. Stanworth, pages 195, 197, 199 reprinted from Siltanen and Stanworth (1984), Women and the Public Sphere (Hutchinson), D. Kavanagh, (1983) Political Science and Political Behaviour, pages 15, 60, 98, 107 (Allen and Unwin, Routledge)

The National Union of Teachers for (1985) Education: investment or impoverishment?, pages 4, 5, 21, 23.

Oxford University Press, New York, USA, for C.W. Mills (original 1970) The Sociological Imagination.

Pergamon Press Ltd. Headington Hill Hall, Oxford OX3 0BW, UK, for W.F. Dennison, pages 28 and 29, K. Jones, pages 241 and 242, reprinted from I. McNay and J. Ozga, (copyright 1985) Policy Making in Education.

Pluto Press, London, 1983, for S. Hall, pages 3, 9, R. Johnson, pages 18, 20, R. Dale, page 42 and C. Benn, pages 119, 121 reprinted from A.M. Wolpe and J. Donald (eds) (1983) Is there anyone here from education?

Stanley Thornes Ltd. for M. Kogan (1986) Education Accountability. An Analytical Overview, pages 18, 19, 22, 23

Times Newspapers Ltd., for material published in the Times Educational Supplement, table published on 29 May and quotations from M. Thatcher, published 16 October 1987.

© Times Newspapers Ltd. 1987

1 Introduction

1.1 Aims

This book takes an interdisciplinary approach to the study of educational debates during the 1980s. Not entirely concerned with the sociology of education, it nevertheless involves a consideration of cultural reproduction and equal educational opportunities. Not entirely related to politics, it nevertheless considers concepts such as partisanship and political participation. The focus is on the ideological framework of educational debate and, in particular, the relationship between voters' attitudes to education and the education policies pursued by British governments during the 1980s. The original aim of the research was to assess voters' attitudes to educational issues by exploring their educational experiences, interests, knowledge and opinions.

A gap in our existing knowledge about educational debates was identified when research themes and trends were considered. Educational research in the 1960s, for example, tended to concentrate on equal opportunities (e.g. Jackson and Marsden, 1963, the Plowden Report, 1967) and we had little information about public attitudes to educational policy until recently [1]. To what extent were the education policy-makers' definitions of reality shared by the public and vice versa? Twenty years on from then, our attempts at finding a satisfactory answer would involve historical research, based on a negligible amount of attitudinal data. It was partly with this in mind, and with a greater accumulation of contemporary survey data to hand, that I chose to study the attitudes and opinions of the voting public in the 1980s and their association with government education policies. This will provide a more substantial understanding of the framework of educational debate, and a more detailed basis for future comparisons as the framework changes over time.

Some pruning was, however, essential as the research had to be reduced to a size that could be managed by one person working to a limited time schedule. Decisions about which sub-issues (see 1.2) should be included and which excluded have mainly emerged from the framework of educational debate. Some sub-issues have been studied out of personal curiosity but have not been reported here in detail because of the pruning process. For example, my interest in and findings about attitudes to progressive education have been shelved in order to make way for such topical subjects as student loans and the national curriculum. This means that the political culture of the time has, to a certain extent, determined what aspects of the research area should be studied, but it does not mean that the current definitions of reality have been slavishly followed. (The framework of educational debate during the 1980s is described in greater detail in 1.3 and discussed more fully in Chapters 3 and 5.)

The Conservative governments of the 1980s also influenced the agenda of political debate and the resulting interest in public participation by promoting a populist image and emphasising the promotion of 'choice', 'accountability' and the 'active citizen'. An inquiry into the nature of the relationship between voters' attitudes and government education policies is therefore a logical response to the agenda set by governments themselves during the 1980s. This study has therefore been extended beyond the usual boundaries of attitudinal research in that it includes the consideration of action as well as consciousness. Social scientists have tended to concentrate on either the study of attitudes or the study of action/participation, but rarely both [2]. Yet it seems to be a short analytical step from one to the other. Questions about participation are frequently asked in attitude surveys (in both the British Social Attitudes Surveys, see 2.3, and the Greater Manchester Study, see 2.4) and questions about attitudes are asked in participation surveys (for example, the British Political Participation Surveys, Parry, Moyser and Day, 1984-9) but the breadth of the individual researcher's subject area often means that only one aspect can be selected for analysis. It was decided to include action/participation in this project because, firstly, only one political issue was being studied, secondly, attitudes and activity were found to be associated in many ways, and finally, the influence of attitudes and action on the process of education policy-making was considered to be an important theme emerging from current political debates.

1.2 The language of educational debate

Definitions are obviously important. The ideological framework, within which debates have taken place during the 1980s and early 1990s, tends to include certain definitions of reality and exclude others that may have previously been perceived as equally 'real'. In Britain, we can see this in the rhetoric of the time. For example, the emphasis on 'equal opportunities', 'child-centred learning' and 'progressive' teaching methods in the 1960s and on the 'consumer', 'choice', 'relevance' and 'accountability' in the 1980s. Such words help to define the framework of educational debate in that the language of one period may be considered odd when moved out of its original context. The language of educational debate can therefore follow certain trends associated with the whole political-cultural context of the moment.

Even the word 'education' can be defined differently according to cultural context and political perceptions. The liberal-humanist interpretation of education (as general self development) that is commonly associated with the 1960s, was replaced in the more utilitarian 1980s by a greater emphasis on vocational skills. Yet this is not to say that the context of educational debate in the 1960s can be identified clearly and unequivocally.

The original aim of the research was to assess voters' attitudes to educational issues by exploring their educational experiences, interests, knowledge and opinions. Theories about common definitions of reality gradually emerged from the data as problems concerning the definition of terms were encountered. Some of the problems involved in defining 'education' have already been mentioned but the difficulties cannot be over-emphasised. In addition to competing functional definitions there are other problems of scope. Does 'education' include all forms of learning or only that learning which takes place within specialized institutions (for example, schools, colleges and universities)? If it is the latter, it is possible to differentiate further by distinguishing between the formal curriculum and the hidden curriculum, formal teaching and individual study? It simply was not possible to find a working definition of 'education' that could be used without severely restricting the exploration of voters attitudes. In practice, as the research progressed, it was found that definitions of the word had political connotations (Chapter 5), as is suggested in the following claim by the Centre for Contemporary Cultural Studies:

> The identification of schooling and education is very conservative in its effects. It tends to present schools as natural rather than historical products. It tends to devalue and marginalize the more spontaneous and more diffused ways of learning. (CCCS, 1981, pp.14-15)

Thus, instead of the definition of education being a problem that had to be resolved at the start of the research, it became an item of interest and a feature of the whole project.

Similarly, a working definition of 'political issue' could not be found and the problems involved in trying to find one also became a feature of the research. This was complicated by the common use of the term 'public issue' to express the same (or similar) meaning. The two expressions emphasise the

3

collective rather than the individual and share the assumption of a common awareness of shared problems. This implied distinction between the private and the public is discussed in greater detail in Chapter 3 (especially in the sections about instrumental interest, and in feminist arguments about the artificiality of such distinctions). However, the preferred use of 'political issue' is intended to highlight a wider debate about educational debates; that is, concerning the extent to which education is or is not part of the political domain. Conservative governments in the 1980s tended to define changes in the education system as technical, rational and non-political. Broadfoot (and others) saw the rhetoric used and its emphasis on administration and efficiency as a means of legitimating Conservative ideology.

> So powerful is the appeal of scientism at the present time that in curriculum, management and finance there is a growing tendency for issues to be defined as simply technical problems, to which an optimum solution exists. The effect of this trend is not only to preclude explicit discussion of the different educational values that might be involved in any particular issue, but also to conceal a growing lack of consensus over educational priorities in general by defining them off the agenda of debate. Arguments couched in terms of efficiency and rationality thus provide a spurious but extremely effective legitimation for the pursuit of particular educational priorities. (Broadfoot, 1985, p.273)

Such definitions of educational issues as political or non-political feature prominently in this research and I will argue throughout that education is part of the political domain, that education certainly is a political issue.

Throughout the research, terms and concepts were therefore used fairly loosely and the formulation of more precise operational definitions were a necessary part of the process. Nevertheless, one working definition was made early in the research process and has been retained throughout. This was the distinction between the singular, education as a political 'issue' and the plurality of 'sub-issues' within the sphere of education. Thus, in speaking of 'education' as a political issue, I am referring to it as a large issue within the public policy domain; to be compared with, for example, 'health', 'unemployment', 'public spending' or 'defence'. The word 'sub-issue' is used to refer to the many issues debated within education as a singular issue. Sub-issues discussed in this book include, for example, educational standards, the curriculum, comprehensive schools, further and higher education. It is immediately obvious that, within each of the sub-issues mentioned, there will be sub-sub-issues (for example within further and higher education there is the question of student loans) but such an expression was regarded as unnecessarily cumbersome and the term sub-issue has been used to refer to any

4

issue within the educational sphere.

1.3 The changing framework of educational debate

Any history of changes in the politics of education is inevitably selective, and runs the risk of being excessively biased and reductionist, but this research needs to be put within some sort of context. In order to do this, and because the topic is mainly about attitudes, the context will be presented as a history of ideas rather than a list of events. It will also be limited to changing ideas during the lifetimes of the people studied here, although it must be acknowledged that the changes are not necessarily peculiar to this country or to this historical moment. Broadfoot emphasised this in her comparison between education in England and France:

> The change in England from the Plowden era (c.1967) to the prevailing climate of utilitarianism and overt accountability may be seen [...] as equivalent to the shift of emphasis from expressive to instrumental goals, from an egalitarian, integrative ideology to an elitist competitive ideology which took place in French education between the French revolution and Napoleon's advent. (Broadfoot, 1985, p.273)

What Broadfoot called the dominant climate, and I have so far described as the ideological framework of educational debate, can be more easily encapsulated in the perception of a normative paradigm. The paradigm is political in that it emerges from an ideological climate and definitions of reality that are nurtured by the political system and the government of the day. Thus, the wide cultural boundaries of the political system limit the range of possible paradigms from which the normative paradigm can emerge. The boundaries of acceptable knowledge provide a normative device by which the prevailing political system can be legitimized: the curriculum can be structured to exclude knowledge that is outside the normative framework and the media can be 'manipulated' or influenced to exclude information that conflicts with the status quo.

Within the cultural boundaries of the political system as a whole, the government of the day adds its own ideals and definitions of reality to formulate a new educational paradigm or to make major or minor changes to an existing one. Where the normative boundaries are currently being radically changed in Eastern Europe, the new and developing ideological framework is reflected in the sales of previously banned books. Thus, knowledge systems, the communication of information, the nature of the political system and its institutions provide an, albeit limited, picture of the ideological framework of debate within a state.

In Britain, the Conservative educational paradigm of the 1980s emphasised market forces and the end of egalitarian ideals. Hall argued that, 'Inequality in education has become once again, a positive social programme.' (Hall, 1983, p.3). Yet he was not suggesting that there ever was a positive social programme of equality in education. From a marxist perspective 'real' equality of educational opportunity is seen as incompatible with a capitalist state and its associated class system. The gradual erosion of egalitarian ideals means, within the context of the capitalist state, a withdrawal of attempts to compensate pupils and students for their socio-economic disadvantages. Instead, the paradigm defines equality as the equal right to compete in a market system, in which poverty is regarded as a spur to greater effort. The main function of education is defined as economic and the rhetoric used ('relevance', 'vocationalism', 'enterprise', 'consumer' etc.) emphasises the training of an efficient workforce, rather than the humanist interpretation of education as the development of the 'whole person'.

It is therefore possible to see a movement away from the more egalitarian paradigm of the 1960s, with its emphasis on the humanist perspective and on equal opportunities, to a vocational paradigm which perceives education as satisfying the needs of the market place. However, as we have very little empirical data about public attitudes to education in the 1960s, theories about the movement from one paradigm to another are rather loosely based. It is possible to describe political changes and other events relating to education but we do not know to what extent the voting public shared government definitions of reality. Thus, any history of the changing educational climate is largely based on events and trends that have been reported by social scientists and/or by the media.

The changing educational climate in Britain since the 1960s clearly had its origins in the 1960s; in the challenges to the dominant paradigm. One challenge was human capital theory (Schultz, 1963). According to this theory the productive superiority of the most technically advanced countries was a result of the superior human capital of knowledge and skills within those countries. From this perspective the main function of education is seen as its economic value as the process by which an efficient workforce is produced. Another challenge came from the writers of the Black Papers (Cox et al., 1969-75) who vehemently opposed the establishment of comprehensive schools and the use of 'progressive' teaching methods. Such ideas would, they claimed, lead to an inevitable reduction in educational standards. Although some of the writers of the Black Papers were 'traditionalists' in that they favoured the continued teaching of Classics and Latin, they joined with utilitarians in their rejection of those subjects that fostered a critical attitude to society (especially Sociology and Peace Studies), dismissing them as irrelevant

6

'non-subjects' (Conquest, 1969, p.13). Such attacks could still be defined as outside the dominant framework of educational debate in the 1960s, the Black Paper writers being regarded as 'cranks' by those who accepted the liberal-humanist/equal opportunities definitions promoted by the then Labour government. During the 1980s, Conservative governments presented many of the arguments promoted by the Black Paper writers as part of a new normative paradigm.

> Ten years ago those Conservatives and other deeply concerned groups who wished to reverse the Socialist tide in education found it difficult to gain a hearing: their campaign for proper standards, high quality teaching and clear tests of ability was frequently derided as a grossly unfair attempt to undermine a broadly successful system. Today the case for fundamental reform is widely accepted. (Conservative Research Department, 1985, p.286)

Even so, it would be wrong to simply associate one paradigm with one political party. Many Labour supporters were also traditionalists or utilitarians and many remain so. Within the Labour party of the 1960s there were still some who supported the idea of maintaining the grammar schools and selection at eleven. (This will be discussed elsewhere, but particularly in Chapters 7 and 8).

During the 1970s, a powerful political reaction began to break down the dominant paradigm and new definitions of reality emerged that were more compatible with both human capital theory and the Black Paper critiques. The economic crisis of the 1970s (and, in particular, the oil crisis of 1973) helped to increase the emphasis on the economic utility of education. Some analysts (e.g. Fowler, 1979) claimed that this was the main reason for the onset of the 'Great Debate' about education in the mid-1970s. At about the same time there was a political reaction to the 'libertarian' elements of the progressive philosophy of the 1960s. Teachers were criticized for promoting an unduly theoretical and academic approach to knowledge and fostering a negative view of industry and wealth creation. The inquiry into standards of education at the William Tyndale School in 1976 also increased public criticism of progressive educational methods and added weight to the arguments in the Black Papers.

The new climate of educational debate was recognized and promoted in the heavily publicized speech given by the Labour Prime Minister James Callaghan at Ruskin College, Oxford, in October 1976. In his speech, Callaghan accorded a higher priority to vocational education and called for an increased state involvement in the education system. This speech is often cited as inaugurating the so-called Great Debate, a succession of speeches and policy documents, leading to a period of structural change in education that continued throughout the 1980s. According to Fowler, the negative view of education in the mid-1970s gave rise to a suggestion that education was failing the nation.

> The emphasis upon the wealth-creating role of manufacturing industry also carried an implied threat to education: that it was clearly a wealth-consuming industry. It must justify itself by the service it provided to wealth creation, through the supply of qualified manpower. (Fowler, 1979, p.78)

Although liberal-humanist arguments were still favoured by many educationalists (some teachers, lecturers, local authority administrators and journalists) those who held such values during the 1980s were increasingly forced on the defensive by the government's promotion of a normative paradigm based on market values. The tone of the paradigm has been represented as 'discourses of derision' (Ball, 1990).

> ...the role of the New Right, as well as its direct impact on policy in some areas, has been discursive, that is it has facilitated a discursive reworking of the parameters of political possibility and acceptability. Some aspects of the once unproblematic consensus are now beyond the pale, and policies which might have seemed like economic barbarism twenty years ago now seem right and proper. (Ball, 1990, p.38)

Theories about a 'British disease', of defects in the 'national character' as the cause of Britain's inadequate industrial performance, were further propounded in Weiner's variation of human capital theory (Weiner, 1981). His thesis was that, owing to the perpetuation of the aristocracy and its associated institutions and values there had been a persistent anti-industrial culture, undermining 'enterprise' and the pursuit of efficiency, and leading industrialists to aspire to the sort of gentrified lifestyles and values associated with a higher status. Public schools with their emphasis on classical liberal education were seen as particularly important for the reproduction of these values. Further reinforcement was secured by privileged access to Oxford and Cambridge and by occupational destinies to high status professions. It is a short step from this identification of an anti-industry culture to blaming education for the 'cultural malaise'.

Once the diagnosis of a 'British disease' (in its various guises) gained acceptance and explanations were established in terms of supposed defects in the education system, the paradigm could be presented as a 'common sense' normative perspective. Its basis has changed very little over time, although the 'solutions' offered by Labour and Conservative governments have varied.

Thus, the assumptions on which many education policies are based are presented by governments as non-controversial, technical and non-political. TVEI, YTS, the Employment Training scheme and various other vocational schemes were built on the assumption that unemployment and other industrial problems were mainly caused by attitudinal and educational defects. Although the problems of unequal access and disadvantage in education are well documented, governments have tended to neglect findings about social inequality and emphasise recommendations that correspond with human capital theory (both types of findings and recommendations being in the Robbins Report, 1963/4). By emphasising the role of education in the production of human capital, the paradigm has neglected its political and social context and excluded those arguments that enable us to see educational issues as both controversial and political.

From an alternative, political perspective it is possible to see that, whilst the importance of the education system as a means of producing an efficient workforce must be acknowledged, the importance of political and economic circumstances and decisions at an international as well as a national level should not be underestimated. At least five arguments support this political perspective.

First, international forces may conflict with the economic interests of individual states. British companies may find that their activities are circumscribed by such transnational forces and that national priorities may have to be regarded as of secondary importance. Managers of multinational corporations will make decisions that transcend national boundaries. The long-term effects of the 1973 oil crisis and of world-wide recession illustrate the critical role of natural resources and political/economic decisions taken at a multinational level. By comparison, the role of the British education system in combatting economic decline has been relatively minor.

Second, British industry is heterogeneous and it is wrong to assume that it has declined in general. Some sectors of industry have declined and some have expanded. It could be argued that it was the decline of some industries (with the resulting need to retrain employees) that caused a perceived lack of skill rather than vice versa.

Third, by focusing on public attitudes, it is possible to obscure the effects of government policies. As both Eatwell (1982) and Leys (1985) pointed out, successive governments have attached great importance to a policy of free trade whilst many of Britain's competitors have favoured protectionism in order to stimulate domestic markets for manufactured goods. Lack of demand for many British goods has naturally affected supply, increased unemployment and generated a problem of credential inflation.

Fourth, the process of credential inflation should not be ignored. In the same way that a currency loses its value when the supply of money exceeds demand, so qualifications are devalued when a glut of highly qualified applicants seek employment in a shrinking employment market. Yet the devaluation of qualifications is not evenly spread. The value of particular qualifications will rise and fall according to the changing character of the labour market. We can, for example, see that students who took degrees in woven textiles during the 1970s found that, during the course of their studies, the opportunities for employment in that field declined dramatically.

Finally, the relationship between education and human capital is also disturbed by the social inequalities in British society. Whilst many unqualified job-seekers are regarded as ignorant and undeserving, others can use social status, family connections or the good name of a school to compensate for lack of paper qualifications. Thus, although there are still severe shortages of skills in some areas, it is wrong to assume that education alone can compensate for national and international, social, political and economic problems.

If events during the 1970s are viewed from beyond the confines of the normative paradigm it is possible to see that political tactics played an important part in the change of direction. Beck (1983) provided an alternative analysis in which the emphasis was on the weak position of the last Labour government (1974-9), the hostile reactions to its industrial strategy and its replacement by a strategy based on closer links between education and industrial policy. Amongst other things, the Labour government's new critique of education dealt with mounting criticism of the education system (from Labour as well as Conservative voters) in a way that did not seem to be an obvious capitulation, it helped to retain some credibility for the industrial strategy and it provided a sphere for cooperation between the government, industry and education. Furthermore, Beck suggested that the educational costs of this policy may have been considerable as it,

> ...had the effect of conferring an unprecedented degree of legitimacy on industrialists - as those best qualified to determine the educational changes needed to reverse the country's economic decline. (Beck, 1983, p.225)

Critics within the Labour government, such as Roy Hattersley and Shirley Williams, apparently feared that the government would be presenting educational reactionaries 'with a whole new arsenal of anti-comprehensive weapons' (Times Educational Supplement, 24 June 1977). Certainly, despite the many changes in education and the economy since 1976, political criticisms of the educational service have continued unabated. During that period there has been a substantial reduction in manufacturing industry and a dramatic increase in youth unemployment. New vocationally orientated

10

schemes such as YOPs, YTS, Employment Training, TVEI and CPVE have been introduced in order to deal with the diagnosis of unconstructive attitudes and lack of skills. Yet, if the paradigm is valid and non-controversial and both the diagnosis and treatment are adequate, why has there not been a substantial reduction in unemployment since Callaghan's Ruskin speech? Any answer will depend less upon 'facts' than upon political perspective.

Reality can be defined by the political system and the government of the day and 'facts' can be presented according to the knowledge and prejudices of the discussant. The intention here is not to reject the idea of a 'British disease' or the important role of the education system within the economy, but to suggest that other explanations need to be considered if we are to avoid misunderstandings and oversimplifications. It can be, and often is assumed that controversial issues are not controversial and one perspective can be legitimized as 'common sense' reality. Whilst certain educational sub-issues (for example, student loans and provisions for schools to opt out of local authority control) may attract public attention, their deeper ideological foundations and assumptions about the function and scope of education, may be taken for granted. It can even be claimed that politics should be taken out of education, as though education were purely a technical problem and solutions could be arrived at objectively (see 5.4).

The argument that education is a controversial political issue is a central theme running throughout this book. It will, moreover, be argued that, whilst the economy has long been emphasised (by politicians, social scientists and the general public) as the most important area of political debate, the importance of education (defined broadly) within the political arena has been underestimated. Operating within a wider political culture, a government will seek to legitimize its authority by restricting debate to a supportive ideological framework. That aspect of education which is concerned with the development of critical awareness is confined within the socially constructed boundaries of a normative paradigm. The boundaries may be very wide or very narrow and the sanctions used by the government (of any state) against illegitimate critiques may vary from disregard or ridicule, to actual physical punishment. In any case, the education system will be used as an agency of social control to reinforce a particular ideological framework (for example, economic, religious, racial or military) and to legitimize the existing political culture.

1.4 The organisation of chapters

An understanding of the context of educational debate therefore helps to elaborate the description, analysis and explanation of attitudes to education during the 1980s. Opinion polls and attitude surveys already provide basic

11

quantitative data about attitudes to sub-issues but statistics are virtually meaningless when taken out of context.

In Chapter 2 it will be shown that reports on quantitative research often include some sort of context-setting and that when several reports of this type are studied they can be seen as reinforcing or challenging each other's findings. This chapter will also describe case studies carried out in the two local authority areas used in the Greater Manchester Study (Edgell and Duke, 1992).

Chapter 3 will describe the different education systems in the two areas studied in both the GMS and the case studies. The local and national context of debate will also be considered.

From Chapter 4 onwards analysis of attitudes follows a rough sequence from interest in educational issues (in general, as well as in particular sub-issues) through to the ability to influence education policy-making; the sequence being, interest, knowledge, attitudes, vote, activity and influence.

Interest. In Chapters 4 and 8 it will be shown that only a small section of the voting public were sufficiently interested in education as a political issue to consider it when they voted. Findings from the literature search, exploratory work and some analysis of survey data, about the independent variables affecting level of interest in education, will be considered in detail in Chapter 4.

Knowledge. Theories about the framework of educational debate and its constraints on public knowledge will be described and applied to case study findings in Chapter 5.

Attitudes. Attitudes to various sub-issues will be discussed in Chapters 6 and 7. As the largest amount of data available is about attitudes to public spending on education, Chapter 6 is devoted to that one subject. Chapter 7 includes attitudes to and knowledge about a large number of sub-issues, ranging from vague concepts such as educational standards to more easily defined sub-issues such as the debate about the bipartite system versus comprehensive schools.

Vote. Relationships between attitudes to education, voting behaviour, radicalism and partisanship will be studied further in Chapter 8.

Activity and influence. In order to deal with the emphasis of Conservative governments on active citizenship and consumer rights, Chapter 9 will consider voters' activity and influence on education policy.

The implications of the findings from this research will be discussed in the concluding chapter. There, questions raised by the findings will be reconsidered and it will be argued that, although the ideal of consumer sovereignty currently prevails in theory, the welfare of children is often not ideally represented by the wishes and effective demands of parents and other voters. Finally, the wider philosophical implications of findings regarding the framework of educational debate will be assessed.

Notes

1. The classic study of political attitudes during the 1960s was 'Political Change in Britain', by David Butler and Donald Stokes, 1969 (with many editions and updates since, it was based on samples of the electorate interviewed between 1963 and 1970). Their main interest regarding education was in the relationship between the type of school attended and partisanship (see this book, 8.3.3), although they also assessed the relative importance of education as a perceived problem for the Government (8.2.4) and asked about the 'warmth' of feeling towards comprehensive schools (7.8). The yearly British Social Attitude surveys (2.3) started in 1983 and have since then provided valuable data about attitudes to educational sub-issues.
2. Edgell and Duke (1986) did not follow this trend. They used data from the Greater Manchester Study to provide a report on radical activity.

2 Research strategy

2.1 Methodological approach

The methods used in this research can be briefly described as a literature search, secondary analysis of survey data, and the execution and analysis of two local case studies. Although it can therefore be seen as consisting of three main phases, the phases cannot be sharply distinguished from each other on any accurate time-scale. It would even be difficult to date the start of the research because, although in theory it has been coterminous with the award of an ESRC grant (starting in 1986) I had already entered the field in my M.Sc. dissertation on the attitudes of parents to education as a political issue (McKenzie, 1986). The literature search dates back several years and press cuttings have been collected since 1983. General reading on the subject has become a habit; the most concentrated period of the literature survey being during the 1986/7 academic year, but the habit of trawling newspapers, journals and books for up to date information continued throughout. Similarly, analysis of survey data was at its most concentrated during 1987, but did not end there.

The gap between ideal types in research methodology and the experience of actually carrying out research will be acknowledged and considered throughout this book. Researchers must often be tempted to sweep apparently untidy methods under the academic carpet in order to impress their potential critics. In doing so they would be not only risking the reliability of their methods but also damaging the morale of their fellow researchers; who are often painfully aware of their own confusion and errors. The gap between theory and practice was particularly felt during the early stages of the research process because the approach and techniques employed meant that it was not possible to identify a clear theoretical area on which to focus. The paradigms and frameworks discussed in Chapter 1 were not considered until a later stage in the research and ideas that emerged from my M.Sc. dissertation could not be formulated into clearly testable hypotheses. My early objectives simply involved finding out what attitudes were and how they related to voting behaviour. As a result, I saw my initial role as that of a cartographer; mapping out a territory, using the tools of the trade in order to eventually discover the shape of the whole in the form of theory grounded on observation. The overall research strategy is summarized in the following model.

Process of theory construction and testing

Observation. Exploratory work (i.e. literature review, interviews with local 'experts').
Theory. Inductive reasoning to identify salient variables.
Observation. Analysis of quantitative data. Crosstabulation of possible independent and dependent variables.
Theory. Search for common factors. Emerging working theories e.g.;
1 The extent of exposure to education affects level of interest in education as a political issue.
2 Voters have a largely instrumental interest; i.e. vote for the policies they believe favour their own interests.
3 Personal problems are considered more important than public issues.
4 Materially deprived groups are least likely to be interested and/or active in education as a political issue. They are more concerned with the immediate problem of survival.
Observation. Case study interviews in Torytown and Labourville.
Theory. Theories about the framework of debate were developed further during analysis of interview data, continued observation (including literature and survey data up-dating), and the writing-up process.

This grounded theory/theory construction approach widens the possible scope of the research and emphasises its relative lack of structure. During the early stages the experience can be rather disconcerting for the researcher, who cannot put the subject being studied into a clearly defined theoretical nutshell. Nevertheless, as the continuous interaction of observation and theory progresses and questions emerge, the grounding of theories on empirical data becomes more substantial and reassuring.

The two types of datasets that have been analysed statistically on computer are the British Social Attitudes' 1984 report (on a survey carried out in 1983, Jowell et al, see 2.3) and the Greater Manchester Study (surveys carried out in 1980/1 and 1983/4, Edgell and Duke, see 2.4). As computer analysis of survey data was at its most concentrated during 1987, later surveys have not been utilized to the full. Nevertheless, attempts have been made to update information via references to more recent British Social Attitudes reports and to studies of the 1987 General Election (Crewe, 1987, Butler and Kavanagh, 1988). Reports emerging from the British Political Participation Survey have also provided a useful source of data for Chapter 9. In common with other researchers I will refer to the people studied in survey research as 'respondents' and the people with whom I communicated at a more personal level in my case studies as 'informants'. This may help the reader to identify references to the more qualitative data emerging from the case studies.

Findings from secondary sources were used in the design of a sample and interview schedule for the local case studies, which were carried out in June and July 1988. This primary research was tied to the secondary sources in several ways. Firstly, a study of independent variables used in the surveys suggested that some variables were more likely than others to affect attitudes to education as a political issue (this is discussed in Chapter 4). Five particularly salient variables were used to construct a sample of voters for the local case studies; these were area, gender, employment sector, experience of further/higher education, and current household consumption of education. Secondly, the operationalization of these variables was made possible by access to the panel already used in two surveys. The Greater Manchester Study was carried out in two areas of contrasting political control and with contrasting systems of secondary education. This provided a particularly useful foundation on which to build the fieldwork stage of my research. Access to information about the panel members meant that salient variables could be built into the sample for the case studies in a way that would not have otherwise been possible. Thirdly, some of the questions asked in the surveys (in the Greater Manchester Surveys and some of the British Social Attitude surveys) were asked in the interviews for the case studies but, in order to expand on the quantitative data provided by the surveys, informants were also asked to explain their responses. In this way qualitative data has been used to clarify existing quantitative data and to explore theories emerging from the study of secondary sources.

The use of panel data also meant that an opportunity for longitudinal research was provided. This was enhanced by the completion of a fourth fieldwork stage at the time of the 1992 General Election. Working with Vic Duke, I returned to informants who had been interviewed in 1980/1, 1983/4 (in Edgell and Duke's Greater Manchester Surveys) and 1988 (my own case studies). As a result, information is available about the changing attitudes of a sample of voters, based on their responses to the same questions asked over a period of 12 years. Details have also been collected about the informants' own education and the education of their parents, thus providing a coherent database for a longitudinal analysis of educational experiences and attitudes. This provides an opportunity to analyse stability and change over a period between four General Elections, combining both quantitative and qualitative

16

data. However, for the moment, this book must concentrate on the findings from the first three stages in combination, rather than on changes over time, which await analysis of all four stages.

2.2 Secondary analysis of survey data

The recent accumulation of attitudinal survey data provides a valuable source of information for researchers working in any of the social science disciplines. In particular, the yearly British Social Attitude surveys (Jowell et al, 1984 onwards) provide a valuable source of data about attitudes to a wide range of issues and allow the researcher to monitor changes over time. However, the use of such data sets means that the researcher is limited by the questions asked; questions that might not have been preferred by the secondary researcher. Trends can be seen in the type of questions asked as well as in the responses given; for example, the nature/nurture debate and the debate about progressive teaching methods are now rarely aired. On the other hand, the standards debate has become so well established as part of the educational field that, although informants are often asked for their views on whether or not education standards have fallen, they are not usually asked to explain what they mean by 'standards'(7.2.1). Yet, despite such reservations, findings from large-scale surveys have provided valuable sources of quantitative data.

In terms of the physical area covered, Northern Ireland has been excluded from large scale surveys and the population studied has been in Britain rather than the United Kingdom. The system of education in Scotland differs in several ways from that in England and Wales, including the examinations taken at 16 and 18 and the length and nature of degree courses. As a specialized study of reactions to the different education systems would be very time-consuming, it is regarded as beyond the scope of the present research. It would, however, be an interesting topic for further research (10.3). Thus, this study of British attitudes does not involve a detailed analysis of differences between the education systems of Scotland, England and Wales. Nevertheless, it is possible to use the combined data from Scotland, England and Wales to study the relationship between independent variables, such as gender and social class, and interest in and knowledge about education as a political issue. As educational systems vary within each of the three regions (according to local political control) but are united by the influence of the same central government, the combined data is valuable in reflecting both local differences and common features.

The first clear question considered in the analysis of survey data was, 'Who cares about education?'. This emerged from the problems involved in defining political issues as such and the realisation that the question was an integral part of the crosstabulation of variables. Simple crosstabulations of independent and dependent variables are, in effect, describing *who* thinks or does *what*. In seeing, for example, that the perceived impact of educational spending cuts was highest amongst those who had young dependents and were in the 30 to 49 age group (see 4.2) it seemed logical to deduce that parents of children currently in full-time education would be more interested in educational issues than those voters who have no current connection with the education system. As the perceived impact of spending cuts was also found to be higher amongst mothers than amongst fathers, it was possible to enlarge the theory by adding the influence of traditional gender roles. The manipulation of datasets therefore became less clumsy and more complex as more questions and theories were clarified.

As the sequence to be followed is roughly - interest, knowledge, attitudes, vote, activity and influence - we can see that each point can be phrased as a simple crosstabulation with the question, 'Who?': who is interested, who knows what, who thinks what, who votes in which way, who is active and who influences. Crosstabulations became more complicated as independent variables were compounded to form pictures of ideal types. This involved a progression from simple cross-tabulations to multivariate analysis of groups of independent variables cross-tabulated with attitude scales created by grouping dependent variables (8.4). Theories developed linking the findings from each point in the sequence, to form a chain of common features rather than a statistically defined causal path. Analysis stops short of a causal model because analysis was of nominal or ordinal variables and separate models would be needed at each point on the chain. For example, the voters who influence education policy-making are not necessarily those who are most active in the educational policy field. Some activists will be more influential than others (9.1). Knowledge about educational issues will vary even amongst influential activists and the role of governments in eliminating interests that conflict with their own can hardly be underestimated. What is presented should therefore be seen as a map rather than a statistically defined causal model. Characteristics are identified, discussed and quantified but a sophisticated causal sequence has not been developed.

Once the emphasis was placed on levels of interest in education, the types of data used and the manipulation of that data became more selective. The British Election Study of 1983 (Butler and Kavanagh, 1984) was, for example, excluded because it did not provide sufficient data about current household consumption of education. Cross-sectional research was favoured over panel data because it was most appropriate for a comparison of the relationship between variables at one point in time. However, the interview schedules used in 1988 were designed to facilitate a future analysis of the longitudinal data available from the Greater Manchester Study panel (10.3).

The GMS, when combined with my interviews and the yearly British Social Attitude reports (Jowell et al, 1984-8) provides a great amount of information about changing attitudes during the 1980s but an intensive study of such changes was regarded as too demanding to be included in the present project. Instead the emphasis has been on the identification of consistencies in both attitudes and the characteristics of the people holding such attitudes.

The context in which attitudes occur is also considered although, as always, the problem remains regarding how much information is needed about the context in order to avoid misunderstandings. Researchers working in all three of the main survey projects used in this book is have provided some sort of context-setting in order to tackle a frequent criticism of surveys for their supposed superficiality. Although a survey's emphasis on quantitative data presupposes restrictions on context-setting, the combination of several surveys, all administered during the 1980s and all including some references to environmental circumstances, results in a very strong foundation on which to build qualitative research. Two of the survey projects (the first two stages of the Greater Manchester Study, 1980/4, and the British Political Participation Survey, 1984-9) have produced reports that are high on theoretical interpretation, thus dealing with another criticism of survey research for its basically empiricist and sometimes rigid nature.

2.3 The British Social Attitudes Reports

In the first British Social Attitudes report Jowell stated (p.1) that one of the aims of future reports and datasets was to provide resource banks for secondary researchers. British Social Attitude datasets are publicly available through the ESRC Data Archive. They are therefore accessible through university departments and are easily manipulated by someone with a basic knowledge of SPSS or SPSSX. Using a time series design, the surveys approach different samples of the population at yearly intervals, collecting some data that is comparable between surveys and some that is particular to an individual survey. The 1984 and 1986 reports each included a whole chapter devoted to educational issues; the 1986 report also noting some of the changes over the interim period. By supplying data from large probability samples (for example, 1,761 in the first survey and 1,675 in the second) they provide a firm basis on which to ground qualitative research and increase the generalizability of my findings.

References to the BSA could be rather confusing as the reports are dated one year after the relevant surveys are carried out. Thus, the 1984 report is based on a survey carried out in 1983. To avoid confusion they will be referred to in this book by the date of the survey and of the report; for example, BSA

1983/4 refers to the survey carried out in 1983 and the report on that survey that was published in 1984. The survey carried out in 1987 has, however, been reported in the 1988 15th report'. It is therefore referred to as either the 1987 survey or the 5th. Report.

2.4 The Greater Manchester Study

Another important source has been data provided by the Greater Manchester Study, which consisted of two surveys carried out in 1980/1 and 1983/4 by Stephen Edgell and Vic Duke, the Department of Anthropology and Sociology, University of Salford. Although designed to study the effects of cuts in public spending, the Greater Manchester Surveys have yielded useful information about attitudes to education.

The two wards in Greater Manchester were chosen by Edgell and Duke because of their equivalent socio-economic structures and contrasting political control. In the GMS reports (Edgell and Duke, 1981-7) they were labelled 'Torytown' and 'Labourville' because of the traditional domination of one party in each area at both local authority level and in Westminster. From my point of view they have been particularly useful because Labourville provides a comprehensive system of secondary education whilst Torytown has retained selection at 11 for grammar schools and secondary modern schools. Education has been high on the political agenda in Torytown for several years as Conservative councils have struggled to maintain a bipartite system despite the sometimes powerful opposition of other parties. The system in Labourville has been relatively unchallenged. (See 3.1 for further details.)

A contrast is therefore provided in terms of political control, educational structure and the level of debate about education - amongst politicians at least. The extent to which the electorate are interested and involved in such debates will be assessed in analysis of the case studies.

2.5 Exploratory fieldwork in Torytown and Labourville

Exploratory work in Torytown and Labourville naturally started with a literature search through reports emerging from Edgell and Duke's Greater Manchester Study. Many of Edgell and Duke's findings are considered throughout this book and their context-setting has proved useful. Their 1981 report to the Social Science Research Council, for example, included a list of local newspaper articles, providing information about the context of local educational debate in 1980 and 1981. They also provided useful contacts who could fill-in the picture of local educational debate with more details. One

20

member of the Torytown Education Committee had for several years collected newspaper articles about local education issues. When I interviewed her she agreed to let me borrow and copy them for my research. The favour was reciprocated as I photocopied them and filed them in an orderly sequence. I also interviewed other 'specialists' and attended meetings in both areas. Labour domination of Labourville was such that the only councillors who could be found with experience on the Education Committee were Labour.

Fieldwork events

15 October 1986 Attended a meeting at girls grammar school (consultation with parents about a proposed merger of schools), Torytown.

3 November 1986 Interviewed a Labour member of the Education Committee, Torytown.

26 November 1986 Attended Education Committee meeting, Labourville.

2 December 1986 Interviewed a Labour member of the Education Committee (also a university lecturer), Labourville.

3 December 1986 Interviewed a Labour member of the Education Committee, Labourville.

8 December 1986 Interviewed a Labour member of the Education Committee, Labourville.

6 January 1987 Attended Town Hall full council meeting, Torytown.

14 January 1987 Interviewed a Conservative member of the Education Committee, Torytown.

15 January 1987 Interviewed the Chief Education Officer, Labourville.

11 December 1989 Interviewed a senior Education Officer, Torytown.

Detailed notes were taken at meetings. Most interviews were, with the permission of interviewees, tape recorded. It was thought that professional politicians and education officers would not find this particularly intimidating. In one case, however, this was not so and the last interview, with a Torytown education officer, was not tape recorded. On that occasion, he was particularly anxious that any report of the interview should not generate criticism from local councillors (of any party) or other local education officers. Confidentiality was an obvious problem and we agreed that, because of their systems of secondary education, it would be easier for a reader to identify Torytown than Labourville. I had expected a certain amount of sensitivity and was not surprised when my offer of a list of questions prior to the interview was taken up. The Torytown Education Department therefore had some time to prepare answers. Questions were mainly about selection at 11+ (findings are reported in 3.1) and the official regarded them as particularly sensitive. Although I asked for permission to tape record the interview, and the education officer agreed, the agreement was so hesitant and the anxiety so obvious that I decided not to do so. In order to allay the interviewee's anxiety even further my note-taking was not as detailed as usual and I cannot therefore provide quotes. However, the interviewee provided some very useful information, including a copy of a Torytown Local Education Authority report on admissions to secondary schools in 1989. The Education Department also provided a copy of a booklet issued to parents; describing educational provision in Torytown, the options available at 11+ and method of selection for a secondary school.

2.6 Case study samples

The case study samples consisted of quotas taken from the 685 who were interviewed twice in the GMS. Salient variables were identified as a result of analysis of national data (Chapter 4) and operationalized via GMS data regarding the characteristics of respondents. Edgell and Duke provided a computerized list of the respondents interviewed in 1983/4 and this was used as my sampling frame. Using a computer, I divided the sample into the relevant subgroups. From each subgroup every 10th (or 5th in small groups) was systematically sampled. Each individual was checked to ensure that s/he was still likely to be in relevant subgroup; for example, that 'parents' still had children of school age. When an individual no longer fitted into a particular subgroup, another was randomly sampled and checked. Forty-two people were approached in each of the two areas in order to get a final area sample of approximately twenty-five and a total of fifty. By checking names against the most recent Electoral Register I found that nine people who had been selected from the GMS panel no longer lived at their 1983/4 addresses. They were replaced by more respondents in order to achieve a sample total of eighty-four. The forty-two finally approached in each area consisted of thirty-six who were interviewed in both of the Greater Manchester surveys and six who have been put on the Electoral Roll since 1983. These few new arrivals were added in order to reduce the average age of the sample and the otherwise disproportionate number of long-time residents.

Quotas representing the following four variables were devised:

1 employment sector (public, private or not in paid employment),
2 whether or not the subjects were parents of children currently in full-time education,
3 whether or not the subjects had had any formal education since the age of sixteen, and
4 gender.

One third of the sample were parents and two thirds non-parents. This was a proportion that roughly corresponded with the findings in the Greater Manchester Study and allowed for a lower response rate from non-parents.

Table 2.1
Case study quotas in Torytown and Labourville,
employment sectors (public, private and unemployed)

	a)*Employment Sector* N=12						
b)*Parents* N=4				*Non-parents* N=8			
c)*Had FE* n=2		*No FE* n=2		*Had FE* n=4		*No FE* n=4	
d)M n=1	F n=1	M n=1	F n=1	M n=2	F n=2	M n=2	F n=2

During the fieldwork stage 52 people were interviewed and 32 of the original sample were not available. When the actual interviews took place it was still found that, due to out of date information, some had been allocated to the wrong theoretical group (some have, for example moved to a different employment sector). After the last interviews were carried out in June and July of 1988 the final sample was as shown in Table 2.2.

No clear explanation could be found for the greater response rate amongst women than amongst men. It is possible that this could be a reflection of greater interest amongst women or an effect of the gender of the researcher. However when reasons for non-availability were listed no particular gender-related (or other) pattern was found.

Table 2.2
Case study final sample

Labourville
a) 7 public sector, 8 private, 9 not employed
b) 9 parents, 15 non-parents
c) 15 had FE, 9 no FE
d) 14 female, 10 male
Total 24

Torytown
a) 8 public sector, 12 private, 8 not employed
b) 11 parents, 17 non-parents
c) 13 had FE, 15 no FE
d) 16 female, 12 male
Total 28

The case study sample was therefore carefully selected to provide theoretical quotas that would add qualitative data to existing quantitative data. They do not, on their own, provide generalizable data but the findings add depth to the more generalizable survey data emerging from probability samples.

2.7 Design of the case study interview schedule

(A full interview schedule is provided in the Appendix)

The design of an interview schedule inevitably involves decisions about breadth and depth. Should the interview include a very wide range of sub-issues or probe more deeply into a smaller number of sub-issues? Should the emphasis be on comparability with existing surveys or on a more innovative approach? Length was also very important because informants could not be expected to tolerate a lengthy interview. The timing of the fieldwork also placed restraints on the design process. These and many other points had to be considered in the design of the interview schedule and its obvious defects must be considered.

The interview was redrafted several times and I was still not totally satisfied with it in its final form (2.9). There was, for example, a temptation to include too many questions, with the emphasis on breadth rather than depth. As a result, the final version is still rather long and some opportunities to probe responses to individual questions more deeply were missed. Many of the questions and responses will not be referred to here, although they do

24

provide useful material for further analysis (2.1 and 10.3). From the interviewees' point of view it must have sometimes seemed a long and tiring experience; although they were very cooperative (2.8).

The amount of time needed to plan fieldwork had also been underestimated. It took so long to design and select the quota sample that the summer was approaching, and with it school and family holidays, when access would have been difficult. As a result I had time to produce several drafts and discuss them with colleagues at the University but did not fully pilot the schedule. A full pilot, involving non-specialists rather than other social scientists, would have been useful. Nevertheless, many of the questions used in the British Social Attitude Surveys and the Greater Manchester Study were replicated in the interview schedule and had therefore already been piloted. Such a small sample (of 52) could in itself be seen as a pilot for future research and one of the aims of the case study, emerging from the grounded theory approach, was to test question-wording. Informants were also asked to explain their responses in order to provide more qualitative information to compliment quantitative data. Some depth was therefore achieved, although a shorter schedule would have allowed more time for probing. The interview schedule was organized into four sections.

In the first section (questions 1 to 15) questions were asked about political behaviour and attitudes. This was covered at the beginning of the schedule in order to avoid leading informants to over-emphasise the importance of education to them as a political issue. Although they already knew that the interview was connected with education, it was still necessary to lead the interviewee as little as possible. For example, informants were asked to explain why they voted for a particular party. If these questions were asked after a series of questions about education there is a greater possibility that attitudes to education could have been used as an explanation. Question 8 about issues could also have been influenced by prior questions about education.

In the second section (questions 16 to 37) informants were asked about their own and their families' experiences, with particular emphasis on education. 'Experience' included not only objective data (such as the type of school attended) but also subjective responses to education. This was intended to lead gently into the more demanding third section of the interview.

The third section (questions 38 to 53) included questions about current debates in education that were intended to assess knowledge of, as well as attitudes towards, educational issues. Some questions about the same subject were expressed in different ways in order to assess the influence of question-wording; for example, Q41a and Q42, Q41b and Q45, Q41f and Q43. The effects of the different approaches offered by the different wording are considered in Chapter 7. Q41h was based on Clause 28 of the 1988 Local

Government Act which uses the word 'promote'. However, it was suggested that 'promote' was too vague and the words 'present a favourable view' were used instead. This alternative expression was also seen by many informants as very vague and it now seems likely that the original term 'promote' would have been preferable in order to test public responses to the original legal statement (see 7.6.1).

The final part of the interview (questions 54 to 68) consists of general questions about independent variables such as occupational and social class. Potentially sensitive questions about income and family spending were left to the end, when time had been allowed for a rapport to develop with the informant.

2.8 Administration of case study interviews

Interviewees were sent a letter fitting the case studies into the context of their past experience as participants in the GMS. Information about the purpose of the research was limited as far as possible in an attempt to avoid leading to the suggestion that their interest in education was greater than it was. Possible exaggeration cannot be assessed, but it can at least be noted that the expressed lack of interest in education as a political issue was so clear amongst most informants (including parents) that any exaggeration on the part of the researcher may lead in the opposite direction.

Interviews took place between 13 June 1988 and 11 July 1988 (inclusive). All took place in the informants' own homes, apart from the police officer, who was interviewed in a private room at a police station (at his request). Their average duration was 88 minutes. This is a rather lengthy period but informants were given prior warning that interviews could take over an hour.

Responses were recorded verbatim whenever possible by a mixture of longhand and shorthand. It was felt that the tape recording of interviews would have been more inhibiting and their transcription time-consuming for the researcher. A mixture of longhand and shorthand meant that the qualitative nature of the data could be enhanced and the interviewer could refer to notes taken (when probing for example) during the interview. Often earlier comments are forgotten when interviews are tape recorded. As I had no previous knowledge of shorthand I simply learned and practised fifty commonly used words before the fieldwork started.

Informants often started the interview with an apology for their lack of interest and/or knowledge about the subject and it was obvious that many were anxious about the possibility of 'loosing face' or 'blowing their cover' to the interviewer. Some actually used such expressions at the end of the interview to describe the anxieties they had before the interview. As schoolchildren, many of them had felt intimidated by the school environment and, as adults they were similarly conscious of the need to make a good impression on a visiting academic. A suspiciously large number of parents, for example, made a point of saying that they had looked at their child(ren)'s school-books the night before the interview.

I used several tactics to put people at their ease, although it is only with hindsight that I am aware of some of them. For example, most of the interviews were carried out during a heatwave. This was a source of conversation before the interview started. Also, as I often arrived looking red, hot and tired, many of the interviewees responded by making an effort to make me feel comfortable (usually with cold drinks). In general my approach was as far removed from the 'ivory tower' academic as possible and an attitude of friendly interest seemed to succeed in putting most informants at ease within the first few minutes (the exceptions were the young voters who had not been interviewed in the Greater Manchester Surveys). Indeed, the average length of interviews reflects a tendency of informants to treat me as an old friend and to prolong my visit. There may be reasons for this other than my personal approach. As this was the third interview for most people, not only were they experienced interviewees but less confident panel members may have dropped out after the first or second Greater Manchester Survey.

2.9 Reflection on research strategy

Of the research problems already mentioned, most seem to fall into one of two categories; those affecting the researcher and those effected by the researcher. Examples of the first category include the exclusion of Northern Ireland and lack of survey data about certain sub-issues (for example, Clause 28, 7.6.2). These could be regarded as the sort of limitations that are inevitable, rather than 'problems' as such. One of the aims of this research was to compensate for some of the limitations inherent in quantitative research methods by providing qualitative data; concerning, for example, informants' knowledge about, and experiences of types of schools.

The problems generated by the individual researcher have, in general, tended to relate to lack of time and lack of expertise. Lack of time could be described as both an external affect and an individual effect in that it relates to both the time limit placed by the Economic and Social Research Council (who financed the research) and the researcher's own time management. Research had to be balanced with teaching commitments and responsibilities to dependents. Failure to pilot the interview schedule can be cited as an example of lack of time and expertise. Preparation for the interviews was probably more time-consuming than it would have been if carried out by a more experienced researcher. However, the use of a 'semi-pilot' did not affect the quality of the data as this was a small sample and the research was not verificational. The data provided by an over-long interview schedule can be analysed and utilized in the future (10.3). Also, the approach was very different to that of a large-scale survey in which design is crucial. Questions were being used tentatively, with a view to applying a qualitative analysis to definitions and perceptions of reality. The case studies could even be seen as a pilot study, of value in the preparation of future large-scale surveys.

Any research project will therefore involve a series of trade-offs, the strengths of the researcher and the research itself being traded with the weaknesses. My previous research training (including the use of SPSS) was a great help in computer analysis, but I was still constantly aware of my incompetence in the use of data packages. A computer 'specialist' would clearly have been more adept in this area, but his/her lack of knowledge of the social sciences could have created a weak element in the alternative trade-off. Efforts to improve my knowledge of SPSS and SPSSX (when the University changed packages part way through the research) were time consuming and often frustrating, and the resulting statistical analysis is not particularly sophisticated. However, if a reasonable assessment is to be made, the balance of weak and strong elements have to be considered.

Studies that are strong on internal validity are often weak on external validity and vice versa. When the emphasis is on qualitative data, findings may not be generalizable to a wide population. Similarly, when the emphasis is on quantitative data, the findings may be lacking in internal validity. This research has tried to provide a balance of both internal and external validity, using a triangulation of qualitative and quantitative methods in order to test findings. It is hoped that the resulting explanatory strengths and the generalizability of findings have therefore been enhanced. However, the British Social Attitudes reports have shown that attitudes have changed even during the relatively short period of this research. The research has not dealt fully with longitudinal changes (2.1) and the field is still wide open for further study.

3 Context of national and local debate

Although the contextual framework of the research is considered throughout, a more condensed picture of the political and educational influences on the case study interviews is presented in this chapter in order to set attitudes clearly in their place.   Changes in the support for various political parties is particularly noticeable, as the press report the latest fluctuations; or at least opinion polls' findings about such changes.   In Table 3.1 (below),   for example, support for the Conservative Party varies between 42 per cent and 49 per cent and for the Labour Party between 36 per cent and 43 per cent. However, opinion polls and other attitude surveys have found that changes in attitudes are not necessarily associated with changes in voting behaviour (8.2.4).   Most voters rarely, if ever, change their vote even though their attitudes to individual issues or sub-issues may change radically.   It is the 'floating voters' or weak identifiers who attract most media interest,   thus detracting attention from the degree of continuity.   Questions relating to continuity and change have not been tackled in depth in this research, as a longitudinal approach has not been followed through (2.1), but the national and local context of debate has been considered.

3.1 National political and educational context

At a national level Labour support was apparently going through a slump when the case study interviews were carried out between 13 June and 11 July 1988. Newspapers blamed this on recent confusion about Labour's non-nuclear defence policy.   In early June disagreements within the party about defence policy led to the resignation of Denzil Davies as the party defence spokesman and one senior Shadow Cabinet minister was quoted (The Observer 26 June) as describing the crisis as, '...the most disastrous ten days since Greenwich.' The same source quoted David Blunkett's (Labour MP for Sheffield

Brightside) comment that, 'Disagreements over policies, and even the sillier thing individuals say and do, pale into insignificance alongside the image we're presenting to the public of a divided party.'

Opinion polls carried out during, and in the time leading up to the interviews, offer a (limited) impression of political party support at a national level. These show a decline in support for Labour and a corresponding increase in Conservative support from early June until Labour started to regain support in mid July.

Table 3.1
Opinion polls at the time of the case studies

Fieldwork for poll	Poll	Sample n	Con %	Lab %	SLD %	SDP %	Con lead
9-13 Jun	Gallup/Telegraph	926	42	43	7	4	-1
22-23 Jun	Harris/Observer	1022	48	36	9	3	+12
22-27 Jun	NOP	1405	49	34	10	4	+15
22-28 Jun	MORI/S.Times	1836	48	38	7	5	+10
24-26 Jun	ASL*	777	45	38	8	5	+7
29 Jun-4 July	NOP	1346	46	36	10	4	+10
2-3 July	Harris/TV-am	1050	47	38	9	3	+11
8-12 July	Marplan/Guardian	1436	45	43	6	4	+2

* Telephone poll

Source: The Guardian, 1 August 1988

The polls showed Labour and the Conservatives as having almost equal support at the beginning and end of the fieldwork period, with public criticism of the Labour Party strongest when my the interviews were taking place. Later in July, as Labour started to recover from its disputes about defence policy, public criticism of the Conservative Government apparently increased. A MORI poll conducted in July (Sunday Times, 31 July) found that more people expected the economy to deteriorate over the next 12 months than thought it would improve. This was the first time since February 1987 that MORI had a mainly negative response to the question.

The average of the last five opinion polls at the end of each month in 1988 shows the apparently fluctuating support for the various parties in the lead up to and during the time of the case study interviews (Table 3.2).

Table 3.2
Average of last 5 opinion polls at end of each month, 1988

	Con	Lab	SLD	Alliance	SDP	Con lead
	%	%	%	%	%	%
January	47	36	-	15	-	11
February	46	38	-	13	-	8
March	45	38	9	-	5	7
April	44	40	8	-	5	4
May	44	39	8	-	5	5
June	47	38	8	-	4	9
July	45	41	8	-	5	4

Source: The Guardian, 1 August 1988

According to opinion polls, the popularity of an individual party can rise and fall dramatically but the reliability of such findings must be considered. Three of the polls listed in Table 3.1 partially overlap in time. A Harris/Observer poll, a NOP and a MORI poll all involved fieldwork starting on the 22 June. Although they each found a strong Conservative lead the lead varied between 10 per cent and 15 per cent. When combined, however, the polls do provide a picture (although limited) of the popularity of various parties and changes in party support. The reported public image of a divided Labour Party was reinforced during case study interviews as even long-term Labour identifiers criticized the party for its lack of unity. One month later, when the Labour Party started to recover from its internal disputes, responses could have been quite different.

Educational debate at the time was centred on the final stages of the Education Reform Bill, which became an Act in late July. At the time of the case study interviews the Bill was passing through the House of Lords and debates in the House were regularly reported in the media. This also followed months of public debate about the various changes to be introduced by the Act; including the National Curriculum, testing at seven, eleven and fourteen, open enrolment, local management of schools, 'opting out', the funding of City Technology Colleges, the abolition of the Inner London Education Authority and several changes in further and higher education. Many of these changes are considered elsewhere (especially 5.5, 6.1 and Chapter 7) and they are particularly important when the context of the research is considered. Public awareness and interest in education as a political issue should, in theory, have been particularly acute at the time of the case studies but the findings suggest general apathy rather than interest (5.5). It is possible that this was a reaction against the saturation coverage of educational sub-issues in the media but it is also possible that there is even less interest when education is not at the forefront of political debate. To use the expression 'public debate' may therefore be misleading as the majority of voters do not participate in such discussions (Chapter 9).

The case study interviews were also carried out after several weeks of media reports about the murder of a Manchester schoolboy. In May 1988 newspapers published leaked findings from the MacDonald inquiry into the murder in 1986 of Ahmed Ullah, a 13 year old pupil at Burnage High School, Manchester. Ahmed was stabbed to death by a (white) fellow pupil. Leaks claimed that the report blamed the school's anti-racist policies for creating racial tension. As a result of its handling by the press, the MacDonald inquiry team published a statement rejecting claims that the report had contained a blanket condemnation of anti-racist policies in schools. The death of Ahmed Ullah, the MacDonald Inquiry and press reports are also considered in Chapter 5 and 7.7.3.. As the murder took place in a Manchester school and Torytown and Labourville are in Greater Manchester, it was possible that case study interviewees would take a particular interest in the ensuing debates. They were, for example, reported not only in the national press but also extensively in the local press. However, again, many interviewees claimed to know little about the debate; although the sensitivity of racism as an issue may have lead some to brush aside the subject as quickly as possible.

In general, therefore, the national political and educational context suggested that respondents would be particularly critical of the Labour Party and particularly interested in education as a political issue. Although the expected criticisms of the Labour Party emerged, few were interested in education as a political issue. Theories about levels of interest are considered in Chapter 4. The next section will consider the context of local educational debate and its association with local political control.

3.2 Local political and educational context

Political control in Labourville changed very little during the 1980s. Labour still has a large overall majority within the council (the majority was 49 after the 1988 local elections) and has maintained its commitment to the existing comprehensive system, generous nursery provision and a tertiary system of further education. Local newspapers have regarded education as a relatively insignificant issue in Labourville politics, debate having been confined to cuts in educational spending and the closure of schools as a result of falling rolls. At the time of the 1988 local elections local newspapers suggested that debates about a proposed gypsy site could pose the biggest threat to Labour popularity, but in the event Labour support was as strong as ever. The Labourville ward from which my interview sample came returned a Labour councillor as usual.

Torytown was, however, in a state of political flux for most of the 1980s. For a long time now the future of education in Torytown has been uncertain, as arguments about the respective merits and defects of the existing bipartite system have been used by politicians at successive elections. When the present research started in 1986 Labour had minority control of the Torytown council, the balance of power being maintained by seven Liberal councillors. A scheme for the reorganisation of education along comprehensive and coeducational lines was proposed by the Labour and Liberal groups. This would have involved a radical change from single-sex grammar and secondary modern schools to coeducational comprehensive schools. As a result of a compromise between Labour and the Liberals, school leavers would be offered a choice of further education including tertiary colleges (favoured by Labour), colleges of further education and sixth form colleges (a combination of the last two being favoured by Liberals). During this research a lengthy period of consultation was taking place and meetings between parents, teachers and LEA representatives were called at various schools. However, the local elections in May 1988 returned an overall Conservative majority of one and the proposals for reorganisation were abandoned. The Torytown ward sampled in this research again returned a Conservative councillor.

Torytown and Labourville's contrasting education policies are reflected in Table 3.3. They are also described in 6.3, where differences in their educational spending are considered.

Nursery provision in Labourville was very generous, its nurseries providing health and community care as well as education, and thus serving the needs of families in particularly deprived areas within the wider Labourville borough. Torytown children, however, could only attend one of the few nursery classes attached to primary schools on a part-time basis. The number of registered pupils at primary schools in Torytown (Table 3.3) included those in nursery classes attached to primary schools. Thus, in 1985/6 Labourville had more than twice as many under fives in full-time education as Torytown, whilst Torytown had nearly twice as many under fives in part-time education as Labourville.

The figures also show that, in Torytown, there was a radical increase in the number of pupils attending schools maintained by other LEAs after the age of eleven. In Labourville virtually equal numbers of children aged under and over eleven attended schools in other areas. Torytown was also loosing pupils overall, when the number of pupils leaving Torytown to go to school elsewhere was compared with the number coming to Torytown schools from other LEAs. Fewer under elevens (-145) and over elevens (-261) were arriving in Torytown than were leaving to go to school elsewhere. The corresponding

Table 3.3
Schools and pupils in Torytown and Labourville, 1985/6

	Torytown n=	*Labourville* n=
Estimated population, June 1985	217800	240000
LEA maintained schools		
Nursery	0	18
Primary	80	97
Secondary	24	26
Registered pupils, January 1986		
Nursery schools	0	870
Primary schools	16076	20508
Secondary schools	14034	17415
Total	130110	38793
Under 5 years on 31 August 1985 (part-time)	607	368
Under 5 years on 31 August 1985 (full-time)	1268	2845
Attending schools maintained by another LEA		
Under 11 years on 31 August 1985	272	392
11 years and over on 31 August 1985	728	390
Chargeable to another LEA, but attending schools in this area		
Under 11 yrs on 31 August 1985	127	714
11 yrs and over on 31 August 1985	467	547
Attending schools not maintained by a LEA		
Aged under 11 on 31 August 1985	0	0
Aged 11 and over on 31 August 1985	1576	11
Pupil:teacher ratio using full-time equivalents		
Primary	22.9	21.6
Secondary	16.3	15.0
Total	19.2	18.0

Source: Education Statistics 1985-86 Actuals, CIPFA, Statistical Information Service, SIS Ref 52.87

figures for Labourville (+322 under elevens and +157 over elevens) showed larger numbers arriving than leaving.

Figures (supplied by the Torytown Education Officer, 2.5) regarding the movements of children from primary to secondary school in 1989 do not support the pattern described in Table 3.3 for 1985/6. According to Torytown LEA's own report, in 1989 102 pupils living outside the area entered Torytown secondary schools (65 of them going to grammar schools and 37 to secondary modern schools) whilst 96 pupils living in Torytown entered schools outside the area (86 of them having previously been selected for a Torytown secondary modern school and ten for a grammar school). However, the absence of any data about movements between areas after the first year of secondary education means that this Torytown report alone is not enough to contradict the CIPFA findings. It is clear that the largest exodus is from secondary modern schools and this sort of movement may continue after the first year of secondary education.

The numbers of children living in Labourville or Torytown and attending schools not maintained by a LEA show a more pronounced difference between the two areas. In 1985/6 only eleven children who were resident in Labourville attended non-maintained schools. The corresponding figure for Torytown was 1,576! Torytown had more children in this category than any other LEA, and the total number aged eleven and over for the whole of England and Wales (in 1985/6) was 6,806. This is explained by the Torytown policy of paying the fees for children to attend independent Roman Catholic grammar schools. The Torytown LEA will pay the fees for Roman Catholic pupils if they pass both the local 11+ assessment and the individual school's entrance examination. In 1989 Torytown paid for 216 first year pupils to take such places at four independent schools. As this figure relates to first year pupils only it provides only a partial indication of the total number of pupils in private education who were financed by the Torytown LEA. In 1989, a further 216 of Torytown first year pupils (153 having previously qualified for grammar school, 63 for secondary modern school) entered independent secondary schools as fee-payers not supported by the Torytown council. Many of these (the figure is unknown) will have qualified for an Assisted Place, financed by central government (see 7.9.3).

Independent schools, with their (usually) low pupil-teacher ratio are not included in the CIPFA figures describing the pupil-teacher ratios in Torytown and Labourville. In 1985 the average pupil-teacher ratio in independent schools (primary and secondary combined) was 11.7 (Statham, Mackinnon and Cathcart, 1989, p.72). The average pupil-teacher ratios for all of England and Wales in 1985/6 were; primary 22.2, secondary 16.1, overall average 17.8. Thus, the Labourville ratios were better than average at each level and the Torytown ratios worse than average at each level (Table 3.3). This tendency for Labourville to provide more generous state education provision is confirmed when the expenditure of the two areas is compared in 6.3. The Education Officer thus presented a misleading impression when, in his interview, he claimed that the selective system generated better than average pupil-teacher ratios in Torytown. Such healthy ratios were more likely to be experienced by the many Torytown children attending independent schools than those attending state schools in the Torytown area.

3.3 Selection at 11+ in Torytown

The methods used in selecting pupils for different types of secondary education are described in detail in this chapter because selection is still a contentious political issue in Torytown. In the Torytown publication, 'Information for parents', (1988) the system of selection at 11+ is described as follows:

> All pupils in their final year of primary education are assessed to establish which type of secondary education will be appropriate for them. As part of the assessment, pupils take two tests known as verbal reasoning tests, one in the Autumn term and one in the Spring term. Before pupils take the first test in the Autumn term they are given two practice tests in order to familiarise them with the type of test to be used. The results of the two tests are supplemented by the Head's assessment of each child's suitability for a particular type of secondary education. A uniform standard is applied throughout the Authority in reaching final assessment decisions.

During an interview in 1986 a Labour member of the Torytown Education Committee complained that (apart from the usual Labour objections to selection at 11+) the Head's assessment of an individual child was unfair because of the way that children were ranked. Teachers placed pupils in a numerical rank order for their class or school. If a child was ranked 10th. by the teacher and came 5th. in the test, his/her actual examination mark would be added to the test mark of the child who actually came 10th. The final mark was a combination of the two and therefore depended on the child's own examination result and the result of the child coming 10th. At the time of the second test in the Spring teachers again placed pupils in a rank order. The averages from the Autumn and Spring examinations and rankings were used to find the final average for the child. This was (the councillor argued) unfair as teachers may underestimate a child and the result of the child who got the mark that teachers predicted for another child could be particularly low. A child's parents would not know this and could not appeal on such grounds.

In 1989 the Torytown Education Officer (2.5) explained that parents were informed of the results of the practice tests but not the actual tests and assessments used for selection at 11+. The ranking system described by the Labour councillor existed until 1989 when numerical ranking was replaced by a system of ranking into three groups by the headteacher; the groups being, secondary modern school, grammar school and borderline cases. There are no standard activities and the assessment is based on observation in class, activities and testing during the last two years at primary school.

If the test result contradicts the Head's assessment the pupil's case is referred to a Review Panel. The Torytown publication, 'Information for parents', describes the following process.

> Assessment of individual children who do not reach the uniform standard, but who were recommended by the Heads of their primary schools for consideration for grammar school education, is made by a Review Panel. The Panel, which consists of two primary school Heads, a grammar school Head, a secondary modern school Head, a primary school teacher, the Senior Adviser for Primary Education and the Assistant Chief Education Officer (Schools), considers written and oral submissions from the pupil's primary school Head, together with examples of the child's own work.

According to the Education Officer, the panel considered a child's coursework again, primarily for verbal reasoning skills rather than for skills in mathematics and science. Each panel member allocated a score of between 0 and 3 to each child considered and the child's scores were added up. The panel then decided what level of total score should lead to a grammar school place and children were allocated accordingly. In 1989 471 cases were considered by the Review Panel in this way. Therefore, a large number of cases had to be considered in a very short time, raising doubts about the amount of attention that could be devoted to each child. Torytown has also (like other areas retaining the 11+) found that differentiation in terms of ability between boys and girls has caused problems.

In 1989 34 per cent of boys in the age group were selected for a grammar school education compared to 41 per cent of girls in the age group (the actual figures were, 393 boys and 476 girls). The different performance of boys and girls in early school assessments is usually attributed to the earlier maturation of girls. In 1967 the Plowden Report even favoured eight (rather than seven) as the most appropriate age for children to transfer from infant to primary schools because the earlier age led to more boys being assigned to remedial classes. An allowance for different stages in development was built into the verbal reasoning tests used in Torytown at 11+. This include weighting for age differences (making extra allowances for summer-born children).

However, this assumed a natural rate of development, consistent for all pupils in an age group and did not take into account different rates of maturation.

Differences between the sexes in educational achievement therefore cause problems in a selective system. If it is decided that the same percentages of boys and girls should be selected for a grammar school, some girls may fail at a level of performance that would qualify a boy for a pass. This method of selection was used in the past and, until quite recently (see 7.5.2) was regarded as acceptable by many educationalists. In Torytown, girls and boys were listed and ranked separately until 1989 when the Equal Opportunities Commission complained that such a separation constituted sex discrimination. As a result the system was changed to one in which girls and boys are listed and ranked together into the three ranks described above, instead of the previous assessment by numerical order.

According to the Education Officer, Torytown had never provided grammar school places that were dependent upon sex, although it still had single sex schools. If there was a shortage of places in the past, pupils could be sent to Direct Grant schools. As in 1989 there was a surplus of places, due to falling rolls, the problem did not (he said) exist. However, he also speculated that more girls would go to grammar schools in the future and that boys would be at a disadvantage, due to the new system of selection. The previous system was, he claimed, more fair because it helped under-achieving boys to get a grammar school place. Yet, if the previous system helped boys, by implication it must have discriminated against girls. If the new system is more fair to girls it also implies that late-developers (of either sex) will be at a disadvantage in the selection process. Torytown pupils can be transferred to a different type of school at the end of their first year at secondary school but this is a major upheaval, rarely done and may still not help the late developer. It has, moreover, been found that there is a slight tendency for girls to perform better than boys until they reach A'level GCE standard (Statham, Mackinnon and Cathcart, 1989).

The proportion of pupils attending grammar school or secondary modern school also varies between different areas of Torytown. Although there was a general agreement amongst councillors and the Education Officer that the proportion varied, no accurate figures were available. The Education Officer said that the collection and maintenance of such figures would require extra work and sophisticated analysis and that the Education Department did not have the time to do more than just respond to instructions from the council. 'Expert' interviewees however, agreed that it was usual for over 45 per cent of the age group to pass in the most affluent, rural areas of Torytown (including the Torytown ward from which GMS and case study respondents were sampled). This can be compared with an overall pass rate of 37 per cent. Estimates offered by Labour and Conservative councillors varied from 50 per cent to 60 per cent in such wards. The same councillors also suggested that in less affluent, urban areas the proportion of passes was likely to be less than 25 per cent. The Education Officer observed that some schools in one particularly deprived area rarely obtained any passes. He claimed that, since the reorganization of local authority boundaries in 1974 (and possibly before then) there had been a standard pass rate throughout the borough, all children having to achieve the same standard in tests and assessment in order to get a grammar school place. The Labour councillor however, produced a press cutting to show that until 1975 different pass rates applied to different areas in order to improve the opportunities for children in particularly deprived areas to get a grammar school place. Thus, a pupil attending one school could (in the past) get a grammar school place on the basis of a lower measure of attainment than a child at another school. (There is also some evidence to suggest that the pass rate in Labourville before comprehensivization varied in a similar way, 7.8.4, Respondent 24.)

Debates about secondary education in Torytown became even more complex when its secondary modern schools were renamed in the late 1980s. They are now called 'high' schools and, in one case a 'comprehensive' school, thus adding to the confusion about definitions that is considered in 7.8.1. Some secondary schools in both Labourville and Torytown are called 'high' schools or 'comprehensive' schools, although the systems are radically different. In Torytown 'high' or 'comprehensive' schools are attended by those pupils remaining after the 'creaming off' of others to attend independent or grammar schools. In Labourville 'high' or 'comprehensive' schools cater for the full range of abilities. It is easy to speculate about the reasoning behind the re-labelling of secondary modern schools in Torytown. The effect of such a change may be to simultaneously reduce the stigma associated with a secondary modern school (7.8.4 Respondent no. 33) and reduce the status of comprehensive schools. As a result the debate in Torytown may become more confusing as comprehensive schools become more closely related to secondary modern schools in the public imagination.

Most Torytown voters were aware of the continuing debate about systems of secondary education but few had any detailed knowledge about the selection process. This is not peculiar to Torytown, or to this point in time, as most of us (the researcher included) who were selected for a particular type of education at 11+, have little knowledge about how the process in which we were involved worked. The foundation of debates on often vaguely constructed definitions of reality is considered further in Chapter 5. Here it can simply be noted that, the local context of education in Torytown adds its own unique dimension to recent national debates about choice, selection and the respective merits of various types of schools.

4 Interest: Who cares about education?

The association between attitudes to education and voting behaviour is considered in Chapter 8. That chapter also includes a more general debate . about the issue model of voting behaviour. In this chapter the discussion is mainly broad and theoretical. It records findings from secondary sources and other exploratory research that was carried out in order to identify salient variable. Some case study data is included but the emphasis is on the early stages of the research (2.1). In asking 'Who cares about education?' I was trying to identify theoretical quotas to be used in the design of the case study samples. More data about interest in education as a political issue is provided in Chapter 6, where arguments provided here regarding the basically instrumental nature of interest are supported by findings about attitudes to public expenditure on education.

4.1 Instrumental interest

Opinion polls often offer respondents a list of issues from which to choose those that they consider most important. This makes analysis relatively simple but weakens the validity of the findings. Those issues that respondents consider to be more important may not be on the list and the use of a list also gives no indication of how interested the respondents are. Some people are very interested in a wide range of issues, whilst others are largely apathetic or interested in only selective issues, and the relative positioning of a list of given topics does not provide a reliable measurement of comparative levels of interest. It does, however, provide some information about the respondents who place education in a relatively high or low position in their order of political interests.

In the British Political Participation Study (Chapter 9 and Parry, Moyser and Day, 1992) the first criticism was dealt with, as respondents were given a free response type question with no prior limitation to a range of issues. They were given a free choice to list the 'issues, needs or problems' which had been most important to them 'over the past 5 years or so.' Other comments in the questions drew attention to the 'public realm', rather than to private issues. Analysis of such responses is time consuming and difficult on a large scale but the BPPS findings have, as a result, both the usual advantages of quantitative data (especially greater generalizability) and qualitative data (greater reliability). The second criticism has also been acknowledged by this method, as the lack of a list of issues means that the disinterested were less able to masquerade as interested by simply toying with the menu. It was easier for respondents to say that no issue has been considered important.

It is not surprising to find that in the BPPS 35 per cent of respondents had no agenda of issues and that the rest had an average of only two issues (Parry, Moyser and Day, 1986, p.40). There was no one dominant issue, although about a quarter of the issues mentioned (including unemployment) could be described as 'economic'. Obviously, the provision of a list would have increased the number of issues mentioned and exaggerated the importance of such issues to some individuals. Respondents were not asked to explain the reasons for their voting behaviour in the Greater Manchester Study or the British Social Attitude surveys. On Parry, Moyser and Day's chart of issue weighting, education scored 6.5 per cent compared to 9.6 per cent for unemployment and 4.9 per cent for health (Parry, Moyser and Day, 1992, Table 11.1). Their findings also emphasised the instrumental nature of interest in individual issues and the compounding of this when active interest is considered.

> One plausible hypothesis, therefore is that action may be a function of the immediacy of the issue or problem, and of the apparent ease or difficulty of finding satisfactory solutions. This would begin to suggest a typical issue agenda rather different from that where 'big issues' provoked 'big action'. (Parry, Moyser and Day, 1992, p.242)

> The evidence suggests, therefore, that when people do step out into the public realm, it is rather more with the defence of their personal and sectional interests in mind, than those of the wider community, or at the very least the two are intertwined. (Parry, Moyser and Day, 1992, p.250)

My 'specialist' interviewees' (2.5) main impression about voters' attitudes to education as a political issue was that what little interest there was in education was mainly instrumental. In his following comments a Conservative councillor (2.5) typified the experiences of all councillors:

. . . as a specific issue it tends to get a lot of publicity because obviously the number of people involved in it tend to be active, articulate people. But the mass of the electorate don't want to know.

He repeatedly emphasised the type of people involved; as '. . . a band of intelligent, articulate people with very strong views'. Where several generations have passed through the same school, '. . . a kind of emotional loyalty', builds up.

> This is particularly so in socio-economic areas like the south [of Torytown] where you've got intelligent, articulate people - but still very parochial. No matter what happens to the rest but 'keep your hands off my school'.

Regarding the effects of falling rolls:

> . . . people are concerned about the effect on their own children. 'Do so and so to everyone else so long as you don't touch mine.' It tends to be a localized effect by the electorate rather than an overall anti-school closure.

An instrumental interest in education as a personal problem rather than a public issue has been noticeable throughout this research. Interest in, and knowledge of, educational issues was generally low but highest amongst those closest to the education system. Educational issues were considered important and interest was stimulated when they invaded respondents' personal lives. If a respondent had a child at school sub-issues became more noticeable: if, for example, that child's teacher went on strike, the political element may take on a previously unrecognised importance and, if the child's school was threatened with closure, the respondent may become uncharacteristically active in defence of what was now regarded as a personal interest. Interviews in Torytown and Labourville reinforced this finding as similar statements were frequently repeated.

> As I'm not directly involved, I've very little interest. This is the whole point of it isn't it? How it affects you - and it doesn't. (Floating voter)

> Education doesn't bother me really because I've got no children of an educational age. I suppose it depends what's important to you. (Informant No.44, Q13)

42

The use of the expression 'educational age' is quite salient in this research (see 4.4) because it reflects a common belief that education is not a lifelong experience. Education was considered less important as a political issue than those issues that were more easily perceived as imposing on personal territory throughout informants' lives.

> Education only lasts a short time but you pay tax all your life. (Informant No.15, comment at end of interview)

The poll tax, National Health Service and a perceived rise in crime were frequently mentioned as being higher on individual issue. agendas than education. This suggests that a lack of interest in education as a political issue should not infer a lack of interest in political issues in general. Although employment in the education system will also lead to an instrumental interest in education as a political issue, few voters are employed in education and it is still the consumption of education that is generally regarded as having priority.

> Our daughter is a school secretary and my wife is a cleaner in the university. Now our sons are married and out of the way we don't need to take as much interest. (Informant No.7, Q5)

An abundance of similar quotes from a small number (52) of semi-structured interviews supports the findings of many political scientists, including Verba, Nie and Petrocik (1976, p.106-9) and Dunleavy and Husbands (1985, p.9), regarding the instrumental reasons why people engage in politics. Moreover, this is closely tied to theoretical approaches to the study of political issues and to feminist critiques of 'male-stream writers' (Siltanen and Stanworth, 1984, p.195) for their definitions of the political and the non-political. The linkage between these elements can be seen in C. Wright Mills' attempt to provide a definition of public issues by contrasting them with personal 'troubles'. Note that he did not call them *political* issues.

> Troubles occur within the character of the individual and within the range of his immediate relations with others; they have to do with his self and with those limited areas of social life of which he is directly and personally aware. . . .
>
> A trouble is a private matter: values cherished by an individual are felt by him to be threatened.
>
> Issues have to do with matters that transcend these local environments

43

of the individual and the range of his inner life. They have to do with the organization of many such milieux into the institutions of a historical society as a whole, with the ways in which various milieux overlap and interpenetrate to form the larger structure of social and historical life. An issue is a public matter: some value cherished by publics is felt to be threatened. Often there is a debate about what that value really is and about what it is that really threatens it. This debate is often without focus if only because it is the very nature of an issue, unlike even widespread trouble, that it cannot very well be defined in terms of the immediate and everyday environments of ordinary men. An issue, in fact, often involves a crisis in institutional arrangements, and often too it involves what Marxists call 'contradictions' or 'antagonisms'. (C.W. Mills, 1970, pp.8 and 9)

If this is applied to education, it can be seen that at a private, personal level troubles can involve the education of oneself or one's children, choice of school, choice of courses, examination results, complaints about the institution, teachers and so on. At an issue level, in which education is a public matter, concern may be about the whole educational system, for example, teaching methods in general, types of school, the finance of schools, types of examinations etc.. One phenomenon can be viewed differently according to the two levels; for example, action by teachers over the loss of their negotiating rights and recent complaints of shortage of cash to maintain schools could each be described as 'a crisis in institutional arrangements' at an issue level. At the level of personal 'troubles' they would be manifest in the difficulties families experience when their children are sent home from school due to the absence of a teacher or in requests for contributions to the school fund.

More will be said about the feminist critique in section 4.3 but, for the moment it can be noted that the problem created by comparing public issues with personal 'troubles' is not simply Mills' habitual use of masculine pronouns, and the critique is not even aimed at him specifically. The problem relates to the tendency amongst 'male-stream writers' to designate the private arena of personal 'troubles' as non-political and to associate women with that private arena. Thus, a problem is only regarded as being political when it enters the public realm and transcends local environments. Yet, if findings about the instrumental nature of interest in political issues are considered, the process appears to be in reverse order; a political problem is more likely to be recognised as such and become meaningful to the individual when it is perceived as moving from the public realm into the private arena (9.8).

A possible reconciliation of this debate lies in considering two models, not one. In considering personal 'troubles' and public issues (in Mills' terms) we are working on a definition of 'issues' at a national level, when an aggregate of personal 'troubles' is perceived as large enough to be regarded as a public issue. In considering definitions of the private and the public we are working on a definition of 'political', where the private domain is regarded as non-political and the public as political. It is with the latter type of model that most arguments have arisen. Education, in particular, may be associated with the private domain in which the family is nurtured and socialized. An 'educational age' may be regarded as a stage in a natural process of personal growth that can be completed and left behind. From this perspective it may be seen as a non-controversial and therefore non-political fact of life.

This image of acceptance of a natural phenomenon is, however, challenged when we consider the involvement of supposedly public political problems in the private arena. Private and individual educational experiences are structured by the social and political environment; by for example, the type of schooling provided, the level of state spending on education, and modes of assessment. Public becomes private and political issues become personal 'troubles' as individuals consume the educational services provided (or not provided) by the state. Even the consumption of a private (i.e. not state) education is a political act, as it is a response to a political issue in the form of supposed defects in the state school system.

When considering the instrumental nature of interests in education as a political issue it is, nevertheless possible to use the image of private and public domains. It helps to explain respondents' greater awareness and concern about those public issues that are seen as having intruded into their personal lives.

4.2 Parents

The state defines parents as a group and is supposed to ensure that all parents have the right and the obligation to send their children to school. In the 1980s Conservative governments also popularized the concept of 'parental choice', the expressed aim being to give parents more power to secure for their children what they believe to be the best education. The image presented is of a coherent group of rational adults who are devoted to the best interests of their children. Differences between parents tend to be obscured even within an individualist political philosophy because, although individuality in terms of demands on the education system (and in particular the demand to opt out) is recognised, diversity of social condition is obscured. Thus, the idealized blanket term of 'parent' invokes a united image that does not acknowledge those differences in culture, ethnic group, class (social or occupational) or levels of affluence that may divide, rather than unite the interests of parents.

Certainly, the rosy image promoted by 'parent power' is not associated with parents who are struggling to provide their children with even the most basic necessities of life, parents who abuse their children (physically or mentally), absent parents who are fathers and mothers in name only or parents who simply are no help to their children's educational progress (10.1.2).

Whilst arguing that the parents of children currently at school are more likely to be interested in education as a political issue it is important to acknowledge that some parents have very little interest in their childrens' education, let alone in the wider political debate (see 7.9.5). It will be shown (4.3) that mothers tend to be more interested and involved than fathers and (7.9.5) that parents' social class and/or attitudes can act as constraints on educational achievement.

Nevertheless, parents are more likely than non-parents to be interested in education as a political issue simply because educational issues make a more obvious intrusion into their lives (8.4.3). At least since the time of Rowntree (1901) it has been recognised that the two most vulnerable stages in the life-cycle are old age and 'early middle life' (Edgell and Duke, 1985, p.1 and p.16). Parents therefore have the overlapping responsibilities of supporting their children financially and promoting their educational development. Awareness of education as a political issue is heightened where the two burdens overlap but, even so it may be a temporary concern and related only to the immediate personal situation. One informant in 1988 said of proposed changes to the education system in Torytown;

> I'm very interested with having children in school and working in a school. (Informant No.42, Q39A)

Her children were at primary school and, when asked about the Assisted Places scheme, she showed little interest.

> I've not really thought about it. I suppose I'm thinking about my children's immediate needs. Its one of those things I might think about if and when it arises. (Informant No.42, Q39B)

Edgell and Duke noticed that the peak of perceived impact of the public spending cuts was amongst the 30-39 year old age group (the group most likely to have children at school) and that the highest level of consumer cuts consciousness was associated with state education users (Edgell and Duke, 1986b, p.2, and see my section 6.4). At the first interview in the Greater Manchester Surveys (1980/1) the level of cuts consciousness among state education users was 47 per cent. This was largely due to the 63 per cent of Torytown residents who attributed changes in educational provision to cuts in educational spending. At the second interview (in 1983/4) it was found that education consumer cuts consciousness had decreased due to a decline in the salience of education cuts over the intervening years. Education cuts consciousness was, however, still relatively high compared to all other services in the area, with the differential between the two Local Education Authority areas remaining large, at 56 per cent in Torytown and 24 per cent in Labourville.

4.3 Gender

The greater cuts consciousness amongst parents in general and amongst mothers in particular was reported by Edgell and Duke after the first Greater Manchester Survey (in 1980-1). They found that the perceived impact of education spending cuts amongst women with dependents in all age groups was greater than that of men in the same situation. It was noticeable that women without young dependents did not report a greater impact of spending cuts. This suggests that the trend is related to mothers (with young dependents) rather than to women in general. The possibility that an awareness of educational changes is related to interest in educational issues is further suggested by Parry, Moyser and Day's (1992, p.262) findings that over twice as many women as men put education at the top of their issue agendas. Also, according to the British Social Attitudes 1986 Report women (but not men) were becoming less likely to choose 'smaller classes' as the main priority for improving primary schools (Jowell et al, 1986, Table 7.2). The writers claimed that the gradual drop in the proportion of large primary classes was a factor that was probably more apparent to women, because of their more direct contact with their children's schools. This impression that mothers knew more than fathers was reinforced during interviews in 1988 when men frequently suggested that I interview their wives or tried to enlist the help of their wives or children in answering questions. The reverse was not the case, and women were generally prepared to deal with questions unaided.

Why did women tend to be more interested than men? More frequent contact with their childrens' schools is one reason, but women tend to be more involved with the welfare state as producers as well as consumers. Edgell and Duke found that cuts in public spending affected women more than men. They found that, although only 44 per cent of all public sector employees were women, three out of four welfare state workers (i.e. in education, health and the social services) were female and three out of five teachers in public sector schools were female. Thus, they argued that,

The restructuring of the welfare state affects women more than men in three ways: first, as producers - three-quarters of welfare state workers are women; second , as consumers - women are the main users of collective social provision, e.g. women are significantly more dependent on public transport; and, third, as the major providers of care in the family - the less the welfare state does, the more is done by women. (Edgell and Duke, 1992, p.118/9)

As women have more frequent contact with public provision than do men, how does this relate to the debate about private and public domains? Feminists criticised 'male-stream writers' (Siltanen and Stanworth, 1984, p.195) for defining and evaluating political activity so as to exclude women's interests. In this way public provision has come to be associated with the home and the family, which is defined as private and apolitical.

Male-stream writers argue that the assignment of women to domestic roles, their primary commitment to home and family, their affective relations, and their indirect relation - through the family - to public life restrict the options for political engagement and limit the development of the political understanding and commitment that would encourage political involvement. By assuming the private is apolitical and that women are private beings, these writers consistently place women in a marginal relation to the public and the political. (Siltanen and Stanworth, 1984, p.195)

If education is defined as a part of the private and supposedly non-political domain in which children are nurtured, it is effectively excluded from the framework of political debate. Educational sub-issues are then seen as non-controversial and the political manipulation of public knowledge is ignored. Yet education is a public issue, its provision is part of the public sector, its costs contribute a great deal to public spending (and form the largest proportion of Local Authority spending) and the public has a vested interest in its generation of public knowledge. Siltanen and Stanworth argued that it was wrong to equate only masculine definitions of the public domain with the political because, '...it ignores the question of why matters that occur in public space are sometimes regarded as political and sometimes not,' and,

...it obscures the extent to which public life in liberal democracies is depoliticized. Routine exclusions of ordinary women and men from the assumption of responsibility for the definition and articulation of political affairs results in apathy and pragmatic acquiescence becoming the foundations of government stability. (Siltanen and Stanworth, 1984, p,197)

Siltanen and Stanworth also argued that, even if the private domain is defined as political, women should not be primarily associated with it or regarded as most responsible for its defence.

> ... to state that women learn political lessons in their 'private' world, even to argue that those lessons are crucial correctives to a 'masculine' political ethos is problematic. It implies that women have a unique responsibility for bringing the humanistic principles derived from the experience of nurturing and caring in the private world of personal relationships and family to bear on the public sphere. This skirts perilously close to recommending that women shoulder responsibility for humanizing a public arena brutalized by men's neglect. It ignores the potential for transformation of men's consciousness, and, far from exploding artificial divisions between public (male) and private (female), it threatens to institutionalize those divisions within the heart of the public sphere itself. (Siltanen and Stanworth, 1984, p.199)

Women do tend to be more interested in educational issues for instrumental reasons, partly because of their closer traditional involvement as mothers and partly because of their greater productive involvement. Using a feminist perspective it is possible to see that this can lead to the downgrading of education in political terms. Other 'masculine' issues, associated with the workplace rather than the home, may take precedence in the public imagination; for example (male rather than female) unemployment, (male dominated) industrial action, and reductions in taxation (which have a greater effect on men's higher average hourly rate of pay, whilst reducing spending on the public services with which women have more contact).

4.4 Educational experience

Informants' educational experiences are described in 7.2.3 where changing educational standards are considered and in 7.9.5 where the influence of parents on educational choice is discussed. However, the many experiences of education are difficult to categorize or quantify. Here the main concern is the extent to which the experience of further of higher education affects attitudes to education as a political issue. Surveys often ask respondents for their school-leaving age and the results can be crosstabulated with other variable. Their findings indicate that the most highly educated take the greatest interest in education as a political issue, tend to be most active in that area and have the least traditional views.

Parry, Moyser and Day's analysis of individual issue agendas indicates the extent of this greater interest:

> Those with college or degree qualifications are twice as likely as the average member of the public to refer to the topic (15.3%). Whilst constituting 20.9% of respondents, those who had received higher education offered 42.3% of the education issues. Hence, although education affects in one way or another a very large section of the population, the voice that authorities are especially likely to hear is that of the well-educated who have gained long experience of the system and can, presumably, reflect on the extent of such benefits as they may have received and may wish to pass on to others. (Parry, Moyser and Day, 1992, p.262)

The BSA report on personal action scores (9.4) verified Parry, Moyser and Day's findings that those who have been longest in education are most willing to become actively involved in education and politics. However, confidence in personal efficacy (as a result of educational achievement) may not have as great an influence on levels of activity in the field of educational politics as personal interest in education (Chapter 9). Voters who have had some sort of further or higher education are less likely to perceive a limited 'educational age' (4.1) that ends at school-leaving age and more likely to view exposure to education as a lifelong process. Thus, education as a political issue can be seen as relevant to them personally. As they regard it as so important, they tend to give it a high priority when considering public spending options (see 6.4 and Table 6.16).

The voting behaviour of teachers and the university educated is considered further in Chapter 8, where it is shown that their support for the Conservative Party declined rapidly during the 1980s, as Conservative education policies took effect. Indeed, the experience of education to degree level seemed to be more closely related to attitudes to education as a political issue than any other independent variable. Not only were the most highly educated least likely to vote Conservative but they were also least likely to stand as Conservative candidates in a General Election (5.4).

This may be associated with indications that the most highly educated have the least traditional and authoritarian attitudes (7.3). For example, the BSA 1983/4 survey found that those respondents with the highest school-leaving age had the least traditional attitudes about women's role in society and that those with the lowest school-leaving age had the most traditional attitudes. In the BSA 5th. Report it was reported that (on a scale of responses to nine general questions) graduates had the least authoritarian responses and Conservative identifiers the most authoritarian responses (Jowell et al, 1988, p.51).

50

Graduates were, for example, least likely to say that homosexuality was wrong (see 7.6.2).

In general, therefore, it seems that the relationship between higher education, attitudes in general, voting behaviour and other political activity deserves more attention than could be given in this research.

4.5 Social and occupational class

It was quite clear at an early stage in the research that extremes of affluence and poverty could effect attitudes to education, either directly or as an intervening variable (associated with educational achievement). During exploratory interviews councillors and officials in Labourville and Torytown frequently commented on the supposed apathy of many low income groups. A chief education officer described the level of interest as a logical reaction to personal circumstances.

> I happen to think that education's the most important thing in the world . . . It's easy for education to be vitally important if you're living in a nice house, you've got a good job and you want to see you children in the same situation; education's vitally important isn't it? If you sit in the inner city where you see a certain amount of hopelessness about your own position and the fact that no matter how well your children might do at school - is that going to get them a job - education may not seem as relevant as it does to the middle class areas. I can understand that. I think that there are issues that are considered important. Housing is obviously important. Employment, or rather lack of employment, is extremely important to many. I think that support for one-parent families - the sort of support they need to sustain themselves in the city - is important. I think that those issues to those people are clearly more important. (Chief education officer, Labourville)

Councillors and officials repeatedly emphasised their impression that it was mainly affluent, highly educated people who took an active interest in the politics of education (see section 9.4) and that the least affluent were the least active.

Obviously the possible association between (social or occupational) class and attitudes to education is worth further·investigation, but I have left this for a future report. There are several reasons for this. Firstly, the present research was heavily dependent on the Greater Manchester Surveys as both a secondary source and a sampling frame from which to select the smaller case study samples. Extremes of affluence and poverty were omitted from the original GMS sample in order to provide wards that had the same socio-economic mix and to test theories regarding the political allegiance of manual worker home-owners. As a result it was found that there were few respondents in some neo-marxist class categories. Edgell and Duke found (1985, p.19, Table 1) that in the census only 2-4 per cent in the two areas sampled could be classed as employers and 4-10 per cent as petty bourgeoisie (on Eric Olin Wright's Mark I, four class scheme). To use such social class categories to structure my small sample (of 52) would have involved working from a small panel base. Secondly, it was found that variations in political orientation were more closely related to consumption location than to social class. In particular, it was found that interest in educational issues was more closely related to the instrumental interests of parents (mothers in particular), sectoral cleavages and educational experience than to social class (whether measured as relationship to the means of production, a manual/non-manual worker division or an occupational hierarchy). Thirdly, problems relating to the operationalization of class in social research create particular difficulties in the present research. These problems include consideration of the following questions.

Who do we consider when measuring class; the individual respondent or the whole household? There are several reasons why the unit of analysis should be the household rather than the respondent. The household acts as a basic unit of economic exchange (both in terms of production and consumption) and the experiences of significant others within the household can clearly effect the attitudes of individual household members. Duke and Edgell suggest that stratification problems could be resolved by combining class categories with a household measure based on dominance or by using multiple indicators. This would answer criticisms about the traditional emphasis on the classification of the 'head of household' by accommodating the influence of various members of the household. However, Duke and Edgell agree with Erikson (1984) who suggested that the nature of the dependent variable should be considered when decisions are being made about the measurement of class.

Erikson proposed two class concepts; 'work position', with the respondent as the unit of classification, and 'class position', with households as the unit of classification. A work-related position is (he argued) concerned with the individual/respondent's behaviour and attitudes, and a class (or market-related) position is concerned with collective/ household consumption behaviour and attitudes. As the respondent's own attitudes to education as a political issue constitute the dependent variable in the present context, Erikson's proposal would suggest that 'work position' is most relevant and that the respondent should be used as the unit of classification (for education producers). However, as collective household consumption of education may influence respondents' attitudes to education the problem of deciding which unit of analysis is most appropriate is not easily resolved.

How are women to be classified? Duke and Edgell found (1992, p.34) that the manual/non-manual divide had little relevance to women's jobs. Such a classification would mean that the majority of employed women would be middle class (non-manual) and the majority of men would be working class (manual). To confuse matters even more, many women frequently move between manual and routine non-manual jobs thus limiting the value of manual/non-manual classification schemes.

Dunleavy and Husbands (1985) found that five out of six employed women were located in routine non-manual or unskilled manual categories. Thus, they noted that gender as a variable is logically prior to occupational class, having major effects on the occupational classes to which individuals are assigned. We can therefore see that social class categories such as Wright Mark 1 are less contaminated by gender effects than occupational class categories. If respondents were classified according to Wright Mark 1, the majority of both sexes would be working class, with women more proletarianized than men. However, it has already been shown that the traditional female role regarding domestic consumption of public services and the greater involvement of women in the production of public services are likely to have a greater effect on female interest in educational provision than is their location (or their husbands' location) within a hierarchy of the economically active. It is possible that class may have a greater effect when attitudes rather than level of interest are considered.

How do we define 'economically active'? If a respondent based measure of economic activity is used we must decide whether or not to include part-time workers. How many hours of work are needed before a respondent can be classified as employed or unemployed? In theory one hour of paid employment per week could classify a respondent as economically active; yet a classification as unemployed may be more appropriate.

Should the research cover all adults or only the economically active? The economically inactive could be classified by their previous class or occupational position. There is a strong case for classifying pensioners and others who have worked previously by their former position but problems arise in the classification of respondents who have never worked. Bechhoffer (1969) has also suggested that only the temporarily unemployed should be categorised by their previous occupation. Another possibility is that the long-term unemployed could be categorized as a separate class entirely. This might prove to be particularly useful when the main emphasis of a research project is on levels of affluence (see 9.8, 10.1.1 and 10.1.2). Indeed, for the case studies, a quota of informants who were not in paid employment was selected. However, the quota included pensioners, people with disabilities, students, housewives who were not seeking paid employment, and people who were actively looking for jobs. The diversity of circumstances and attitudes within that group suggested that a common classification was not entirely appropriate. Whatever solutions are attempted, the unemployed are a problematic group to categorize.

Thus we can see that an accurate picture of social class is less likely when the unit of class analysis is the respondent rather than the whole household. Edgell and Duke favoured Eriksons suggestion that households should be classified according to the highest occupational or social class in the family unit. This seems to solve several problems but other problems remain.

Which measure of class should be used? The options are varied but mainly relate to either occupational class schemes (in which primacy is given to manual and non-manual boundaries) or social class schemes (in which divisions are related to the means of production). If occupational class schemes were used in the present research a hierarchical structure could be identified, whereas social class is not totally hierarchical. However, the classification of women would cause particular problems. It has already been noted that social class categories are less contaminated by gender effects but the use of neo-marxist categories would also cause problems in this research as few respondents can be labelled as either employers or petty bourgeoisie.

Dunleavy and Husbands have used a scheme that combines the two approaches. They used the basic Eric Olin Wright scheme of four social classes and then sub-divided the controllers and workers by the manual/non-manual cleavage. By combining social class and occupational class they provide a possible framework for future research into the relationship between social class and attitudes to education as a political issue. However, the many operationalization problems have meant that social class has not been incorporated in the design of the theoretical sample used for the 1988 case studies.

Some of the data collected can nevertheless be used in a future study of the relationship between social class and attitudes to education. Findings reported in 6.4 about the relationship between income levels, social class and occupational class and attitudes to educational expenditure (Table 6.16) deserve particular attention. There it is shown that the tendency to favour increased spending on education declined as Marxist class categories were scaled, but increased as the level of income was scaled. This inverse relationship between the effects of social class and income levels may be explained by the importance of level of education (4.4) and its closer relationship to income than to social class.

4.6 Sectoral cleavages

It has already been noted that the parents of schoolchildren (mothers in particular), are likely to have an instrumental interest in education as a political issue (4.2). The consumption of a service either directly or indirectly (as in the case of parents) is likely to increase interest in that service. Employment that is either directly (for example, teachers) or indirectly (for example, other local authority employees) related to the education system is also likely to increase interest in educational provision and related issues. Such findings about the instrumental nature of political interests have been elaborated into a concept of sectoral cleavages that can be used in the analysis of attitudes to education. Dunleavy in particular (1980) has used the work of O'Connor (1973), Habermas (1976) and Castells (1977) to argue that consumption sectors exist wherever consumption processes involve a competition between private/market and public/state forms of provision. Edgell and Duke noted:

> Sectoral theory refers to divisions between those who are dependent upon the public for their employment (i.e. as producers) and/or for certain services (i.e. as consumers), and those who produce and/or consume in the private sector. (Edgell and Duke, 1991, p.40)

Parry and Moyser explained quite clearly why, although sectors may cut across class they can also be seen as being related to levels of affluence:

> The upshot of the theories [of consumption sectors] is that those who are able to use private services (which means that they are able to pay, often highly, for them) will tend to support those party policies which favour their maintenance and extension and will have less interest in support for costly public provision. This leaves a large body of, usually poorer, persons who have to rely on public services and thus appear to have an interest in policies for the support of the national health service, or state education. (Parry, Moyser and Day, 1992, p.138)

My research detracts slightly from consumption sector theories at this point as, although the current consumption or non-consumption of education has been built into the theoretical sample (for the 52 interviews), no attempt has been made to build in a distinction between consumption of a private or a state education. This would require a more specialized piece of research involving sampling from a relatively small proportion of privately educated children (about 7 per cent, see 7.9). Not only was it easier to split informants into just two groups of consumers and non-consumers, but the emphasis on electoral behaviour in general suggested that minority groups of this size should be excluded from decisions about the structural design of the research. As information about the people to be interviewed in 1988 was four years out of date, predictions about consumption or non-consumption were likely to be inaccurate in some cases. It would have been even more difficult to predict the type of service consumed. Findings about the type of education and other services consumed therefore appeared at random.

Duke and Edgell recognised the problems involved in utilizing educational sector in their analysis of findings from a randomly produced sample for the Greater Manchester Surveys. They included education in the analysis of their first hypothesis about the relative degree of fragmentation of social classes but excluded it from the latter stages of their analysis, using only health, housing and transport (Duke and Edgell, 1991, p.42). Education was excluded for three reasons; firstly because the private education sample was very small, secondly because formal education is usually consumed by households only at particular stages in the family life-cycle (i.e. only by 35 per cent of the households in their 1980/1 survey) and thirdly because the 1983 British Election Study (used by Duke and Edgell for secondary analysis) lacked appropriate data on educational sectors.

Duke and Edgell found that both,

> . . . social class and consumption sector influence the ideological structuration of public spending issues but differences between consumption locations remain within social classes. (1984, p.28)

Thus, of the GMS respondents who were owner occupiers, 80 per cent owned their own car, 71 per cent were in an occupational pension scheme, 13 per cent were in a private health care scheme and 8 per cent were using private education. The equivalent percentage for local authority renters were 43 per cent, 45 per cent, 7 per cent and 4 per cent respectively (Edgell and Duke, 1986a, p.494). Controllers emerged from both GMS datasets as more privatised than workers and employers were the most privatised of all (Duke and Edgell, 1984, p.18). We can therefore see that consumption locations tend to be cumulative and related to social class but that there are differences between cumulative consumption locations within social classes. This 'cumulative sectors' approach can be contrasted with a 'fragmented sectors' approach in the context of education. Education sector can be classified as one of several consumption sectors to generate a scale of private or public consumption; or cumulative sectors. This approach was favoured by Duke and Edgell, and Dunleavy and Husbands who argued that attitudes to various policy areas could be studied by establishing an overall consumption sector location.   Involvement in mainly private or mainly public modes of consumption generates group interests that can be incorporated into political party differentiation.   According to Dunleavy (1980), the fact that the non-manual middle class is mainly privatised reinforces its class identification and its links with Conservative privatisation policies.   However, he noted that working class consumption locations are more fragmented (between private and public sector) and that this weakens the links between the Labour party and the working class.   Duke and Edgell confirmed this when they found that variations in political orientation were more closely related to overall consumption location than to social class (1984, p.175/7, and see 8.3.2).

Another 'fragmented sectors' approach has been suggested by Saunders (1981) who noted that individual experiences of public and private provision do not entirely overlap, but can vary according to the policy area involved. Education as a political issue can then be seen to have its own distinctive political identity and individual educational experiences may be quite different from experiences of other consumption sectors.   Dunleavy acknowledged this to a certain extent when he subdivided consumption processes into those which are predominantly public (education is an example) and those which are predominantly private (for example housing).   Nevertheless, he also claimed that although education is predominantly a public process, the educational cleavage has had a political impact far beyond its numerical significance (1980).   All of this leads me to conclude that a fragmented approach in which education is considered as one political issue and one consumption sectoral location (as opposed to part of a scale of cumulative sectors) is most appropriate in the present context.

The theoretical approach is more straightforward when production sector is considered.   In this case respondents are categorised as public employees, private employees/self-employed, or not in paid employment.   Edgell and Duke found that respondents' production sector proved to be more stable over time than respondents' class, however defined.   At the time of the 1983/4 survey, 93 per cent of their panel were still in the sector that they were in in 1980/1 (Edgell and Duke, 1985, p.322).

4.7 Local political control

Duke and Edgell found that, although consumption locations for four services (education, housing, health and transport) varied according to social class, the class differences were less pronounced in the Greater Manchester Survey than in a national sample, mainly due to the socially mixed nature of the two GMS wards (Duke and Edgell, 1984, p.18).   They suggested that, although local state issues are frequently consumption based, political action in response to these issues may also involve an important class component. Protest against the spending cuts in Labourville was found to be overwhelmingly trade union based (class) whereas in Torytown action groups tended to focus more on single issues (sectoral) such as education. In the present context such findings can more readily be interpreted as a reflection of the different emphasis on educational debate in the two areas (3.2). Edgell and Duke also found that, although in both areas most knowledge about spending cuts was about education, education was reported more often as a sphere of impact in Torytown than in Labourville. In Torytown 21 per cent of all respondents and 41% of households with children in full-time education saw themselves as affected by education cuts whereas the corresponding figures for Labourville were only 13 per cent and 23 per cent.

It will be shown (6.3) that educational spending cuts were more severe in Torytown than in Labourville and that this reflects the influence of local political control rather than simply central government dictat. Both local authorities were subjected to central government pressure to cut spending but their responses were quite different. The Labourville council was particularly reluctant to cut any educational spending and retained its commitment to not only spending on state schools and further education but also to the continued maintenance of its excellent nursery facilities. In Torytown however, where nursery facilities were minimal, the council was prepared to make radical cuts in its spending on state schools whilst (unlike Labourville) paying the fees for pupils to attend private schools.

ʹEducation has therefore been more prominent as a political issue in Torytown, where cuts in educational spending (on state education) were more visible and debates about the future system of secondary education continued throughout the period of this research. We can therefore see that local political control and the different foundations of educational debate may have a pronounced effect on public interest in, and attitudes towards, education as a political issue.

5 Knowledge: Bias and the framework of educational debate

5.1 The framework of knowledge about education

The images associated with the words 'knowledge' and 'bias' suggest that there is some absolute notion of truth that can be understood, communicated and accurately reproduced; yet in the framework of educational debate the 'truth' is a very illusive concept. Knowledge of educational sub-issues is acquired after a process of communication in which some facts are omitted (intentionally or not), some distorted and many are reinterpreted several times. If we imagine a game of Chinese whispers (in which a message is passed in a chain from person to person) we can get an impression of the potential for distortion in the transmission of knowledge about education as a political issue. This was particularly noticeable when, in the case study interviews, informants' 'knowledge' about the murder of a schoolboy from an Asian family was assessed. Myths emerged, based on distorted media reports, hearsay or sometimes half understood messages about an unpublished official report.

Yet, even closer to original sources our knowledge is not necessarily of some absolute 'truth'. Foucault (1972-1977) showed how areas of knowledge which are often taken to be natural have been socially constructed and how the 'discourses' and 'discursive practices' that are usually associated with professional practices can imply that socially constructed knowledge is knowledge of some sort of truth. Several writers (including Bourdieu and Passeron, 1977, Young, 1971, Bowles and Gintis, 1976) have also argued that, if any knowledge is regarded as superior, it is because those in power have defined it as such and imposed their definition on others. This is so in the case of public claims about the current state of the education system as well as in the knowledge transmitted within the classroom.

The implication is that there is no objective way of evaluating knowledge, that the researcher's knowledge is as restricted as anyone else's and that

59

perhaps the debate should stop there. However, it is common, when views on education are expressed, for the writers to claim as 'fact' their own, subjective views. Arguments about a supposed fall in educational standards are, for example, contradicted by statistics concerning the proportion and level of examination passes but supported by subjective views about discipline and literacy (7.2 and 7.3). Before a debate on that subject could be reasonably attempted, agreement would have to be reached about how to measure 'standards' and elements of bias identified. Yet the identification of bias again assumes some recognition of the truth, some firm ground or framework within which the debate can take place, and this poses problems of its own. It is common for favourable/unfavourable measures (the firm ground) of 'standards' to be chosen according to the perspectives of the combatants; examination passes may, for example, be considered sufficient evidence from one perspective but not from another.

Thus, definitions of truth often involve the subjective exclusion of values that are defined as extreme or irrational. Definitions can be seen as layers covering some inner definition of 'truth', each definition being used to justify the next. We can see this in the case already mentioned of the Macdonald investigation into the fatal stabbing of a pupil from an Asian famiIt by a white pupil at Burnage High School, in Manchester (see 7.7). Although the authors of the report and the Government at Westminster favoured publication, the local authority refused to publish the report because of anticipated legal problems. Parts of the report were released to the press and some newspapers (who had already defined the concept of anti-racial education as wrong) interpreted the released parts as a criticism of anti-racial education in general. Limited information about the report was therefore distorted by a biased media before reaching the public, who then imposed on it their own definitions of reality. We therefore need to consider the way that messages are internalised by the public and the conceptual frameworks they employ in the process if we are to try to understand what education as a political issue means to voters, both individually and at a macro level (see 5.5).

5.2 The researcher's personal bias

It is unlikely that anyone can produce a totally objective study of education as a political issue. We are all influenced by our own experiences, in school, in the home and in society at large. The writer's perspective can be partially explained by her social and educational background and some knowledge of this may help the reader to identify and understand any bias in this book. It may, therefore be useful to note that this work is the product of a woman who is a mother (with children attending a state comprehensive school during the

1980s), the daughter of working class parents and the product of a certain pattern of education herself (a description of this would note attendance at state primary and secondary modern schools and further and higher education as a mature student). Simply by assigning herself to a social class, a writer is open to criticisms of bias, because readers may consider that social class is the figment of a biased imagination. The writer's personal perspective must be clarified together with the perspectives of the people being studied in order to identify subjective interpretations. Interpretations may differ from those produced by, for example, a man with no children, the son of middle class parents, and the product of a different type of education (perhaps public school and Oxbridge).

A grounded theory approach has been used in this research in order to maximize the influence of empirical findings and minimize the effect of the researcher's existing theoretical perspective. Such an aim can never be perfectly achieved but the principles on which social research is founded have been utilized to deal with the problem of bias in research. These principles were most succinctly described by Patricia Broadfoot, when president of the British Educational Research Association.

> In the most general terms these ethical principles centre on the pursuit of truth. This does not mean that we embrace any absolute notion of truth since for most of us in the social sciences, this cannot be; but rather we seek to describe, illuminate, portray and hopefully sometimes, even explain, that small section of reality that serves as the focus for our particular enquiry. Recognising that we can never divorce ourselves from our own values - some of which we may not even be aware of overtly - we try to generate insights which are dictated as closely as we can make them by the data themselves. These data are in turn collected according to detailed canons of procedure which years of experience within the various disciplines have consecrated as the most impartial and illuminating basis for scholarship in that field. (Broadfoot, 1988, p.5)

The recognition of personal values can also be used as a tool in the pursuit of objectivity. Wright Mills provided another clear exposition of the approach I have followed in this study:

> I am hopeful of course that all my own biases will show, for I think judgements should be explicit. But I am also trying, regardless of my own judgements, to state the cultural and political meanings of social science. My biases are of course no more or no less biases than those I am going to examine. Let those who do not care for mine use their

rejections of them to make their own explicit and as acknowledged as I am going to make mine! Then the moral problems of social study - the problem of social science as a public issue - will be recognized and discussion will become possible. Then there will be greater self-awareness all around - which is of course a pre-condition for objectivity in the enterprise of social science as a whole. (Mills, 1970, p.21)

Problems arise when writers claim that they have no personal bias and present as fact their own, subjective interpretation of events. For example, arguments about the existence of a private, fee-paying alternative to the state school system often centre upon subjective notions of morality and freedom. Freedom of choice and the immorality of privilege are both presented as facts. Is it not useful to look at the educational/social backgrounds of those involved in the argument? Thus, I can state that I am opposed to the provision of a privileged education for the children of parents who can afford to pay for it and opposed to the bipartite system of secondary education. These might be considered the natural (but subjective) conclusions of someone from the sort of background described above. Is it not a similarly understandable reaction if someone who had a happy childhood in a public school or a grammar school is in favour of their continued existence? In 7.9.4 it will, however, be shown that such reactions are not inevitably associated with the respective types of educational experience.

It should also be noted that attitudes change over time and that this can apply to the researcher as well as the people being studied. My own attitudes changed during the course of this research and personal biases have not been consistent. As a personal bias against the privileged education of a minority of advantaged children has remained, the reader can safely assume an incompatibility with one of the distinguishing features of right-wing perspectives. Experience has also given me a strong, feminist perspective, although, like many busy women, I am ridiculously ignorant of feminist literature. However, as findings have gradually emerged to challenge or support various alternative perspectives, some personal sympathies have also swung from pluralism, to Marxism, to theories of a power elite and finally to the scepticism of politically established definitions of reality described in Chapters 1 and 10. As this scepticism is a core element in this book we can see that many of the researcher's reasoned conclusions and personal attitudes have emerged from empirical findings rather than vice versa.

A rational and sceptical approach also means that a personal antipathy towards private education has not led to an inevitably Marxist bias, as it is acknowledged that educational privilege has existed in both capitalist and non-capitalist societies. The established political system in any state has the power to define reality and the framework within which educational debate takes place. This applies to communist states as well as capitalist states and has been used most effectively in totalitarian states of all types; whether based on left-wing, right-wing or religious ideologies. Conservative (not in a party-political sense) supporters of the status quo will, in any of these states, accept political definitions of reality and thus confine public knowledge within socially constructed boundaries.

5.3 Bias in research methodology

Criticisms of bias in research are dealt with here in terms that relate to the central thesis about the restrictive framework of educational debate. Philosophical and methodological debates regarding bias in social research are so tortuous that they cannot be considered here in any depth. However, three of the main charges are acknowledged and briefly considered. First, feminists have argued that political research has been pervaded by the sexist attitudes of male writers. Second, social scientists in general are criticised for their left-wing bias. Finally, social researchers themselves have complained that interference by Conservative governments in the selection and completion of research projects and in the dissemination of findings has generated a right-wing bias in both the input and the output of social research.

Feminist critiques have already been mentioned (4.3) and the association of women and education with a private and supposedly non-political domain has been considered. Bourque and Grossholtz (1984) go into greater detail by suggesting four categories of distortion in studies of political socialization and political participation. Firstly, they complain of 'fudging the footnotes'. By this they mean that statements about women's political orientation are either misleading versions of the original arguments or are unsupported by the references cited. They claim that,

> . . . political scientists have very clear and decisive beliefs about women's attitudes and roles which they are using in lieu of evidence. (Bourque and Grossholtz, 1984, p.118)

In particular they accuse Lane (1959/64) of doing this by claiming that when partners disagree about politics the wife is most likely to be persuaded by the husband. Their reference to Lane is rather dated but they defend this by noting Lane's later comment that the book had 'weathered well' (Bourque and Grossholtz, 1984, p.108).

This leads to their second complaint that there is a tendency to assume that men influence women's opinions but not vice versa. It had been found that conjugal pairs usually vote alike and have similar political opinions. From this it is concluded that women vote according to their husband's dictates. Duverger is picked out for particular criticism for his remarks that,

> While women have legally ceased to be minors, they still have the mentality of minors in many fields and particularly in politics, they usually accept paternalism on the part of men. The man - husband, fiance, lover, or myth is the mediator between them and the political world. (Quoted by Bourque and Grossholtz, 1984, p.115)

However, no study of female political attitudes supports this idea (Bourque and Grossholtz, 1984, p.117) and it can equally be reasoned that partners are attracted to each other in the first place because of their similar attitudes. I found no evidence of such male domination in my research. Indeed one example of conjugal influence discovered in the research was of a husband whose political views were influenced by his wife's experiences as a teacher: he complained that her long hours and poor pay resulted in his opposition to Conservative education policies.

Bourque and Grossholtz' third complaint is of an unquestioning assumption that the political attitudes that are characteristic of men are used to define mature political behaviour. If female attitudes do not match the resulting definition they are described as either politically naive or apolitical. Again they criticize Lane for arguing that women should devote themselves entirely to their children and not '...extra- curricular activities of an absorbing kind' (1959/64) and for his claim that the effects of the feminist movement on mothers' attitudes had led to a rise in juvenile delinquency. Bourque and Grossholtz counter that,

> ... women are caught in a damned if you do and damned if you don't situation: they do not behave politically like men because of their social roles - and as a result they do not behave very well; but you cannot change their social roles because, if you did, the fabric of society would be torn asunder. (Bourque and Grossholtz, 1984, p.111)

Yet, if the social role of the mother enhances interest in educational issues, the interest may be labelled as private and (using biased logic, see 4.3) not political. Therefore, Bourque and Grossholtz argue that definitions about the nature of politics tend to exclude those attitudes that are characteristic of women.

> Those characteristics and enthusiasms which supposedly sway men (war, controversy, electoral manipulation) are defined as specifically

political, while those characteristics and enthusiasms which supposedly sway women (human need for food, clothing, shelter, adherence to consistent moral principles, the pre-emption of national by human concerns, a rejection of war as rational) are simply not considered political. (Bourque and Grossholtz, 1984, p.118)

A fourth complaint is that women's political contribution is equated with their role as mothers. It has already been shown (4.3) that women with young dependents were more likely to be aware of educational changes than their male counterparts. However, this does not mean that women are only drawn into the educational arena when they become mothers. It has also been observed (4.3) that three out of four welfare state workers and three out of five teachers are female. Thus, their roles as employees may also enhance awareness of and interest in education as a political issue. Furthermore it can be claimed that workplace experiences as well as family circumstances may widen women's political potential in general and not just their interest in education.

Other complaints relate to the supposed left-wing bias in research methodology. Marsland has been particularly vociferous in making such complaints through the pages of 'Network' (the newsletter of the British Sociological Association, for example, No.40, October 1987). He also studied sociological textbooks, found that they were typically premised on socialist values and claimed that they were obsessed with problems of inequality rather than personal freedom, exaggerated the extent to which poverty exists, and were ambivalent towards private enterprise (1988). Saunders has also complained that, although social scientists consider competing perspectives, right-wing theorists tend to be either neglected or not seriously considered.

The 'New Right' is caricatured and broadly equated with 'Thatcherism', and this enables sociological critics to attack and dispense with it through slogans like 'authoritarian populism', rather than addressing the ideas and arguments to be found in the writings of people like Hayek. It is as if Marxist theory and analysis were dealt with simply through an analysis of Stalin's purges or Pol Pot's massacres. (Saunders, Network No 44, May 1989)

Although Saunders here seems to have succeeded in creating an unusual equation between Thatcher, Stalin and Pol Pot, his criticisms are both supported and qualified when we consider the third major criticism of bias in research methodology.

Research methodology has been criticized for sexist bias, left-wing bias and finally (in this summary at least) for right-wing bias. An explanation for this apparently odd combination of extremes lies in what Broadfoot described as two cultures; the scientific culture and the commercial culture. Broadfoot associated the scientific culture with the world of academe and hence with social research.

> It is this scientific culture that we seek to teach our students when we urge them to distinguish between fact and opinion, evidence and value-judgement. When we teach them the skills of systematic enquiry, interpretation and analysis. (Broadfoot, 1988, p.5)

The commercial culture favoured and promoted by recent Governments has, however, tended to use social research in ways that are considered to be compatible with capitalist principles but not with the researcher's criteria of worth. According to Broadfoot the commercial culture,

> ...represents the elevation, and hence imposition, of one set of value criteria - those of the sponsor over those of the researcher with which it may well be at odds. The former is likely to look for maximum pay-off for minimum investment, the resolution of short-term goals and specific problems. Sponsors may even look for research to support a particular policy stance or product. By contrast the researcher's criteria of worth will lie in the care with which the study is carried out, the sensitivity of the conclusions drawn and the relevance of the findings produced to the larger body of scholarship in a particular field. The distinction is fundamentally a question of whether the researcher is there to serve science or whether science exists to serve particular interests. Whilst the two are not mutually exclusive they nevertheless represent a fundamental difference in emphasis at least and arguably in values as well. (Broadfoot, 1988, p.7)

Thus, the researcher's scientific principles of rational and sceptical enquiry are not compatible with either the elevation of the sponsor over the researcher or with a conservative reluctance to challenge established definitions of reality. Researchers can therefore be described as having a left-wing bias simply because the ethical principles that they employ in their work clash with those advocated by the New Right.

> The world of academe is quite literally another world, or . . . another culture. It is characterised by values, goals, ways of working and rewards which are fundamentally at odds with those of laissez-faire

individualism and profit, market-forces and competition. It cannot
. . . be squeezed into a conformity with the prevailing political culture.
(Broadfoot, 1988, p. 4/5)

In view of the pressures on research that have been imposed by the
Conservative governments it is not surprising that Saunders accuses social
scientists of treating right-wing theorists with indifference or ridicule.
Government departments (for example the Department of Health and the
Department of Social Security) now automatically retain possession of the
work of their contract researchers and bar researchers from publishing their
findings in learned journals unless they have express permission. The
Economic and Social Research Council is increasingly funding research that
is related to policy and rejecting proposals that do not satisfy the government's
(normative) definition of worth. It has also been claimed that educational
researchers are '..sick of having their surveys into age-related testing, assisted
places and so forth shelved or snubbed' (New Society, 29 April 1988).

5.4 Political bias in the education system

As in research methodology, it is also usual for right-wingers to detect a left-
wing bias and for left-wingers to detect a right-wing bias in the education
system itself. At the moment the most widely publicised pressure to keep
politics out of education appears to come from the right-wing because a long-
established government (of over 12 years now) has the means to persuade
(rather than coerce) voters to accept its definitions of reality through its
determination of the agenda for educational debate. Two years into the first
Thatcher government Donald suggested that,

> . . . implicit in the restructuring of education [at the present time]
> . . . is the question of how the state exercises its power in part through
> the production of 'truth' and knowledge about education. (Donald,
> 1981, p.100)

We can see this production process in many government pronouncements. For
example, in a speech made to the Conservative Women's Conference in 1988,
Thatcher claimed a monopoly of traditional virtues for the Conservative party
and interchanged expressions of truth and value to suggest that they had the
same meaning.

> We shall be strengthened by our Conservative values: self-reliance,
> personal responsibility, good neighbourliness and generosity to others.

Most of us were brought up to respect these values. I respect them today, for they are the traditional values of British life. And as the false values of Socialism fade, so those true and traditional values are returning to our country. (Thatcher, at the Conservative Women's Conference, 1988, quoted in The Guardian, 26 July 1988)

In his critique of what he called the 'economic utility challenge' to education, Bailey argued that, by virtue of its implicit assumption of consensus about society, the economic utility model of education is essentially indoctrinary (Bailey, 1984).

Set in sharp relief with this new 'consensus' or politically sponsored normative paradigm is the previous normative paradigm (1.3).

The false prophets of the 1960s gravely damaged British Education. Instead of concerning themselves with standards and skills, they preached the virtues of 'progressive' education and 'spontaneous self-expression'. They tried to use schools as an instrument of social engineering. They assumed that large quantities of money, however spent would produce desirable results. (Conservative Research Department, 1985, p.282)

Thus, the rhetoric used and methods favoured in the past were presented as false and 'social engineering' was equated with spurious attempts to generate a supposedly unnatural level of social equality rather than with the Conservative government's version of social engineering via an increase in parental (and therefore social class) influence on educational outcomes. Critics of the New Right therefore argue that government representations of non-controversiality are simply a pose and Marxists, in particular, argue that Labour governments have similarly administered an education system that was politically defined. Hall, for example, claimed that Labour's attempts to equalise educational opportunities went no further than the promotion of comprehensive schools.

It attended to the machinery of reform - the comprehensive school - but not to its actual conditions of existence, its real practices and strategic social purposes. Fabian-like, it assumed that all these 'details' were best left to the experts and professionals. Believing ultimately in the neutrality of the state, Labour does seem to have subscribed to the erroneous view that 'Education should really be taken out of politics'. It is not an error Margaret Thatcher's government is likely to make. They know only too well that a vision of what British society should look like in the future is incapable of mobilizing populist support or being realized without a 'politics of education'. (Hall, 1983, p.3)

However, as some 'details' have been left to educational experts and professionals, the implementation of government education policies has been aggravated by Broadfoot's scientific culture, as Labour's policies (for example, Educational Priority Areas) were hampered in the past by unsympathetic administrators. Conservatives will therefore continue to complain about a left-wing bias in educational administration and in the classroom.

In 1987 the Salisbury Review described the Department of Education as, '. . . rotten with leftist ideology, and well-stocked with conspirators anxious to impose that ideology throughout the world of education.'. Baroness Cox, a Conservative education spokeswoman in the House of Lords, claimed that,

> Education has been turning into indoctrination. There are a growing number of education authorities and teacher groups who are committed to politics in the classroom. (Baroness Cox, Addressing the Freedom Association in 1987, [1])

When making such criticisms Conservatives tend to ignore or sanction possible right-wing indoctrination. For example, during the 1987 General Election campaign, Margaret Thatcher visited Waldersdale secondary modern school, where Conservative hats, stickers and flags were handed out to pupils. In 1988 attempts were made to swamp school governing bodies with Conservative members. In 1989 [2] there were attempts to recruit sixth form pupils as Conservative agents.

Whilst Conservative traditionalists are likely to complain about the influence of left-wing teachers (9.7), criticisms emerging from the commercial culture will emphasise the failure of the education system to produce adequately skilled workers and criticisms emerging from the scientific culture will centre on the influence of the current normative paradigm. More specifically, within the social sciences the main criticisms of political bias in the education system relate to cultural reproduction, the associated exclusion of many working class people from higher education, the Conservative Party's emphasis on parental choice, and the nature of the school curriculum.

Bourdieu and Passeron (1977), in France, and Young (1971) in Britain have written extensively about the reproduction of the ideals and values of the dominant culture through the education system. They argued that the dominant classes are able to impose their definitions of reality as the basis of knowledge and thus legitimate and perpetuate their own domination within the status quo. As the school acts as an agency of political socialization, so nationalism and a benevolent image of established authority is cultivated.

Bourdieu also claimed that a social function of the education system is the exclusion of members of the working class from higher levels of education. This is accomplished by examination failure and/or self elimination as working class pupils assume that they have little chance of success. Mann (1970) produced a similar claim when he argued that subordinate classes tend to accept their position at least to some extent either by the (pragmatic) belief that there is no realist alternative or by internalizing the (normative) expectations of the ruling class and viewing their own inferior position as legitimate. Similarly Parkin (1971) distinguished between three meaning-systems each promoting a different moral interpretation of class inequality. First, the dominant value system endorses the existing order and emerges from the dominant institutions in society. Second, the subordinate value system is a negotiated version to fit the realities of working-class life and this encourages accommodative responses. Third, the radical value system promotes an oppositional interpretation of class inequality. The normative acceptance described by Mann and the subordinate value system described by Parkin both provide explanations of how the privileged position of the dominant class is legitimized by educational success and the relatively underprivileged position of others is legitimized by educational failure. Although the education system may present itself as politically neutral and based on meritocratic principles, it is seen by many social scientists (especially, but not only, Marxists) as a means of perpetuating the domination of one social class and legitimizing unequal opportunities.

Some of the social constraints on educational opportunities are shown quite clearly later in this book as informants' education experiences are described (especially in 7.9.5) and their responses are considered. It will be shown that Parkin's three meaning systems provide useful analytical tools (7.11). Informants did often accept the definitions of reality that legitimate educational and social advantages and disadvantages, or believed that, although the system had faults, they were powerless to change it, or oppose the definition of inequalities as a natural phenomenon.

The emphasis of recent Conservative governments on parental choice (10.1.2) is criticized by many social scientists for justifying the elimination of the disadvantaged from higher education by the use of clever rhetoric. It is argued that, if the legitimation of unequal opportunities is successful, some parents will actually 'choose' an inferior education for their children. The case has been put very forcefully by Johnson.

> Educational Thatcherism, like all educational conservatisms, works back from adult destinies and their gross inequalities, in order to construct appropriate 'educational' regimes. So we have 'hewers of wood' and 'drawers of water' again, except that they are now called

70

'trainees'. But Thatcherism's particular brainwave is to find a further way of justifying the enforced underdevelopment of humans. It cultivates the realism of parents! What better solution than that parents, or those least well placed to compete, should actually 'choose' the educational under-privileging of their children. (Johnson, 1983, p.18)

Here ('educational conservatisms') we can see a reference to differences between Conservatives and it should be noted that, although Conservatives who favour the 11 Plus examination will usually also favour the freedom to 'choose' private education, it cannot be argued that the present emphasis on parental choice is compatible with the 11 Plus. Lynn highlighted a fundamental incompatibility between the Conservative policy of promoting parental choice and the policy of some local Conservative authorities (such as Torytown) in promoting selection.

> . . . the 1944 Act was profoundly alien to Conservative philosophy. The idea that state officials should allocate children to different kinds of school, on the basis of the decisions of experts about what kind of occupation they are best fitted for, is part of the philosophy of socialism and the planned society. The Conservative tradition is surely one of individual families making such decisions for themselves. (Lynn, 1970, p.32)

By allowing the local authority to allocate their children to a secondary modern school (rather than 'choosing' to either send their children to a comprehensive school outside the LEA area or to pay the fees for a private education) some parents are, in effect, relegating their children to what most voters consider to be an inferior education. Some parents will perceive such a choice whilst others will accept, without question the result of the 11 Plus examination and resulting decision made by state officials. We can therefore see that parental choice is incompatible with selection by state officials, although both policies are associated with Conservative authorities. In Torytown, for example, the majority of children attended schools selected for them by the local authority whilst a minority of parents 'chose' to send their children to independent schools (3.3).

The decisions made by parents are often based on financial constraints, lack of information about the possibilities available or sometimes convoluted reasoning. In section 7.9.5 for example, it will be shown that some parents regarded their daughters' education as less important than that of their sons' and that a child may choose to go to one particular school at the age of eleven simply to remain with familiar schoolfriends.

In studying the policies espoused by politicians, their own education and the sort of educational choices that they make for their own children should be considered. Knowledge of the social and financial constraints that limit parental choice effects the attitudes of politicians no less than it effects the attitudes of voters. The type of education that individual politicians received will effect their opinions, although they cannot justifiably be admonished by their opponents for the choices made by their parents or the type of education system (mainly selective) that existed during their schooldays. However, Kenneth Baker, when Secretary of State for Education, described 18 members of the Shadow Cabinet as 'sanctimonious hypocrites' for having been to independent or selective schools (The Observer, 7 June 1987). Mr Baker was himself criticized for having little personal knowledge of the state system.

Of greater significance are the experiences and the attitudes of politicians as parents. To what extent do they share common experiences with parents in the electorate? A large proportion of Conservative politicians are the products of private schools themselves and the majority choose to send their own children to private schools. Most (68 per cent) of the Conservative MPs elected in the 1987 General Election attended private schools, compared to 14 per cent of Labour MPs (Butler and Kavanagh, 1988, p.202). Fifteen out of the 21 members of the new cabinet established after the election had been to a public school (Times Educational Supplement, 5 June 1987). None of the pre-election cabinet (which included Kenneth Baker) sent their children to state schools, whilst none of the shadow cabinet sent their children to private schools (study by ISIS reported in The Observer, 7 June 1987). Furthermore, the lack of experience as state consumers of education was not compensated by experience as state education producers. At the time of the 1987 General Election 50 Conservative candidates were teachers or lecturers; compared to 146 Alliance candidates and 188 Labour candidates (Times Educational Supplement, 5 June 1987).

The rationale behind the decisions of politicians as parents is debatable, as conclusions will be mainly conjecture. Whilst it is generally assumed that Labour politicians send their children to state schools because of their personal antipathy towards private education, Conservative politicians cannot admit to a similar antipathy towards the state schools 'chosen' by about 93 per cent of British parents and experienced by the vast majority of voters. Thus, Conservative explanations emphasise the word 'choice' although the reasons for that choice are not clarified.

> The Labour left - hard, soft and in-between - hate the idea that people should be able to choose. In particular, they hate the idea that parents should be able to choose their children's education. The Conservative party believes in parental choice. (Mrs Thatcher's speech to the Conservative Party Conference, reported in the Times Educational Supplement, 16 October 1987)

After over 12 years of Conservative government and Conservative attempts to shape state education into what it regards as a satisfactory system, the majority of Conservative politicians still choose not to send their children to state schools. They and their children are thus buffeted from the effects of government policy; for example, cuts in public spending which effect educational provision, teachers' strikes and teacher shortages, the introduction of a National Curriculum for state schools only, open enrolment ('popular' schools taking as many pupils as space will permit whilst 'unpopular' schools face a gradual decline), the abolition of the Inner London Education Authority and the introduction of City Technology Colleges.

Obviously governments cannot publicly argue that private schools are superior to the state schools over which they have a greater influence. Instead the argument presented relates to the freedom of individual parents to make their own private decisions. The private family arena is, as Elshtain argues (1981), to be preserved as a non-political refuge from the 'force of the public'. Family relationships, and parents in particular, are defined as caring and responsible, the ideal being presented as a reality when parental choice is considered. Parents who neglect or in other ways abuse their children do not appear in government pronouncements about the promotion of family values or parental choice in education. They thus have the freedom to make the wrong choice, to be indifferent to or obsessed with their child's efforts, to ignore or to bully. Siltanen and Stanworth argud that where the ideal, caring family does not exist there must be an opportunity for public intervention (by state officials) into the private arena.

> Far from political intervention undermining the intimacy and warmth of private lives, the morally reconstructed private world that Elshtain recommends could be guaranteed only by upholding the obligation to intervene into private situations, to protest against abuses of freedom and dignity. Intimacy and privacy are neither licenses for, nor

73

protections against, inhuman conduct. There may be no violence in Elshtains's ideal family, but this offers no solace to battered women and children who suffer from the neglect of our political institutions in the name of personal freedom. Whose freedom is being protected? Whose freedom from physical abuse is being denied? Campaigns around such problems are bringing about a gradual transformation in public- private relations. To hold up a vision of an ideal, loving and caring, family is to avoid the issue of existing coercive relations. (Siltanen and Stanworth, 1984, p.207)

The present Government continues a policy of legitimizing its idealization of the family and traditional values through its determination of the curriculum for state schools. As private schools for privileged children are exempt from the National Curriculum, are we to assume that the government does not feel the need to determine the required value system to be transmitted there? Possible faults in our, past or present, social and political environment (for example, inequalities relating to poverty, racism, gender or sexual orientation) have, from a New Right perspective, been over-emphasised in the school curriculum, whilst Marxists would argue that they have been under-emphasised.

Our children need to speak and write clear English if they are to compete later in life. They need a good grounding in basic mathematics. They need to know all that is best in the history of their country. Children need to be taught traditional moral values and to understand our religious heritage. We cannot leave them to discover for themselves what is right and wrong. (Mrs Thatcher's speech to the Conservative Women's Conference, quoted in The Guardian, 26th May 1988)

Too often, our children don't get the education they need - the education they deserve. And in the inner cities - where youngsters must have a decent education if they are to have a better future - that opportunity is all too often snatched from them by hard-left education authorities and extremist teachers. Children who need to be able to count and multiply are learning anti-racist mathematics - whatever that may be. Children who need to be able to express themselves in clear English are being taught political slogans. Children who need to be taught to respect traditional moral values are being taught that they have an inalienable right to be gay. Children who need encouragement - and so many do - are being taught that our society offers them no future. (Mrs Thatcher's speech to the Conservative Party Conference,

1987, reported in the Times Educational Supplement, 16 October 1987) © Times Newspapers Ltd. 1987

Parents and employers are rightly concerned that not enough children master the basic skills, that some of what is taught seems irrelevant to a good education and that standards of personal discipline and aspirations are too low. In certain cases education is used for political indoctrination and sexual propaganda. (From 'The next moves forward', The Conservative Manifesto, 1987, p.18)

From a New Right perspective, political indoctrination involves the raising of criticisms about the existing political system and political slogans are related to claims of inequality. Marxists (and other critics) would, however, argue that political indoctrination involves cultural reproduction and the elimination of the working class from higher education, whilst political slogans include the rhetoric of 'enterprise', 'choice' and the 'market'.

Similarly sexual propaganda can be interpreted differently by the two perspectives. The New Right argues that homosexuality should not be presented in schools as a viable alternative to the traditional heterosexual family (see 7.6). From other perspectives the education system would be failing to defend individual rights to individual lifestyles if it defended such intolerance. However, findings in the British Social Attitudes surveys (see 4.4 and 7.6.2) indicate that respondents with the highest school-leaving age tend to be most tolerant of homosexuality and to have the least traditional attitudes towards the role of women in society. Thus, it could also be claimed that the consumption of a higher level of education could lead to left-wing or moderate views. Alternatively (or concurrently), it could be argued that voters with a higher level of education are simply better informed and more likely to question basic assumptions. Research by Denver and Hands [3] indicates that teachers' political preferences were not likely to rub off on their pupils. Sixth-formers taking A'level politics courses in England and Wales had significantly higher levels of political knowledge and sophistication than those who did not study politics and were more likely to support a party because of its politics than to take a lead from their parents. Therefore, the education system as a whole cannot simply be accused of promoting intolerance and traditional attitudes, and the effects of further and higher education on attitudes in general deserves further research.

Nevertheless, whatever perspective assumes greatest influence over the school curriculum, the result will still be a political bias. The curriculum is not a natural phenomenon but, '. . . the outcome of past struggles for cultural authority, for the intellectual, moral and ethical leadership of society' (Donald and Grealy, 1983, p.94). Decisions about what sort of history should be taught in our schools are most obviously political, as history has to be selective and the same events (for example, the French Revolution) can be interpreted in several ways. Martin Walker noted that increased government control over the knowledge that is to be reproduced in schools is incompatible with the New Right philosophy of 'rolling back the state'.

> There is an irony in the way that a government which is deeply committed to ending nationalization in industry should be promoting the nationalization of its history teaching. For that is the direction in which centrally-directed curricula and the insistence on the British dimension to history are heading. (Martin Walker, in the Guardian, 21 June 1983)

The idealisation of Britain and the British (past and present, families and the political system) could, if the emerging definitions of reality are internalized, lead to a rise in right-wing extremism. The New Right's fears that political education can result in the propagation of left-wing views have not been supported by research findings and are countered by fears that political ignorance could make young people particularly vulnerable to fascist arguments [4]. Analysis of the interviews in Torytown and Labourville in 1988 showed that it was the interviewees with the least knowledge about the murder of Adbul Ullah (see 7.6.3) who tended to make racist comments, when asked about recent 'events' at Burnage High School.

Thus, if efforts to remove political bias from the education system mean that pupils are not offered a curriculum that is based on the scientific culture's ethics of rational criticism, they may emerge from schools without the knowledge or ability to communicate effectively with people representing alternative political, cultural or religious ideologies.

5.5 Public knowledge about educational sub-issues

Some efforts have been made to assess knowledge about educational sub-issues amongst case-study informants. The qualitative nature of that part of the research, testing findings from quantitative data and evaluating the attitudes of the 52 people interviewed, required an understanding of the knowledge and reasoning on which such attitudes were based. Assessment of respondents' knowledge is rarely part of attitudinal research and in doing this I was following the example set by Edgell and Duke in their study of attitudes to public spending cuts. Indeed, in questions 38 to 40 (see Appendix), I adapted the format they used in their second survey. This involved first asking the informants if they had heard anything about certain educational sub-issues, then how much interest they had in discussions about them and, finally, what they knew about the sub-issues. Questions asked elsewhere in the schedule about sub-issues also involved probing to find out the reasons for the answers given. In some cases two similar questions were asked about the same subject in order to test for the effects of question-wording.

Psychologists might relate this approach to Kelly's construct theory (1955) and would note in particular the use of a repertory grid for Q41 (in which some of the questions asked in the Greater Manchester surveys were repeated). As the panel used for the case studies was very small and the intention in that part of the research was to collect mainly qualitative data, the repertory grid was not applied for its usual purpose of collecting quantitative data. However, the approach has been influenced by Kelly's theory about the personal construction of reality. Just as the dominant culture will try to define reality and legitimize its own values, so will individuals actively try to make sense of their environment. Kelly argued that, in a real sense, each of us is our own construct system, as only through that system can we interpret ourselves. One method of finding out how a informant constructs reality is to ask, really listen to the answer given and resist the temptation to translate what is said into one's own construct system, thus imposing one's own definitions of reality. This is naturally a methodological ideal to be aimed at but not necessarily achieved, and it is hoped that a discussion about the researcher's own bias (in 5.2 in particular) will help the reader to assess the extent to which it has been achieved.

Kelly noted that, because of the effort we put into creating our construct systems, we might feel the need to protect them from changes which might seriously disrupt them. This is close to Bourdieu (1973), Parkin (1971) and Mann's (1970) arguments about the way that working class people in particular try to accommodate their experiences to fit the dominant class's legitimation of inequality. It has a particularly close relationship to Festinger's theory of cognitive dissonance (1957). Festinger argued that in making a decision we create dissonance rather than resolve a conflict. Before making a decision we are aware of the arguments for and against the various options which we are considering. However, once a decision has been made to choose say Y, then the points favouring the alternative options of X and Z and the snags associated with Y are dissonant with the fact that we have chosen Y. According to the theory, dissonance is therefore a negative motivational state and the decision-maker will try various ways of reducing his or her level of dissonance.

One example taken from my research illustrates both cognitive dissonance and the accommodation of working class attitudes to the values of the dominant culture. In answer to question 41I about the introduction of student loans a retired man answered that he was in favour of them. Had this been a large-scale survey, his response would have been noted, added to others and associations may have been drawn from the resulting statistical analysis. However, in this case notes had already been taken (Q27) about his experiences of further education. During the 1930s he had paid his own fees for a course evening classes, spread over five years at a college of technology.

> They thought I was a penny marvel. Seventyfive started the course and it got down to fifteen. I was the only one guaranteed to get through. (Informant No.34)

He was expected to pay 7s.6d. for the final examination but had money problems at the time, could not pay and therefore did not get the qualification. He has had no further education since.

> I never dared go back and face them again. They thought I was going to do something for the college. (Informant No.34)

Such an experience might suggest an interest in reducing the financial constraints on students. However, the experience was not mentioned when he explained the reasons behind his attitude to loans. Instead he added to this the example of a man who was educated in Britain until he was 30 and then emigrated. That man should, he argued, have paid for his education to let someone else benefit.

> Why should I pay for someone to get a better education than me? If they get a good job they can afford to repay it. (Informant No. 34)

Arguments in favour of the alternative option of increasing student grants could be seen as representing the dissonance emerging from his decision about loans. This dissonance may have been reduced by his resentment towards successful students, who had achieved what he did not achieve.

Another retired informant provided an example of both cognitive dissonance and the possible impact of government definitions of reality. When asked question 41C about the redistribution of income and wealth she replied,

> Do you mean bring us all down to the lowest common denominator? If I earn money I won't share it with those that won't work. If you don't earn you don't eat. It isn't human nature in any department. Even the biggest socialists in the country wouldn't do it. (Informant No. 23)

The interview was dated 13 June 1988, which was three weeks after Mrs

Thatcher's speech to the General Assembly of the Church of Scotland. This speech was widely reported in the press and, in particular, her quote from St. Paul that, 'If a man will not work he shall not eat' [5].

Whether or not the informant's words were directly influenced by the speech, we can reasonably assume that many government statements about self-sufficiency had influenced her attitude. This is particularly interesting in view of the fact that this informant had not had any paid employment since 'before National Insurance was introduced' and that she and her husband were totally dependent on a state pension. Her argument that 'If you don't work you don't eat' would seem to be at variance with her experience. However, as her husband was formerly a self-employed butcher, the emphasis on payment for food and the traditional association between small shopkeepers and the Conservative party may be seen as reducing the level of dissonance.

Some attitudes also seemed to be inconsistent, but the question-wording and the place of the statement within the flow of the interview must be considered. Another informant who agreed with statement Q46B about the welfare state later expressed concern about inadequate welfare provision.

> That goes for these hangers on that have no intention of getting a job and all those people that abuse it. That's why it's gone to pot, because it's been so badly abused. (Informant No. 20, Q46B)

When asked for any other comments at the end of the interview, she said she was concerned about how young people on the dole managed.

> It must be disheartening having no future and wanting what other people have, constantly struggling to make ends meet. It's no wonder that some steal things. (Informant No.20)

She said that she and her husband had enough money to manage at the moment and it must be awful not to know that. However, she was concerned about how she and her husband would manage once he retired. They had enough at the moment, but listed their regular payments (rates, electricity, gas etc.) and said they would not be able to afford them once he retired.

Attitudes to educational sub-issues were not therefore simple representations of knowledge or experience. Indeed strong opinions often emerged from a very weak knowledge base and were often apparently unrelated to personal experience. Attitudes to comprehensive schools and private schools show this quite clearly. Many interviewees had no personal experience of comprehensive schools but had negative attitudes towards them. Definitions of a 'comprehensive' school are problematic (7.8.1) and not helped by the ambiguous use of the word in Torytown (3.3). The two questions asked about attitudes to comprehensive schools in the British Social Attitudes surveys and the Greater Manchester Study (7.8.2) also lead to apparently contradictory responses.

The majority of informants were against the abolition of private schools, without any personal experience of them and although many thought of them as out of reach for low income families (7.9.4). Few had heard about Assisted Places, either by their correct name or as an opportunity for children from less affluent families to go to independent schools.

Some people claimed to have heard of various sub-issues but said that their recollection was very vague. For example, when asked about City Technology Colleges, one informant replied;

> I don't really know. I'm sure if somebody jogged my memory it would bring it to mind. I've got a feeling that it's to do with youngsters being taught things that are more practical and to do with going back to the old style technical schools. (Informant No.51, Q40C)

It has already been noted that, unless a sub-issue was perceived as being personally relevant, little interest was likely to be taken in it. Impressions were therefore in many cases vague or erroneous and some informants obviously tried to imply knowledge that did not exist (hence the inclusion of probes and question 40 about details). Nevertheless, a lack of knowledge about current educational sub-issues should not be interpreted as reflecting a lack of knowledge about other aspects of education or of other political issues. Informants often provided fascinating accounts of their own education and the education of family members (7.9.5). These sometimes included experiences that now seem rather dated; for example, elementary schools and a school-leaving age of 14. Some showed a detailed knowledge of some educational sub-issues whilst having virtually no knowledge of others. For example, one man was able to say very little in answer to question 40 but, at the end of the interview detained me for a stimulating discussion about the work of A.S.Neill (1962). He first read some of Neill's books during the 1940s and had been interested in debates about teaching methods ever since.

Efforts were made to discover the source of informants' knowledge about education but responses to question 52 were often vague. The most common response was that information about education was obtained from newspapers, and no-one (including the 'fan' of A.S.Neill and the teachers) said that they had got their information from books. It was found that the most commonly read newspapers were those that are generally described as having a Conservative bias (the Sun, Star, News of the World, Express, Mail, Times, Telegraph). I classified the Mirror, People, Guardian, Observer and Independent as being non-Conservative and finally noted that eight informants read a mixture of Conservative and non-Conservative newspapers (for example, the Mirror mid-week and the News of the World on Sundays). The frequencies are shown in Table 5.1.

Although twice as many informants read newspapers with a Conservative bias as read non-Conservative newspapers, it should not be inferred that readers internalize the political allegiances of the publishers. One informant, for example read the Sun, the Star, the Mirror and the News of the World and admitted that,

> I only buy them for the scandal, the crosswords and so on. I never read the news. I enjoy trivial things. The News of the World because I love their crossword. That's the only reason I buy it. (Informants No.44, Q53)

Table 5.1
Newspapers read by the case study informants

National Conservative	4
Local + National Conservative	18
Total Conservative	22
National non-Conservative	2
Local + National non-Conservative	9
Total non-Conservative	11
Mixed allegiance	4
Local + mixed	4
Total	8

(Note: This makes a total of 41. Of the remaining 11 informants, four read none, three rarely read a newspaper, three read only a local newspaper and one read only a job-related journal.)

Media studies specialists cannot define a simple causal relationship between political attitudes and the political perspective of the newspaper read, and my research has added little to that particular debate. Does the type of newspaper effect political attitudes or do political attitudes effect choice of paper? Butler and Kavanagh analyzed the role of the press in the 1987 General Election and, although they argued that press reporting would be remembered for the smear campaigns against Labour and Alliance politicians, they concluded that the effect of newspaper reports may simply have been to reinforce existing loyalties (1988, pp.186-7).

In order to assess knowledge of some educational sub-issues some questions adapted a format already used by Edgell and Duke to assess knowledge of four public services and the level of authority responsible for each of eight services. The four services were education, transport, health, and the social services. They found that 25 per cent wrongly attributed the Greater Manchester Council with responsibilities for education (Edgell and Duke, 1985, D23). In the context of the present research, this suggests that many voters did not associate education as a political issue with either the Torytown or Labourville councils, and that they would not regard education as a political issue in the elections of the Torytown and Labourville councils.

The case study informants were asked (Q38), 'Have you heard anything recently about any of these subjects?' The seven subjects emerged from current local and national events (3.2 and 3.3) and were as follows:

a) Changes or proposed changes in the provision of education in (Labourville or Torytown)
b) The Assisted Places Scheme
c) City Technology Colleges
d) The Education Reform Bill (currently passing through Parliament)
e) Proposals to let schools opt out of Local Education Authority control.
f) The proposed abolition of the Inner London Education Authority.
g) Recent events at Burnage High School, in Manchester.

Frequencies were crosstabulated with the variables that were likely to influence interest in educational sub-issues.

Although the panel of 52 is very small (and the findings therefore not generalizable) analysis of the findings has proved instructive. For example, although there were fewer public sector employees than private sector employees, there was an inverse relationship between the two, public employees having heard of more sub-issues. Although more of the households consuming some education had heard of six or seven issues, there is little indication here of a consumption effect. Again, although the informants who had heard of the most issues were mainly female and in Torytown, their greater number in the sample meant that no inference could be taken from the finding.

Table 5.2
Number of sub-issues case study informants' heard of

	0 or 1	2 or 3	4 or 5	6 or 7Total
Production sector				
Private sector	5	7	6	119
Public sector	1	5	3	817
Unemployed	2	4	9	116
Consumption sector				
No education household	4	8	10	224
Some education household	4	8	8	828
Educational experience				
No school-leaving qualification or FE	5	5	6	218
A school-leaving qualification or FE	1	10	5	117
A school-leaving qualification and FE	2	6	2	717
Gender				
Male	4	6	8	422
Female	4	10	10	630
Area				
Torytown	4	9	10	528
Labourville	4	7	8	524

In question 39 I asked - 'How much interest do you have in discussions about these subjects?' Interest is an extremely vague concept and some of the answers were very vague. However, many simply answered 'None' and any professed interest (however minor) was counted as interest in order to construct **Table 5.3**. Here the most obvious difference was related to consumption sector.

Table 5.3
Number of sub-issues case study informants expressed
any interest in

	0 or 1	2 or 3	4 or 5	6 or 7	Total
Production sector					
Private sector	17	2	0	0	19
Public sector	10	2	3	2	17
Unemployed	14	0	2	0	16
Consumption sector					
No education household	22	0	2	0	24
Some education household	19	4	3	2	28
Educational experience					
No school-leaving qualification or FE	17	1	0	0	18
A school-leaving qualification or FE	13	2	2	0	17
Some school-leaving qualifications and FE	10	2	3	2	17
Gender					
Male	17	1	3	1	22
Female	24	3	2	1	30
Area					
Torytown	24	2	2	0	28
Labourville	17	2	3	1	24

In question 40 I asked - 'Can you tell me briefly, in your own words, what you know about these subjects?' Again answers were difficult to quantify. For Table 5.4 any correct knowledge about a subject was counted. Where informants gave some false information (sometimes together with correct details) the answer was classified as wrong. Therefore, although an individual might give some correct details about seven subjects, if some of the information given for two of them was wrong the number of subjects that the informant would be classified as having knowledge of would be reduced to five.

Table 5.4
Number of sub-issues case study informants gave correct details of

	0 or 1	2 or 3	4 or 5	6 or 7	Total
Production sector					
Private sector	10	8	1	0	19
Public sector	5	4	5	3	17
Unemployed	7	6	3	0	16
Consumption sector					
No education household	13	7	4	0	24
Some education household	9	11	5	3	28
Educational experience					
No school-leaving qualification or FE	11	4	3	0	18
A school-leaving qualification or FE	6	8	3	0	17
Some school-leaving qualification and FE	5	5	4	3	17
Gender					
Male	8	9	3	2	22
Female	14	9	6	1	30
Area					
Torytown	10	12	5	1	28
Labourville	12	6	4	2	24

Again an inverse relationship between private and public sectors could be seen. There is also the indication of a possible relationship between consumption and knowledge about educational sub-issues. In addition the three tables (5.2, 5.3, 5.4) indicate a greater interest in and knowledge about educational sub-issues amongst the most highly qualified informants. Again findings cannot be generalized from such a small sample, but the salience of educational attainment is emphasised when survey data is considered in Chapters 6, 7, 8 and 9 (and especially in 8.3.3).

Raw frequencies, excluding independent variables, also indicate that, although most informants claimed to have no interest, more of them could provide some details and more still claimed to have heard of sub-issues.

Table 5.5
Knowledge and interest frequencies (from case studies)

Number of debates	Heard of	Interest	Detail
0	3	32	8
1	5	9	14
2	6	3	13
3	10	1	5
4	11	2	5
5	7	3	4
6	4	0	0
7	6	2	3

The lack of interest and difference between having heard of a sub-issue and being able to provide some accurate information about it suggests a general indifference to education as a political issue, even amongst the majority of the consumers of education. If the twelve people who were both public employees and education consumers are considered, we can see (in Table 5.6) that again their awareness of educational sub-issues exceeded their interest in them. They nevertheless demonstrated a greater awareness and general knowledge of current educational sub-issues than other informants.

Table 5.6
Public consumers/employees' interest and knowledge

	Educational consumers/ public employees n=	Other informants n=
Heard of		
0 or 1	0	8
6 or 7	7	3
Interest		
0 or 1	6	35
5 or 7	4	1
Detail		
0 or 1	1	21
5 or 7	5	2
Total	12	40

Notes

1. 'The standard bearers', p.20, New Society 15 May 1987.
2. The Guardian, 11 May 1989
3. Denver and Hands, reported in Talking Politics, Vol.1, No.1, Autumn 1988, p.32
4. ESRC, 'Youth', Newsletter, No. 61, November 1987. The issue dealt with research initiatives concerned with the problems facing young people in Britain. It described area studies tracing the processes of the development of ideas about economic and political understanding in adolescence, and how these influence the young person's sense of identity and personal effectiveness.

6 Attitudes: Public spending on education

6.1 Central government policies on educational spending

During the 1980s no particular proportion of local authority finance was earmarked for education, but it usually accounted for about half of each authority's budget and local authorities controlled over 84 per cent (Statham et al, 1989) of all public spending on education. However, the proportion spent on education declined, from over 54 per cent of all English authorities total expenditure in 1978/9 to 49 per cent in 1986/7 (CIPFA, 1988). This is partly explained by the falling birth-rate during the 1970s and corresponding reduction in the number of pupils being educated. Between 1981/2 and 1985/6 the total number of pupils in maintained schools fell from 7.95 million to 7.23 million (full-time equivalents). However, a reduction in spending does not inevitably follow falling rolls and although demographic trends have started to move in the opposite direction a corresponding increase in educational expenditure seems unlikely. This is because the relationship between school rolls and educational spending is not so finely tuned as to adapt to changes as and when they occur; resources and the management of those resources are the deciding factors. During the 1980s Conservative governments restricted the level of local authority income and limited the freedom of local authorities to choose how resources could be allocated although, as can be seen in Torytown and Labourville, local authorities reacted to the changes in different ways.

In 1985, the Association of Metropolitan Authorities conducted a survey of the 43 metropolitan LEAs (including Torytown and Labourville) to evaluate the changes in educational provision between 1980 and 1985 (Crispin and Marslen-Wilson, 1985). Commonly reported changes included increased parental contributions and poorer school maintenance (27 Local Authorities reported that their interior maintenance programme had worsened and 20 that their exterior maintenance programme had worsened). Additional evidence from other sources shows that expenditure in real terms per pupil per annum on books and equipment also declined. In secondary schools this was from £50 in 1975/6 to £45 in 1985/6, although it dropped as low as £39.8 in 1980/1 and 1981/2 (Statham et al, p.131). Paradoxically, the Association of Metropolitan Authorities reported that in 1985 expenditure per child (unit cost) was at its highest for 10 years and the pupil:teacher ratio was at its lowest. This can be explained by noting the extra expenses involved in recent changes in education. Such conditions could include; the need for expensive materials and equipment such as computers, higher costs associated with falling rolls, more pupils identified as having special educational needs, new curricula developments, and the effect of high youth unemployment.

Although local authorities had the main responsibility for the collection of rates (now the Community Charge) to pay for their educational spending, and for making decisions about how finance was allocated, their freedom in terms of both income and expenditure was severely constrained by central government. Central government policies effected the process of determining the level of local rates, and now of the Community Charge. They also effected the amount of additional support that central government provided in the form of various grants. In the mid 1970s the rate support grant from central government was 66.5 per cent of local authority income. This fell to 61 per cent in 1979 and 46.3 per cent in 1987 (Statham et al, 1989, p.116). Whilst the proportion provided by government grants fell, local authorities found that their ability to levy rates to compensate had also been severely constrained. In this respect the effects of central government policies were been similar to those on other welfare state services. However, in the case of education, the degree of change was particularly great. From being the most rapidly expanding service within the welfare state its relative position compared to other services started to decline within a contracting welfare state (Dennison, 1985, p.34). As a percentage of total government expenditure on public services, education fell from 14.4 per cent in 1978/9 to 13.3 per cent in 1986/7 (White Paper, 1988, Chart 1.10). Education spending also declined as a percentage of the United Kingdom gross domestic product, from 5.5 per cent in 1981/2 to 4.8 per cent in 1985/6 (DES, 1987, Table 1).

⋆ During the 1980s central government policies had the effect of reducing local authorities' control over public spending on education both from above and from below. Central government gave itself more power to determine both authority income and expenditure and transferred some responsibilities to other agencies; for example, increasing individual institution's control over their own spending and giving the responsibility for some courses to the Manpower Services Commission. This pattern can be seen in the following brief chronology of some of the relevant changes during the 1980s.

Chronology of changes in the financial management of education

1980 The Education Act
- Removed the obligation to provide free school milk and provide school meals. Allowed local education authorities to provide milk or meals or not as they wished, at whatever cost or standard they chose. This included free milk or meals for families on low incomes. Responsibilities remained to provide free meals for the children of families receiving Supplementary Benefit or Family Income Supplement.
- Created the Assisted Places Scheme, whereby pupils can be transferred from maintained schools to selected independent day schools, with central government paying part or all of the tuition fees (on a means tested basis).

1980 The Local Government and Land Planning Act
Introduced a new system for allocating grants to local authorities. The amounts received in grants are no longer based on local authorities' previous expenditure patterns but are calculated according to the authority's score on a range of factors which the government decides are likely to affect its expenditure. Penalties were introduced for spending above the recommended level. Introduced the new block grant and grant related entitlement (GRE).

1982 The Local Government Finance Act
Formalised the system of financial penalties to be imposed on authorities who overspent (explained below).

1984 The Rates Act
Gave the government the power to set an upper limit to rate increases where these were judged to be excessive.

1984 The Education (Grants and Awards) Act
Enabled the government to allocate directly a small proportion (up to 1 per cent) of the block grant for specific educational projects which the Secretary of State judged to be important (thus reducing local authorities' control over how the block grant was spent). These are called education support grants (ESGs).

1985/6 The government took 25 per cent of the funding for non-advanced further education from the local authorities' budgets and gave it to the Manpower Services Commission (MSC) which was attached to the Department of Employment.

1986 The Social Security Act
Local authorities no longer have the power to supply free school meals or milk to any children other than those from families receiving Income Support; and they no longer have any obligation to supply free meals or milk to any children (even those from families receiving Income Support).

1988 Education Reform Act

- Polytechnics, the larger colleges and those schools which choose to 'opt out' of LEAs control will be financed directly by central government, not by local authorities. This reduces the percentage of educational expenditure under the control of local authorities.
- Required LEAs to delegate certain responsibilities for financial management to the governing bodies of the larger colleges remaining under LEA control.
- Required LEAs to delegate certain responsibilities for financial management to the governing bodies of schools. This has been called local management of schools (LMS).
- Introduced a National Curriculum for pupils in maintained schools. Attainment targets in each of its constituent subjects are set for pupils at the age of 7, 11 and 14. The implementation of these plans suggested the need for increased expenditure for the necessary standardization process and the testing of pupils. However, central government did propose to significantly increase its grants to local government.
- Abolished the Inner London Education Authority, transferring its responsibilities from April 1990 to the inner London boroughs.

The abolition of the ILEA (9.1) was an almost inevitable consequence of the government policy of reducing local authority spending powers. Once a local authority oversteps its grant related entitlement by more than 10 per cent the government pays a progressively smaller proportion of the extra spending and ratepayers pay an increasingly large proportion of it. Added to this is a more costly penalty known as grant holdback, whereby overspending authorities have a proportion of their grant withheld. The ILEA estimated that it needed about £1,000 million in 1987/8, compared to a government estimate of £560 million. As a result the ILEA lost all of its block grant. In 1987/8 it would have had to reduce its spending to £469 million in order to get any grant at all.

Central government policies during the 1980s not only reduced the role of local government in the determination of educational spending, but also indicated the direction in which education priorities should move. As more public funds were to be channelled into the provision of private education (via the Assisted Places Scheme) less was to be spent on school meals, milk and other ancillary services formerly provided as part of state education. Many schools are now experiencing difficulties in arranging field trips and other educational visits. Under regulations introduced in 1989, schools can no longer charge parents for trips which take place mainly during school hours. If parents do not make sufficient contributions voluntarily, the trip has to be cancelled. Local authority efforts to create central hardship funds, to help in such cases, were blocked by the funding formula defined by central government (see The Times Educational Supplement, 11 August 1989).

The introduction of a funding formula meant that, when local management of schools was introduced, some schools faced drastic cuts in their income whilst others benefitted. For example, Wymondham County High school in Norfolk was told that its budget for the 1989/90 academic year would be cut by £68,120 whilst Earlham Comprehensive school in Norwich expected to gain £106,220 (reported in the Times Educational Supplement, 11 August 1989). Schools pay actual teaching costs, although these are funded on the basis of average salaries in the country. This means that those schools with a majority of teachers who are on or near the bottom of the salary scale benefit, whilst those schools employing mainly teachers near the top of the scale lose.

✗ Local authorities also face a shortage of teachers of particular subjects and in some individual schools. The introduction of a National Curriculum highlighted the shortage of teachers in certain subject areas; notably languages, mathematics and science. Low wages and the apparently low morale in the teaching profession resulted in many qualified teachers leaving the profession to work elsewhere and made teaching less attractive to new graduates. In the late 1980s the effects were particularly noticeable in Inner London, where some children were prevented from starting primary school at the mandatory age because of a shortage of teachers.

6.2 Theories about public spending

This research did not demand a detailed study of theories about public spending, but a brief resume of four particular theories is included because they each help to clarify the relationship between attitudes to education as a political issue and public spending outcomes. The first theory emphasises the importance of ownership of resources in the relationship between central and local government, the second emphasises the contradictory principles behind the functions of local and central government, the third considers public confidence in the education system, and the fourth challenges the need for high levels of spending on state education.

6.2.1 Resource dependency theory

Educationalists often use resource dependency theory as a model for their analysis of the balance of power between central and local government. Resources are broadly defined as finance, authority, work and services and to monopolize ownership of resources is to create dependencies, exact compliance and accrue power (Ranson, 1985). The theory originated in a study of competing welfare agencies in the U.S.A., where the competition was relatively equal and it could be used to explain the fine balance between agencies. However, in Britain we can see that the balance of power between central and local government is so unequal that, in a conflict with central government over the allocation of resources, local government is likely to lose. Moreover, its emphasis on the actors involved rather than the whole environment means that resource dependency theory tends to underestimate the importance of political policies and economic and social constraints. It has been shown (6.1) that, in this instance, political policies and the power of central government are prior to the ownership of finance, authority, work and services and can lead to the accumulation of more of these resources.

6.2.2 Dual state thesis

Also relevant is Saunders' (1981) dual state thesis which, like resource dependency theory, provides an analytical framework for studying the relationship between central and local government. Saunders argued that central government is typically concerned with social investment, corporatist politics and private sector profitability whilst local government is mainly concerned with social consumption, competitive politics and social need. This results in tension between the two contradictory principles of profit and social need. Although local authorities are similarly constrained by central government powers, individual local authorities will respond in different ways according to their own political identification and circumstances.

The emphasis is therefore on an increasing financial dependence on central government and, although critics (for example, Ashford, 1974, Clegg, 1982, and Martlew, 1983) have argued that Saunders exaggerated the dominance of central government and the differences between the two levels, we can see that during the 1980s financial dependence on central government increased. Moreover, the description of government policies provided in 6.1 tends to support the dichotomy between profit and social need. Conservative governments have emphasised the assumed need to pare back spending on state education as much as possible whilst encouraging parents to make alternative arrangements for their children's education. Social need (for example, in the form of free milk and school meals) is not regarded as a priority. Yet, at the same time, central control of education increased enough to contradict the government's professed principle of minimum state intervention. Duke and Edgell conclude that, '...what is taking place is a rolling back of the welfare state rather than a rolling back of the state per se.' (Duke and Edgell, 1986, p.21). The approach favoured by Conservative governments can clearly be seen in the policies of the Torytown local authority. Torytown spent less than Labourville on state education but a vast amount of its public income was spent on providing a private education for some Torytown children (6.3).

Saunders' theory therefore seems to provide an explanation for the

94

relationship of conflict between a Conservative central government and a Labour controlled local authority, where each has policies that are related to the respective concerns of central and local government. Findings in 6.3 also lend support to this theory regarding a situation where the roles were reversed. During the Callaghan government in the late 1970s, a Labour central government was torn between its ideological concern about social need and its pragmatic concern with social investment, whilst the Conservative local authority in Torytown faced a potential conflict between the local principle of social need and its market-based ideological concerns. The result was that the spending restrictions introduced by the Labour government were interpreted and applied more zealously in Torytown than in Labourville.

6.2.3 Decline of public esteem

The third theory relates to the public esteem given to the education system and the effects of this on public spending. Dennison argued that,

> . . . there has been a reduction in confidence in relation both to the processes and outcomes, and a resultant decline in public esteem, reflected in the translation from top to bottom placing in public sector resource distribution. (Dennison, 1985, p.28)

He claimed that there was sufficient qualitative evidence to support his point even though he acknowledged that, without the establishment of sophisticated research techniques before the supposed transition, changes in the public standing of the education service could not be evaluated. To Dennison the education service in the 1980s was disadvantaged compared to other services for three main reasons; firstly, because of the demographic factors mentioned in 6.1, secondly, because its aims, objectives and outcomes were too diffuse and intangible to be widely understood or evaluated and, thirdly, because an effective opposition to central government policy did not emerge. Government criticisms of the education system were, to Dennison, closely related to government spending policies; the criticisms being used to justify the need for spending cuts (Dennison, 1985, p.34). In particular Dennison emphasised the role of the government in defining a framework for educational debate that supported its policies,

> Of course it can be argued that the DES sponsored the erosion in public confidence to justify the new approach. There is, perhaps, no better way to further lessen esteem for a service, than by publicizing a 'debate' in which reasons for reductions in this esteem receive scrutiny. (Dennison, 1985, p.29)

However, Dennison argued that, more important than this publicised debate, was the lack of a positive lobby to question its assumptions and the policy implications. This argument can be challenged by evidence of opposition to government policies (see Chapter 9) but it is difficult to evaluate the extent to which the opposition gained popular support. The teachers' unions (see 9.7), for example, launched an assault on government education policies but, as the unions were also demanding more pay for their members, their general complaints about the education system received less public attention than did their occasional strikes. In 1985 the National Union of Teachers published a pamphlet in which it attacked government policies in vehement tones, claiming that, '. . . not one of our major international competitors treats education and training with the contempt we currently do in this country.' (NUT,1985, p.9).

The arguments were forcefully put even though, as Dennison claims, they did not succeed in overruling the government sponsored definition of reality.

> At a fundamental level we believe it is important to recognize that the education system has been 'hijacked' by a narrow market-determined view of what 'education' should provide. In doing so, schools and teachers have been scapegoats for the broader failings of governmental policy. Education has thus become easy prey for expenditure cutbacks and has laid itself open to the introduction of specious tests of effectiveness and performance. We disagree with this way of looking at the role of education in society. In our view, the so called 'great debate' of the mid-1970s which was supposed to have provided pointers for a more responsive education system, in fact began the process by which schools and the teaching profession officially got a disproportionate share of the blame for Britain's deteriorating economic performance. In effect the 'great debate' has provided a false prospectus upon which the government has launched its attacks on state educational provision. [. . .] In the last few years it would not have mattered how much schools had turned out youngsters according to the model supposedly laid down for them by industry in the 'great debate'. The jobs for these youngsters had simply disappeared. Yet schools and teachers have somehow continued to be singled out for the failures of an economic system that is wholly outside their control. (NUT, 1985, pp.4-5 and 21-23)

This theory is complex and more difficult to clarify than the competing accusation that the education system, and teachers in particular, were inefficient. Some inefficiency can be proved in any system, however well managed, whereas Dennison's theory about a manufactured reduction in public confidence is not easily supported or falsified by empirical research. Moreover, a lack of interest in education as a political issue amongst the majority of voters (see Chapter 4) means that only a small minority were likely to read such pamphlets.

6.2.4 Natural inequality

The fourth theory justifies the reduction in public spending on education by presenting social inequalities as though they are natural differences or the result of a meritocratic education system. According to Scruton, Conservatism, '. . . involves the maintenance of a hierarchy, and the attempt to represent the unpleasant fact of inequality as a form of natural order and legitimate bond.' (quoted in Wolpe and Donald, 1983, p.88). Interpretations of this natural inequality tend to emphasise either an idealized image of a meritocratic system of education, in which social and economic inequalities have no effect, or a socio-biological perspective involving the inheritance of intelligence. In either case, if inequality is 'natural' and an unpleasant 'fact' increased spending on the education of some children will be wasted; it would be more profitable to provide those who have been classified as able with the largest share of resources.

Such arguments about natural inequality were propounded in the Black Papers, published during the 1960s and early 1970s to counteract 'progressive' trends in education and to defend the bipartite system of secondary education. In one Black Paper Richard Lynn produced an explanation for educational inequality, and its consequences in terms of public spending, that many Conservatives would now regard as very extreme. It might also be damaging in terms of electoral support if the Conservative party were to adopt the same rhetoric.

> By blinding themselves and others to the truth, the progressives raise false hopes that much more can be done for slum children than is actually possible. No amount of money poured into the 'educational priority areas', enthusiastically espoused in the Plowden Report, is likely to bring any appreciable proportion of slum children up to the standards of university entrance [. . .] If it is thought desirable to improve the intelligence of the population, money would be better spent on helping less intelligent people to limit the size of their families [. . .] The suppression of these truths by progressives leads to a whole series of false deductions. One of the most serious is that it is the fault of society that slum dwellers are impoverished and their young do badly at school. To the young red guards, it follows that society is unjust and must be overthrown. They do not realize that slum dwellers

are caused principally by low innate intelligence and poor family upbringing, and that the real social challenge is posed by this. (Lynn, 1970, p.30)

Conservatives today tend to prefer an emphasis on 'parental choice', or market-place analogies involving the 'consumer', but the effect is still to pass on educational advantages or disadvantages from one generation to the next. As Dale argues,

> If we probe beneath the slogan [of parental choice], it becomes apparent that 'parental choice' would be exercised only by sufficiently wealthy parents and for appropriately concerned parents. And, to complete the circle, that expression of concern would be an index of parents' moral deservingness to receive any superior offerings, or to benefit from unequal treatment. Parental choice and parental concern, then, may be seen as mechanisms for justifying the unequal treatment that would result from privatization. The people who morally deserve - or, of course, can afford - more, get more. (Dale, 1983, p.42)

By implication, children are regarded as deserving or undeserving according to the status of their parents, and unequal educational opportunities are passed from one generation to the next. However, although the concept of inequality has been espoused most vigorously by the Conservatives, theoretical support for the concept of parental choice belongs to no particular political party (Stillman, 1986). To boldly support the opposite extreme of the forced allocation of children to particular schools would, in the recent political climate, be regarded as politically naive, even though most children are still (in effect) allocated to a school by their local education authority (see 3.3 and 7.8.5).

The effects of the nature/nurture debate can be observed in practice in the spending policies of the Torytown and Labourville local authorities. Although both have operated within the restrictions imposed by central government we can see that their reactions have been radically different. In Torytown the emphasis has been on the measurement of existing intelligence at the age of eleven and the rights of parents to send their children to private schools. In Labourville, however, the emphasis has been on starting the child's education as early as possible, in some cases to compensate for social disadvantages. Thus, one local authority has been primarily concerned with outcomes and the assessment of existing intelligence to differentiate between children, whilst the other has been primarily concerned with inputs and the process of developing every child's abilities to the full.

6.3 Expenditure in Torytown and Labourville

Duke and Edgell showed that between 1975/6 and 1982/3, when Labourville and Torytown were under pressure from central government (first Labour, then Conservative) to limit their spending, Torytown reacted by making more radical cuts in its education spending than did Labourville. Between 1975/6 and 1978/9 net expenditure on education in both districts fell by almost 9 per cent. However, their income from specific grants (which contributed to gross expenditure) increased significantly during that period making the fall in gross educational expenditure less pronounced. Nevertheless, in Torytown there was a real cut of 2.4 per cent in educational spending between 1975/6 and 1978/9, whilst in Labourville there was no real cut (Duke and Edgell, 1986, p.9, Table 1).

The same sort of trend can be seen during the 1980s. Although both local authorities experienced reductions in net and gross education spending between 1978/9 and 1981/2 the level of real cuts was greater in Torytown (Duke and Edgell, 1986, p.10, Table 2). In Torytown gross expenditure declined by 12 per cent compared to only 3 per cent in Labourville. Duke and Edgell considered the possibility that the lower level of spending in Torytown reflected low resource levels, but found that Torytown had the highest average rateable value in Greater Manchester, whilst Labourville had the fourth (Duke and Edgell, 1986, p.17). It is also interesting to note that by comparison, central government did not reduce its educational spending between 1979/80 and 1982/3 (Edgell and Duke, 1986b, Table 4), a finding that is explained by its increasing involvement in local authority spending via the contribution of specific grants.

Duke and Edgell's conclusion was that local political control was the key factor, explaining the different responses of local authorities to central government restrictions on their spending. Although net educational expenditure per head was higher in Torytown in 1975/6 (£88.03 in Torytown compared to £80.00 in Labourville) by 1982/3 it was much higher in Labourville (£161.39 in Torytown compared to £204.28 in Labourville). The usual method of comparing educational spending levels is, however, to calculate net spending per pupil (otherwise referred to as unit costs). When this is done the possible effects of variations in age distribution between areas is excluded. Duke and Edgell found that the higher level of spending was confirmed by this calculation. Net spending per pupil in Labourville was 26 per cent higher for nursery schools, 7 per cent higher for primary schools and 11 per cent higher for secondary schools. By 1985/6 Torytown had stopped providing nursery schools and was still spending less per pupil in primary and secondary schools.

Table 6.1
Unit costs in Torytown and Labourville 1985/6

	(1) All schools in Metropolitan LAs	(2) Torytown	(3) Labourville	(4) (2) as a % of (3)
	£	£	£	%
Nursery	1253	0	1321	-
Primary	823	739	797	92.7
Secondary	1214	1172	1239	94.6

Source: Education Statistics 1985-86 Actuals, CIPFA, Statistical Information Service, SIS Ref 52.87

In column (4) of Table 6.1 we can see that net spending per pupil in Labourville was 7.3 per cent higher for those attending primary schools, 5.4 per cent higher for those attending secondary schools and that Torytown spent nothing on nursery schools. (Some primary schools in Torytown have nursery classes, attended on a part-time basis. The costs for these are included in Torytown's primary school unit costs.) In column (1) we can see the comparative averages for all school within Metropolitan local authorities. Torytown was below the average at all levels whereas Labourville was only below the average for its spending on primary pupils.

Comparisons involving actual expenditure on education services are more difficult as the different size of the population has to be considered. When reading the Table 6.2 it must therefore be remembered that the population of Torytown was 90.1 per cent the size of Labourville and that the number of registered pupils in Torytown (30,110) was 77.6 per cent that of Labourville (38,793). Those pupils who were attending schools maintained by another local authority (1,000 from Torytown and 782 from Labourville) or attending private schools at no cost to the local authority were excluded from the table (see 3.2 and 3.3).

By subtracting from column (3) the smaller proportion (77.6 per cent) of pupils in Torytown it is possible to see the different spending of the two authorities more clearly in column (4). The provision of school meals in Torytown was particularly low (-21.2) when compared to that in Labourville. Similarly expenditure on teaching staff in further education was much lower in Torytown than in Labourville (-19.2) whilst Torytown spent much more on mandatory student grants than did Labourville (+130.4). This may be explained by the 1,576 pupils from Torytown attending schools that were not

Table 6.2
Torytown and Labourville Expenditure 1985/6

	(1) Torytown	(2) Labourville	(3) TT as a %ofLV	(4) (3) - 77.6%
	'£000	'£000	%	%
Nursery schools				
Teachers	0	274	-	-
Other staff	0	504	-	-
Other expenditure	0	171	-	-
Total	0	949	-	-
Net expenditure	0	947	-	-
Primary schools				
Teachers	8512	11587	73.5	-4.1
Other staff	1129	1979	57.0	-20.6
Other expenditure	2421	2665	90.1	+12.5
Total	12356	16657	74.2	-3.4
Net expenditure	11818	15853	74.5	-3.1
Secondary schools				
Teachers	11400	15337	74.3	-3.3
Other staff	1888	2324	81.2	+3.6
Other expenditure	5820	3996	145.6	+68.0
Total	20240	22241	90.0	+12.5
Net expenditure	19171	21353	89.8	+12.2
Special schools				
Net expenditure	2241	3365	66.6	-11.0
Milk and meals				
Net expenditure	1652	2929	56.4	-21.2
Further education				
Staff (teachers and others)	5480	9389	58.4	-19.0
Mandatary student grants	4625	2223	208.0	+130.4

NOTE. Adjustments with other LEAs are excluded from the figures given for nursery, primary and secondary schools but included in each total.

Source: Education Statistics 1985-86 Actuals, CIPFA, Statistical Information Service, SIS Ref 52.87

maintained by a local authority. Pupils who attend private schools are more likely to move on to higher education than are pupils who attend state schools. The large proportion of privately educated pupils in Torytown may have reduce demand for further education courses (many of which do not qualify for a mandatory grant) whilst increasing the demand for higher education courses (most of which do qualify for a mandatory grant).

Another noticeable difference between Torytown and Labourville can be seen in 'Other expenditure' on secondary schools. The difference may be explained by Torytown's spending on the fees of pupils attending independent Roman Catholic schools. When 'Other expenditure' is added to expenditure on staff, Torytown spending on secondary education looks particularly generous, but the unit costs given in Table 6.1 do not describe differences (or similarities) between the LEA's spending on private, grammar and secondary modern schools.

An impression of how expensive private school fees are can be gleaned from information about the Assisted Places scheme (financed by central government and therefore excluded from Table 6.2). The 1987 edition of Social Trends gave the estimated yearly cost to the government of each pupil with an Assisted Place as £1,600. This does not represent the full cost of fees paid for a private education but merely the government's contribution after parents had been means tested. In 1987 full fees for day pupils attending Headmasters' Conference schools averaged £3,500 and for day pupils at Girls' Schools Association and the Governing Bodies of Girls' Schools Association schools averaged £2,900 (ISIS, 1987). If such costs are compared with the net expenditure per pupil attending the secondary schools financed by the Torytown LEA we can see that, in 1987, taxpayers' paid more for each Assisted Place (average £1,600) than Torytown ratepayers paid, in 1985/6 for each place in a local secondary school (average £1,172). Although the dates given are not directly comparable, it is unlikely that Torytown increased its spending by nearly 50 per cent between 1986 and 1987. The Torytown average also conceals variations in expenditure on different types of secondary education and the possibility that spending on some types of education may be far below the overall average.

6.4 Attitudes to public spending

The best supported finding regarding attitudes to public spending in general is that most voters were not in favour of the spending cuts. This has been a consistent response in the British Social Attitude surveys and in the Greater Manchester Surveys. Each year, for example, the BSA has asked respondents to choose from three options regarding taxation and spending on the welfare state. Table 6.3 shows that, when respondents were asked to choose between three options, the vast majority were consistently opposed to any further reductions and increasingly in favour of more spending.

Table 6.3
Attitudes to taxation and spending options,
BSA 1983/4, 1987/8

	1983/4	1987
	%	%
Reduce taxes and spend less on health, education and social benefits.	9	3
Keep taxes and spending in these services the same.	54	42
Increase taxes and spend more on health, education and social benefits.	32	50

Source: Jowell et al, 1984 and 1988

Edgell and Duke's findings were similar. In 1983/4 they found that 63 per cent of their respondents preferred to keep up services rather than cut taxes (Edgell and Duke, 1985, p.14) and that many of the minority who approved of the spending cuts in general still favoured more spending on education. Even amongst those strongly approving of the cuts, 25 to 29 per cent favoured more spending on education (Edgell and Duke, 1981, Table 16).

There were majorities in favour of more spending on five out of the eight services mentioned by Edgell and Duke, with the National Health Service and education as the most frequently supported services (health 83 per cent, education 74 per cent, see Edgell and Duke, 1991, p.77, Table 4.3). Defence was the only service for which the majority (50 per cent) favoured less spending, with only 20 per cent favouring more spending. Moreover, the British Social Attitude surveys have reinforced Edgell and Duke's findings, as here again we can see that only the NHS was placed higher than education.

My interviews in 1988 again confirmed the high rating for education. The number favouring more spending was subtracted from the number favouring less to give an index for comparison with government policies (see Table 6.5 and Chapter 8). A minus sign in the index means that the number of interviewees who were opposed to government policies on that sub-issue exceeds the number in favour by that figure. A plus sign means that the number favouring government policies on that sub-issue exceeds the number opposed by that figure. This meant that in the case of general spending on education the index came to -32, a clear majority therefore being opposed to government policies on this particular sub-issue.

Table 6.4
Highest priority for government spending,
BSA 1983/4, 1987/8

	1st.Priority		2nd.Priority	
	1983/4	1987	1983/4	1987
	%	%	%	%
Health	37	52	26	27
Education	24	24	26	31
Help for industry	16	5	13	7
Social benefits	6	4	6	7
Housing	7	8	13	16

Note: The rest of the 10 items came lower.

Source: Jowell et al, 1984 and 1988

Table 6.5
Favouring more or less spending on education
(case studies, 1988)

	n=
Spend less	2
Spend more	34
Other answer	16
Less - more	-32
Total	52

Unlike the British Social Attitude surveys and Greater Manchester Surveys I found that more of my informants favoured extra spending on housing (-33), as well as the NHS (-42), than extra spending on education (-32). However, benefits (-25), industry (-24), the police (-16) and defence (+28) came below education. Once again a large majority favoured a reduction in defence spending. In answer to question 12, where informants listed their priorities, education was again placed second. Forty informants placed it in the top three of their priorities for extra spending (10 placed it first, 19 second and 11 third). Only the National Health Service received more support.

Table 6.6
Priorities for extra public spending
(case studies, 1988)
Number placing an option in their top 3

	n=
Health	49
Education	40
Housing	18
Police	16
Industry	15
Benefits	14
Defence	8
Total	52

The strength of support for extra public spending cannot be isolated from events in 1988 prior to the case study interviews. At the time of the budget in 1988 there was a great amount of public debate about the reduction in taxation at high income levels. This was reflected in the views expressed by informants at an individual as well as a cumulative level. For example, when one informant was asked if he had any further comments at the end of the interview, he responded with an attack on the government's priorities.

> I think that with all the publicity and pressure put on the government at the time of the budget this year, to carry on with tax cuts when the NHS is short of money was a very poor thing to do. (Informant No. 50)

It would, however, be an oversimplification to simply state that voters favoured more public spending on education without acknowledging different attitudes to different educational services. British Social Attitude survey respondents have also been asked to prioritize different types of educational spending. In the Table 6.7 we can see that, by 1987, secondary schools had overtaken special needs as the service that was perceived as most in need of extra government spending.

Edgell and Duke also found that schools received the most support when respondents were asked if they would be prepared to pay more in taxes or rates for individual education services. 75 per cent were prepared to pay more for schools, 65 per cent for universities and 60 per cent for the Youth Training Scheme (Edgell and Duke, 1985, Appendix IV A224). These findings were again supported in the 1988 case studies when the same question was asked. Out of the 52 informants, 38 were prepared to pay more for schools, 33 for colleges, 29 for the youth employment or job training schemes and 23 for

Table 6.7
Priority for extra government spending on education,
BSA 1983/4, 1987/8

	1st.Priority		2nd.Priority	
	1983/4	1987	1983/4	1987
	%	%	%	%
Special needs	32	28	27	25
Secondary schools	29	37	25	26
Primary schools	16	15	17	17
Nursery/pre-school	10	8	12	9
Further/higher education	9	9	15	19

Source: Jowell et al, 1984 and 1988

nurseries. The relatively low level of support for employment training schemes could reflect the cynical attitudes of those informants who saw them as having little value. The local level of nursery provision had an effect on some responses as Labourville was well-known for its excellent nursery facilities and extra spending was regarded as unnecessary there.

Existing knowledge of educational provision clearly influences attitudes to education. Edgell and Duke assessed knowledge of four services (including education) and questioned respondents about the level of authority responsible for each of eight services (see 5.5). As 25 per cent of their respondents wrongly attributed the Greater Manchester Council with responsibilities for education, we can question the extent to which they associated their local authorities in Torytown and Labourville with decisions about educational spending. Personal assessments of the impact of cuts in educational spending may also be unreliable. For example, in their second survey, Edgell and Duke found that only 32 per cent of those households resorting to private tuition specifically because of the spending cuts had mentioned it previously under impact. They also found that only 27 per cent of those using private nursery facilities specifically because of the local cuts had given this answer earlier (Edgell and Duke, 1986b, p.12).

The effect of recent events on attitudes has already been noted (Chapter 3, 5.5 and this section). Edgell and Duke also observed the effect of recent events on knowledge of and attitudes towards public spending. Their first survey followed a prolonged teachers' strike and school closures dispute in Torytown, where the cuts in educational spending were frequently reported in the media. After monitoring the local press before the 1980/1 survey they found that nearly a quarter of all press reports on spending cuts in Torytown were related to education whereas the comparable figure for Labourville was nearly one in ten (Edgell and Duke, 1981, F1/2). In Torytown education was the most frequently mentioned area of impact amongst respondents but in Labourville it was work or jobs. Educational spending remained a controversial issue in Torytown in the second survey but health replaced it as the service about which respondents had the most knowledge overall. An increased awareness of health cuts may have resulted from the lengthy NHS pay dispute in 1983.

In both of the Greater Manchester Surveys, Labourville respondents were better informed about changes in public spending in general than were Torytown respondents, despite the greater level of cuts in Torytown (Table 6.8). However, Torytown respondents were more aware of spending cuts in education than Labourville respondents.

Table 6.8
Specific knowledge of spending cuts in education by area:
panel at first and second interviews (GMS)

	Labourville (n=334)			Torytown (n=351)		
	GMS1	GMS2	Change	GMS1	GMS2	Change
% specific knowledge	67	50	-17	70	52	-18
Most frequent mentions at GMS2	fewer staff		72	fewer staff		91
	school closures		36	school closures		69
	universities		35	school books		47

Source: Edgell and Duke, 1991, p.121, Table 6.1 amended

Edgell and Duke noted that specific knowledge was higher at the first interview because of particular events at the time (e.g. disputes over the education cuts of 1980/1). The decrease in specific knowledge at the second interview was balanced by a fall in the percentage who expressed no knowledge. On both occasions fewer Labourville respondents expressed no knowledge but more Torytown respondents expressed some specific knowledge. The most frequently mentioned effects of the spending cuts were different in the two areas.

The actual effects of the cuts in educational spending were less apparent in Labourville and, unlike in Torytown, the most frequently mentioned effects were not entirely local. Universities came third in the Labourville list and these are institutions that are not financed by the local authority. Their higher priority in Labourville may, however, be explained by the fact that there is a university situated in the Labourville borough but none in Torytown. As we can see in the following table, more of the specific knowledge about spending cuts in Torytown was local.

Table 6.9
Perception of spending trends, specific knowledge
of spending cuts and proportion of specific knowledge by area
1983/4 (GMS)

	Spending trend			Specific knowledge	Specific knowledge
	cut	same	increase		
	%	%	%	%	%
Labourville	84	8	1	50	37
Torytown	83	4	2	52	52

Source: Edgell and Duke, 1991, p.123, Table 6.2 adapted

Edgell and Duke noted that education was the 'area of greatest knowledge viz-a-viz the cuts and the area of provision with the most salient use-knowledge-impact-reaction nexus of relationships' (Edgell and Duke, 1981, C21). Here we can see instrumental interest in education (4.1) related to knowledge and attitudes. Only about one third of households currently consumed state education (Edgell and Duke, 1985, p.14) but it was the main consumer impact in the first survey, accounting for over half of such impacts. The extra impact in Torytown was apparent at both interviews (24 per cent and 17 per cent respectively) and, although education consumer salience decreased in the second survey, it was still relatively high compared to all other services.

Table 6.10
Perceived impact of spending cuts on household
as consumers and producers by area

	Labourville (n=334)			Torytown (n=351)		
	GMS1	GMS2	Change	GMS1	GMS2	Change
	%	%	%	%	%	%
Reporting any impact	55	49	-6	55	55	0
Consumer education	16	9	-7	24	17	-7
Producer education	6	2	-4	3	4	+1

Source: Edgell and Duke, 1991, p128, Table 6.5 adapted

Support for extra spending on education was also mainly instrumental, those respondents with children at state schools tending to be most in favour of increased educational spending (in 1983/4 this was 85.4 per cent compared to 44.1 per cent of those without children in state schools). It is interesting to note here that the few parents with children at private schools were most in favour of increased educational spending (83.9 per cent in 1983/4). This may be seen as a generous attitude to state schools or (amongst those parents who receive an Assisted Place for their children or have their fees paid by the Torytown LEA) as a similar self interest to other parents. Whether education is funded by the local authority or by central government in state or private schools it still counts as part of public spending. However, the small number of respondents in any survey with children at private schools (7.8) means that any generalization about such motives is open to doubt.

The British Social Attitudes surveys have similarly reported that support for extra spending on education is instrumental. If life-cycle is used as an additional indicator, we can see (Table 6.11) that those respondents at the point in their life-cycle where they were most likely to have children at school or college were most strongly in favour of increased expenditure on education.

Table 6.11
Age group, school-leaving age and income group:
% favouring increased expenditure on education,
BSA 1984/5

	%
Age group	
18-24	47
25-34	68
35-54	57
55 & over	33
School-leaving age	
under 16	46
17-18	56
19 and over	62
Household income	
under £5,000	37
£5,000 - £7,999	52
£8,000 - £11,999	59
£12,000 and over	59

Source: Jowell et al., 1985, p.25

School-leaving age was also associated with attitudes towards expenditure on education, those longest in education being the most likely to favour increased spending on education. This tendency could lead to gender differences, as more men than women stay in education after school-leaving age. However, the findings about this are contradictory. The BSA found that, in almost all age groups, men were slightly more in favour of increased expenditure on education. Edgell and Duke found that men were more likely (38 per cent) to approve of spending cuts in general than women (30 per cent) but that opposition to the cuts related to level and involvement in the labour market rather than gender. They also found that women were better informed than men about cuts in educational spending. In households with nursery and school age children over 80 per cent of women and about 68 per cent of men expressed specific knowledge of cuts in education compared to 60 per cent of respondents in households without school age children (Edgell and Duke, 1983, p.14). Overall, when all types of households were considered, 67 per cent of women and 62 per cent of men expressed specific knowledge of cuts in education; 19 per cent of women and 13 per cent of men perceived an impact of cuts in educational spending.

When the effects of social class on attitudes to public spending on education are considered an inverse relationship between income and economic class is found. The British Social Attitudes survey 1985, for example, found that the tendency to favour more spending on education increased as income increased. However, the tendency to favour increased expenditure on education decreases as we scale Marxist class categories. Edgell and Duke found that the percentage wanting more spending on education decreased from 76 per cent of workers, 71 per cent of controllers and petty bourgeoisie, to 60 per cent of employers. This apparent anomaly may be explained by the classification of highly educated, highly paid workers. Level of education is not clearly represented in Marxist class categories, as employers and the petty bourgeoisie may not necessarily be highly educated whilst well qualified professionals are likely to be classified as workers or controllers. Thus, occupational class categories may provide a better, but still inaccurate, representation of educational attainment, which is clearly associated with attitudes to educational expenditure.

The picture emerging of the ideal type of supporter of increased spending on education is that of a highly educated parent of a child, or children, currently being educated. Conversely, supporters of educational spending cuts are characterized as employers who are not highly educated and have no children currently being educated. Few respondents fit these ideal types (and the number favouring the cuts is quite small) but, as indicated in Chapter 4, these variables affect interest in education. Chapter 8 will also show that they are associated with voting behaviour. If we consider the relationship between voting behaviour and attitudes to educational spending we can see that the same independent variables affect both attitudinal areas. In 1983/4 (GMS2) 58.0 per cent of Conservatives, 87.4 per cent of Labour voters and 80.5 per cent of Liberal/SDP voters favoured increased expenditure on education. Although the percentage favouring increased spending had risen for each type of voter by the second survey, the basic pattern remained the same. In 1980/1 and 1983/4 (GMS1 and GMS2) over half of all Conservative voters favoured increased spending, but a greater proportion of Alliance voters and (even more) Labour voters favoured an increase.

⋌ 6.5 Summary of findings

During the 1980s educational expenditure fell as a percentage of total government spending on public services and as a percentage of the United Kingdom's gross domestic product (6.1). Central government reduced local authority control over its own expenditure, by increasing control from above (central government) and below (individual schools). Conservative governments' policies effectively put market orientated economic principles before social need; this being most clearly seen in the introduction of Assisted Places and the removal of local authorities' obligation to provide free meals or milk.

Local authorities still have some freedom to determine how their dwindling resources should be spent and their political identity is a key factor in determining how this is done. Torytown, for example, been more zealous than Labourville in following central government policy on educational spending. It promoted Assisted Places and paid the fees for some local children to attend independent schools, whilst spending less per state educated pupil than Labourville and spending less than Labourville on school meals and milk. Labourville, on the other hand, provided generous nursery facilities although it had no obligation to do so.

The majority of voters, however, have consistently claimed to be opposed to spending cuts and prepared to pay more in taxes to increase public spending. More than half of the relatively few GMS respondents who approved of the spending cuts were in favour of more spending on education. This poses problems for theories of decline of public esteem (6.2.3) and natural inequality (6.2.4). Even if there has been a decline in public esteem and/or a common belief in natural inequalities, such attitudes have apparently not led to the public legitimation of Conservative spending policies. In terms of Saunders' dual state thesis (6.2.2) voters strongly emphasised social need (the 'local' state) rather than profit (the 'central' state). This apparent support for increased spending was so strong that what has been measured here has been the comparative strength of support rather than the balance between those in favour and those against the spending cuts. The ideal types described in 6.4 must therefore be considered carefully.   Although less likely to favour increased spending than other groups, 60 per cent of employers, 54-8 per cent of Conservatives, 46 per cent of respondents who left school below the age of 16 and 44-66 per cent of respondents who do not have children at school all favoured more public spending on education.   They may have given relatively less support than respondents in other categories but such large percentages cannot be ignored.

The general impression is still one of support for public services, but an apparent contradiction remains, to be considered later (8.2.4). If there is so much support for public spending on education (and other services) why have so many voters continued to vote for a political party that is committed to cuts in public spending?

7 Attitudes:
Various sub-issues

7.1 Selecting sub-issues

The word 'sub-issue' is used in this book to describe each of the many issues debated within education as a singular political issue (1.2). As such, a sub-issue is a vague concept and the selection of sub-issues for analysis is partly subjective. Selection has, however, been based on a continuous trawling of the current framework of educational debate (Chapters 1 and 5), the context being examined at both national and local levels (Chapter 3).

The criteria used to identify sub-issues and decide which should be analyzed were mainly determined by topicality. First, could it be identified as a sub-issue? Definitions are important and are considered at the start of each of the sections of this chapter relating to an individual sub-issue. For example, discussions about educational 'standards' constitute a large, and apparently permanent, feature of educational debates but the concept of 'standards' is very vague (7.2.1). Secondly, was it a topic about which voters were likely to have opinions? In the case study interviews a question was asked about the level of teachers' pay but few informants had any knowledge of teachers' rates of pay. Lack of accurate knowledge did not necessarily mean that an informant had no opinion about a subject (5.5) but, in the case of teachers' pay, many claimed that they did not have the knowledge on which to base an opinion. Thirdly, was quantitative data available about attitudes to a sub-issue? Very little survey data was available with which to make comparisons about attitudes to teachers' pay, provisions for schools to 'opt out' of local authority control (see 5.5) and proposals for the local management of schools. Although such subjects could be included in the case study interview schedule (and the first two were) the generalization of findings would have been severely limited by the lack of comparable survey data. Finally, sub-issues were assessed overall for topicality. Some failed to satisfy all three criteria but were included because of their topicality. For example, no directly comparable questions about Clause 28 were asked in the British Social Attitudes surveys or the Greater Manchester Study (although some related questions were asked) but the sub-issue was included because of its topicality. The emphasis within the research was on the current framework of educational debate at both national and local levels and sub-issues were selected accordingly.

Some sub-issues seemed to emerge from national rather than local debate: for example, the standards debate, National Curriculum and student loans. Others could be more closely associated with local debates, in Torytown in particular: for example, the comprehensive versus bipartite system of secondary education and coeducational versus single sex schools. Yet to define a sub-issue as primarily local or national would be an over-simplification. Parental choice was, for example, a key sub-issue during the 1980s at both national and local level. Chapter 6 also showed that not only was public spending on education a sub-issue that had relevance at both national and local level, but perceptions of spending trends and attitudes towards them could differ according to local context.

7.2 Standards

A supposed rise or fall in the standard of education is a regular feature of educational and political debate, but it is also a notoriously illusive concept and participants in the debate will often have their own competing definitions of the term. If, at a very simple level, we see standards as degrees or measurements of quality it is quite clear that quality is a subjective expression and that degrees or measurements are social constructs. People will disagree about what constitutes a high standard of education in much the same way that they will disagree about the quality of television programmes, art, music or literature. Yet some art forms will win the distinction of becoming 'classics', having been assessed as such, not on the basis of a measurable characteristic, but because they have been socially defined as such. Similarly, the general public will tend to regard certain educational institutions, such as public schools and the universities of Oxford and Cambridge, as superior to others, not on the basis of measurable characteristics but on the basis of subjective perceptions of quality.

7.2.1 Defining standards

My approach to the standards debate involved asking informants what standards meant to them and whether they thought that standards of education had fallen or risen. Their families' educational history and changes in the

114

provision of education and in measures of attainment were also considered because such debates are often carried out on the flimsiest of empirical bases. The subjective nature of the debate and its alliance to competing perspectives is emphasised throughout.

A small sample of the definitions provided in the 1988 case studies reveals the nature of the problem. Informants generally reacted with surprise when they were asked what they meant by standards and many had difficulty in formulating a clear response.

> At least every child should be able to read and write when they leave school. (Informant No. 48, Q47 Illiterate non-voter)

> Basically respect for their parents, the school and the teachers and the environment. (Informant No. 28, Q47 Police officer)

> What the average reaches. (Informant No.01, Q47 Teacher)

> I don't think it's got anything to do with passing examinations (though education's got a lot to do with that) but it's got to do with people's attitudes. (Informant No.25, Computer consultant)

> The whole education. Not only academic but the virtues of developing things in children; the talents and respect for other people, adapting the needs of the child and preparing them for a job, their next school or whatever. (Informant No.12, Teacher)

The responses were diverse and an attempt to categorize the aspects of education mentioned by the 52 informants (Table 7.1) revealed two central themes; the 'overt' curriculum (course contents, qualifications etc.) and the 'hidden' curriculum (discipline, attitudes, effort etc.). As some informants mentioned more than one aspect the total is more than 52. Some of the aspects mentioned are measurable (for example pupil:teacher ratio), or may at least be assessed (breadth of the curriculum, knowledge of English and Mathematics) but the methods used in doing this are often disputed. Other aspects are virtually impossible to measure or compare over time. Discipline, for example, was frequently mentioned and sufficient emphasis was placed on it throughout the case study interviews for it to warrant particular attention (7.3). However, if standards of discipline are to be assessed we need reliable measurements of data recorded both before and after the supposed decline in school discipline. The lack of answers to such practical problems means that there is no solid basis on which to judge the extent to which discipline has been a problem in the past and how it compares with the present.

Table 7.1
Definitions of 'standards' (case studies)

	n=
Wider curriculum	18
Discipline	17
Know more	14
English/Maths	11
Society/jobs	7
Qualifications/exams	6
Effort/homework	6
Pupil:teacher ratio	2
Other	9

Moreover, it is not possible to determine the cause of discipline problems in schools. To what extent is it caused by the schools and the teachers and to what extent by external influences on the pupils? Critics of recent governments have argued that discipline has been integrated into discussions about educational standards to support Conservative claims about a decline in traditional values (5.4). A concise Marxist critique of the Government's approach to the standards debate can be taken from Hall.

> Standards ...This is a conservative codeword for regressing to the past. It means social discipline, conformity to tradition, respect for authority - the hallmarks of a tamed and subordinated population. Nevertheless, the word is pointing at something real, not imaginary. The left ran away from the standards debate (or made a present of it to the other side, as in James Callaghan's and Shirley Williams's Great Debate), when we should have stood and fought. Of course a comprehensive literacy - and the deepening and enrichment of literacy as a so-called 'life skill' - must be a socialist goal. When did you last see a working person who profited from being ignorant? (Hall, 1983, p.4)

Yet the influence of the Black Papers (Cox et al, 1969-1975) and Conservative governments during the 1980s (5.4) is more noticeable in the standards debate than that of socialist educationalists and politicians. Thus, after 13 years of Conservative government, there is a certain irony in the championship of standards in state education by Conservative politicians who do not themselves choose to consume it (5.4).

If standards are pointing at something real and not imaginary, that something could be assessed by looking at the leaving qualifications gained by school pupils. This sort of procedure is not straightforward because in order to appreciate individual achievement (output) we need to consider the whole circumstances of a child's life (input). Some children will be at a disadvantage because of social inequalities, physical or mental handicaps or the lack of a supportive family. Thus, the achievements of a child with mainly disadvantageous inputs cannot be directly comparable to the achievements of a child whose circumstances are entirely favourable. What may be classed as a major feat of achievement for one child may be regarded as a minor achievement for another. Educational researchers are therefore tending to concentrate their efforts on the measurement of inputs as well as outputs in their attempts to assess educational attainment and comparisons between individual schools.

However, paper qualifications are often regarded by employers and parents as the simplest way of assessing the educational achievements of school-leavers and the quality of the education system as a whole. If such outputs are considered without regard to inputs it is possible to see a continuous rise in educational attainment during the past thirty years. In 1961/2 73 per cent of pupils in England and Wales left school without even attempting a school-leaving examination (Ministry of Education, 1964). The introduction of the CSE, the raising of the school leaving age and the growth of comprehensive schools increased the number of pupils taking examinations. By 1973/4 only 20 per cent of pupils left school in England without a graded GCE or CSE result and by 1980/1 this figure had fallen to 11 per cent (DES, 1982, Table 3).

Between 1980/1 and 1985/6 the proportion of school-leavers with no GCE or CSE passes again fell, but there is evidence that school-leavers qualifications reached a standstill in 1983. For the first time since 1945 official figures showed no rise in the qualifications obtained. Figures for the 1985/6 academic year show that the same proportion of pupils as in 1983 left school with nothing, the same proportion gained one A level and there was no perceptible sign of improvement on some other indicators (for example, the number gaining at least one O level or at least 5 O levels). As the effects of government education policy tend to show up in the statistics three or four years later, these statistics show the effects of government policy during Mrs Thatcher's first term of office. They do not include the effects of the large scale teachers' strike in 1987, when children were likely to have suffered more severely.

In the early 1990s reports from the examination boards indicate a substantial rise in the number of pupils getting the equivalent of a GCE O level pass since the introduction of the GCSE. Yet, another illustration of the illusive nature of standards can be seen in continuing debates about both GCSE and A'Level GCE results. Are the increasing numbers of passes and high grades an indication of improved standards, or a result of teachers and examiners being less scrupulous in their work?

7.2.3 Family educational histories

In the 1988 case studies informants were asked questions about their families' educational history. They were also asked to compare the standard of education and teaching when they were at school with current standards. In this way it was possible to compare current attitudes with past experience. Although 24 thought that educational standards had improved, and this was the modal response, 28 did not. Yet looking at the long term changes in their families' education (Table 7.2) we can see that every indicator suggests a long term improvement. Many of the informants' parents had no secondary school education and left school at 14 with no qualifications. Informants and their spouses were more likely to have had a secondary school education, left school later (the modal age was 15) and obtained a qualification, although the majority still obtained none.

Table 7.2 does not take into account the effects of age cohorts and some informants were older than the parents of other informants. It is, however, possible to see informants' ages reflected in their responses; for example, only the older informants attended elementary schools. Attendance at a secondary modern school was the modal response for informants and their spouses. This reflects not only the type of secondary school provision in Torytown but also the fact that it was the most common form of secondary education elsewhere when middle-aged informants were attending school. Younger informants could not leave school below the age of 16 because of the raising of the school leaving age in 1972. Informants' age is also reflected in their highest school leaving qualification. The School Certificate (matriculation) was a group examination. Pupils had to pass in 5 subjects: English, mathematics, Latin and/or a foreign language, a science and one other. It thus established a core curriculum. In 1950 it was replaced by the GCE, a single subject exam. Heads could then allow pupils to choose previously unacceptable combinations of subjects. Pupils who would have been unlikely to pass the School Certificate could obtain 4 or more GCEs or (from the 1960s onwards) several CSEs.

Table 7.2
Family educational history (case studies)

	Father n=	Mother n=	Spouse n=	Informant n=
Type of school				
No spouse	-	-	12	-
Don't know or foreign	23	19	2	2
Special	-	-	1	1
Elementary	19	23	7	7
Secondary modern	2	2	19	22
Grammar	4	3	7	8
Technical or 'Central'	-	1	-	4
High/Comprehensive	2	2	2	5
Private/Direct Grant	2	2	2	3
School leaving age				
No spouse	-	-	12	-
Don't know	20	16	-	-
11	1	1	-	-
12	5	3	-	-
13	3	4	-	1
14	22	24	10	10
15	-	1	16	24
16	-	2	10	12
18	1	1	4	4
19	-	-	-	1
Highest school leaving qualification				
No spouse	-	-	12	-
Don't know	18	12	-	-
Unspecific (eg 'report')	-	2	4	1
None	31	35	25	32
ULCI	-	-	-	2
RSA	-	-	-	2
CSE	-	-	1	3
O'Level or 16+	1	-	6	6
Matriculation/school cert.	1	2	1	2
A'Level	1	1	3	4

To get a clearer picture of informant's educational histories I split them into three age cohorts according to their educational context (Table 7.3). Informants born before 1930 could have left school before the changes introduced by the 1944 Education Act, those born between 1930 and 1949 would have had their education largely determined by the 1944 Act (i.e. in a tripartite or bipartite system), and those born from 1950 onwards would have been most influenced by the changes since the 1960s (including comprehensivization for some).

Table 7.3
School-leaving qualifications by age cohort (case studies)

	1910/29	1930/49	1950/69
	n=	n=	n=
Unspecific	-	1	-
None	11	16	5
ULCI	-	1	1
RSA	1	1	-
CSE	-	-	3
O'Level or 16+	1	-	5
Matriculation	2	-	-
A'Level	-	3	1
Total	15	22	15

Over two thirds of the informants in each of the earliest age cohorts left school with no qualification compared to about one third in the youngest age cohort. Such findings and the findings from the previous table therefore support the national statistics already given about the long term decrease in the proportion of pupils leaving school with no qualifications. They certainly do not support the claim that educational standards (if defined by qualifications) have fallen since most of the informants were at school.

Informants often took a fatalistic approach to their own educational experiences, blaming themselves and supposed innate deficiencies for lack of achievement. One particularly memorable informant was illiterate but had nevertheless managed to make a reasonable living by converting cars. When asked what type of secondary school he attended he answered that he thought it was a secondary modern but was unsure (and he was similarly unsure what type of school his daughter had attended). Several informants were not sure about how to categorize their school (see 7.8.1).

> It wouldn't have made any difference [what type of school it was]. I was left handed and they tried to make me write with my right. I didn't stand a chance. I couldn't read when I left school so it would have been a waste going anywhere else. I was clever in different ways.

I had a photographic memory. I could picture something before I made it. If I'd been able to read and write I could have gone right to the top. (Informant No. 48, Q22)

This man was particularly proud of the way that he had coped with his illiteracy. He showed me the home improvements he had made and explained how he dealt with letters, finances and officials. However, he seemed to have mixed views about his illiteracy. Although he complained about his treatment at school and the lack of support from his parents (7.9.5) he also spoke of it as a natural rather than a socially constructed problem. Most informants regarded educational failure as personal failure, apparently unrelated to the education system as a whole or to the wider social system. Thus, educational and social constraints could be perceived as natural. Most obviously, the school leaving age was to many people an automatic time of transference to work (7.9.5). One informant for example left school at 14 because it was regarded as the natural thing to do.

It seemed to be the thing to follow. You just left school and went to work. (Informant No.50, Q25)

The effect of social influences tended to be underplayed when informants spoke of their own educational achievement but, when the educational experiences of all of the case study interviewees were compared the constraints imposed by individual families (7.9.5) and society in general could hardly have emerged more forcefully.

7.2.4 Comparing standards

It has already been noted that the most common response in 1988 to the question about educational standards was that they were currently higher (an index of -12, although the majority disagreed). The frequencies are shown in Table 7.4.

Table 7.4
Current educational standards compared with those during informants' school-days (case studies, Q47)

	n=
Lower now	12
Higher now	24
Same now	4
Mixed views	8
Don't know	4
Lower - higher	-12

The British Social Attitude surveys found that respondents opinions were quite evenly balanced, although slightly more believed that standards had fallen.

Table 7.5
Current educational standards compared with those during respondents' school-days (BSA)

	1983/4	1984/5
	%	%
Higher now	39	37
About the same	15	18
Lower now	41	38
Not educated here/DK	5	6

Source: Jowell et al, 1984 and 1985

In 1987 BSA did not ask the above question. Instead it asked; 'On the whole, do you think school-leavers are better qualified or worse qualified nowadays than they were 10 years ago?' (Table 7.6).

Table 7.6
Are school-leavers better or worse qualified now? (BSA)

	%
Much better now	11.7
A little better	24.8
About the same	25.6
A little worse	21.2
Much worse now	15.3
Don't know	0.6

Source: Jowell et al, 1988

It is possible that my earlier questioning about families' educational histories may have affected responses by reminding informants of educational provision in the past. Questions about educational standards are also affected by the time scale adopted. For example, in his 1987 General Election survey Crewe (Crewe, 1987) asked respondents for their perceptions of recent changes. Sixtyeight percent of his respondents believed that the quality of education had got worse compared to 10 per cent who thought that it had improved. Much depends on what respondents define as recent and what they define as standards. If Crewe's respondents were referring to changes introduced by Conservative governments during the 1980s and only to the proportion of school-leavers gaining qualifications, the official figures for 1983 to 1986 only point to a standstill and not a decline. The question I asked implied a longer time scale and included a period (1945 to 1983) when secondary education was extended to all, the school leaving age was raised twice and more pupils took examinations.

> They must be higher because there's far less children in classes than when I was at school. I'm talking about 43 children in a class when I was at school so they must be better. (Informant No. 44, Q47)

Some informants saw the emphasis on reading, writing and arithmetic as a credit to educational standards in the past and complained of school-leavers' deficiencies in that respect whilst others saw the emphasis on the three Rs as a defect.

> It was just a matter of reading, writing and arithmetic when I went to school. There's a lot more goes on now. (Informant No. 49, Q47)

They're far better. They've got it at their feet. In them days there was nothing. There was just the 3 Rs and that was your lot... [About teaching standards.] Fabulous today but not then. I've been in schools and I've seen it. The teachers put it over to the kids better. In them days it was all the cane and God knows what. I think we learned more about religion but I think, with the teaching standards, they've got everything today. (Informant No. 20, Q47)

The contrast between the two school cultures left some people quite amazed and out of their depth with their own children.

They're higher now because I don't know half the things that they're doing now. They leave me standing. When our [eldest] was doing Maths I hadn't a clue what she was going on about. They're definitely higher. ...[About teaching standards] Higher. They seem to go into depth more with everything. They don't seem to just give them set work to do. They stretch their minds more. They're not just satisfied with an answer. They ask why or how they reached that answer. (Informant No. 16, Q47)

To another informant it seemed that educational standards must have increased in order to equip school leavers for the fierce competition for jobs.

When I left school you could choose from hundreds of jobs in 1954 but now you've got to be well educated to stand a chance of a job. There used to be that much industry in [area near Torytown] that anyone could get a job. (Informant No.41, Q47)

7.2.5 Summary of findings

The concept of 'standards' therefore covers a wide range of indicators but is so well established within educational debate that it had to be considered as a sub-issue. Individual definitions of the word vary, as do perceptions of recent and long-term changes. Such definitions tend to fit into two types of categories; those emphasising the overt curriculum and those emphasising the hidden curriculum. When the overt curriculum is considered we can see that more children now obtain more qualifications than in the past (although there some are indications that the increase in qualifications came to a standstill between 1983 and 1985). Standards, when defined as the overt curriculum, have therefore clearly improved and claims that comprehensivization would inevitably result in a reduction in standards (Lynn, 1970) have not been supported. Informants with personal experience of and the most knowledge of the education system are, moreover, most likely to believe that standards have risen since they were at school.

However, have standards increased enough to satisfy the demands of the economy and in comparison with educational standards in other countries? This research has not generated data about such related questions and possible answers cannot be contemplated. The sort of public debate about standards that has been considered so far is, in any case, based on limited knowledge, and knowledge about the demands of the economy and education in other countries is likely to be even less substantial. As the debate is based on such weak foundations it can easily be manipulated by politicians; hence Dennison's theory (6.2.3) that Conservative governments in the 1980s have criticized the state education system in order to reduce public confidence in it and thereby justify educational spending policies. At the moment the apparent (see 6.5) lack of public support for spending cuts does not verify Dennison's conclusion, although attitudes towards teachers (7.3.3) lend support to his claims about low public esteem. It is also reasonable to conclude that a Government led drive towards privatization is likely to benefit from a common belief that the standard of education in state schools has declined and from the associated increase in the consumption of private education (7.9.2).

7.3 Discipline

It has already been observed that some of my informants based their judgements about changing educational standards partly or entirely on their perceptions of the management of discipline in schools. Again, discipline is such a well-established feature of educational debate that it has to be considered a sub-issue, but again it is a notoriously vague concept. Unlike educational qualifications, it cannot be quantified and there is no reliable method for making comparisons over time. Individual teachers will be reluctant to admit to having severe problems in maintaining discipline in class. Some members of the public may make assumptions about discipline in schools that are based on the behaviour of just a few pupils outside the school gates. Thus, the lack of a substantial knowledge base from which to formulate opinions means that hearsay is often labelled as fact. Speculation may be more closely related to the 'generation gap', amplified fears or political attitudes than to objective, empirically grounded debate.

7.3.1 Political definitions and attitudes

Political attitudes towards discipline in schools tend to vary between two extremes; right-wing concern about a supposed deterioration in moral values that is inextricably linked with egalitarianism, or a left-wing view that equates discipline with an authoritarianism that is inextricably linked with inequality of opportunity. Thus, Hall was (1983, p.4) concerned about the 'tamed and subordinate population', that is necessary for the maintenance of a capitalist system, and its socialization through the education system. Many left-wingers (including pluralists and Marxists) will acknowledge that some sort of discipline is necessary in all schools if they are to actually succeed in educating pupils, but their concern is about the use of discipline as a form of authoritarian control. The problem for the left lies in distinguishing between authoritarianism and the discipline that is needed if pupils are to actually learn and work effectively with other people. Wolpe claimed that,

> In order not to be tainted by the label of 'authoritarianism' the left has turned a blind eye to some of the questionable aspects of libertarian policies and has avoided recognition of the relation of discipline to social problems within schools. We know perfectly well that schools reflect the social conditions of the wider society, and what factors contribute to these. We know how pupils react and the form their alienation takes. But we also need to consider and assess the role of discipline as both a short-term and a long-term measure in order to produce an effective educational system... (Wolpe, 1983, p.112)

If a fear of authoritarianism were to result in parents and teachers failing to teach children self-discipline and effective working practices, individual pupils and the education system as a whole would inevitably suffer.

Right-wing concern varies from a supposed excess of freedom in schools, which results in not enough being learned, to a belief that society in general has deteriorated and that only major changes in moral values can solve discipline problems. Rhodes Boyson has played a major roll in expressing the case about the deterioration of society in general. In the 1975 Black Paper (Cox and Boyson) he argued that egalitarianism, lack of discipline in schools and the decline of the traditional family (5.4) has resulted in a deterioration of the whole moral order of society. He claimed that parents often failed to be 'real' parents (Cox and Boyson, 1975, p.51), 'real' parents being fathers who go out to work and mothers who do not go out to work. According to Boyson, if mothers were discouraged from entering the workforce, discipline in the family, and consequently in the school, would improve. Egalitarian ideals are, according to this view, responsible for lack of discipline because they breed discontent and foment social disorder. However, this authoritarian stance does not take into account the many families who are totally dependent on a woman's earnings or suggest changes that would lead to all men being both willing and able to support their families financially. It tends to ignore

126

the perpetuation of severe social problems as a result of unequal opportunities and presents an unrealistic image of the past as a time when discipline was not a problem.

> [About his father] He told me about how he was cheating once because he copied a lad's work. They found him out and I think he must have got into real trouble. It seems funny because you don't think your parents are capable of doing things like that. (Informant No.16, Q32)

Again we can see that, if either the left-wing extreme that associates discipline with authoritarianism or the right-wing extreme that associates egalitarianism with lack of discipline were to be assimilated into the education system, children would not benefit. Some discipline is needed, but a harsh discipline that pupils perceive as unfair and associate with social injustice could lead to resentment and social disorder rather than social conformity.

7.3.2 Topical debate in 1988

During the summer of 1988 a government sponsored committee of inquiry into discipline in schools (the Elton committee) was collecting evidence from teachers' unions. The committee's report was not published until the beginning of 1989 but the evidence being collected was widely publicised during the weeks leading up to and including the case study interviews. The National Association of Headteachers (NAHT) for example, submitted its findings from a survey of 1,600 headteachers in England and Wales (Times Educational Supplement, 17 June 1988). In the survey a majority of headteachers reported either no increase or only a marginal increase in disruptive behaviour since 1985. However, 14 per cent of nursery school heads, 15 per cent of infant school heads and nearly 20 per cent of secondary school heads reported an increase in violence, disruptive behaviour or vandalism.

The NAHT blamed the child's whole environment, observing that many parents failed to develop proper social habits in their children and some parents reacted with open hostility to requests for cooperation from their child's school. The media and peer group pressure were also regarded as partly to blame and the abolition of corporal punishment in state schools was regretted, with reservations,

> ... it is its loss as a deterrent rather than a weapon which is mourned in the majority of cases, particularly since there appears to be little or

nothing to offer as an alternative in the eyes of pupils. (NAHT quoted in The Guardian, 17 June 1988)

Similarly, evidence from the National Association of Schoolmasters/Union of Women Teachers (NAS/UWT), which included copies of thirteen publications it had issued since 1972, described problems that were generated from both inside and outside the school system. External problems such as lack of discipline in the home, alcohol and drug abuse and internal problems such as over-sized classes and badly resourced government initiatives were also mentioned.

Media reports on the evidence presented to the Elton committee in the weeks leading up to the case studies could therefore present discipline as a major or a minor problem. The BSA 5th. Report tried to provide a balanced resume of the conflicting evidence presented in the summer of 1988.

> Another survey in 15 LEAs, carried out on behalf of the National Association of Head Teachers and published in June 1988, found that teachers face one assault every four minutes; and overall 18,000 acts of violence annually, with 30,000 children suspended every year for bad behaviour. However, the findings of other recent surveys have been disputed by bodies such as the Children's Legal Centre, and by the national Children's Bureau in its evidence to the Elton Enquiry. (Source: Jowell et al, 1988, p.30)

Findings about the number of acts of violence therefore present a different impression than the NAHT findings that most headteachers reported either no increase or a marginal increase in disruptive behaviour. Informants' perceptions of discipline problems in schools could therefore be influenced by the information selected by the newspapers they read. As twice as many case study informants read 'Conservative' newspapers as 'non-Conservative' newspapers (**Table 5.1**), their attitudes were most likely to be affected by the Conservative definition of discipline as a major problem.

7.3.3 BSA findings in 1987

The 1987 BSA survey asked three questions about attitudes towards teachers in state secondary schools:

d) Do you think parents have more respect or less respect for
   teachers nowadays than they did 10 years ago?
e) And do you think pupils have more respect or less respect for
   teachers nowadays than they did 10 years ago?

f) Do you think teachers are more dedicated to their jobs than they were 10 years ago?

g) And, on the whole, do you think the job of a state school -teacher is more difficult or less difficult nowadays than it was 10 years ago?

Table 7.7
Responses to questions about teachers, BSA 1987

%	More now %	About same %	Less no %	DK
d)	5.2	22.8	71.3	0.2
e)	2.2	9.5	87.6	0.2
f)	5.7	33.5	60.0	0.4
g)	62.1	15.7	21.6	0.2

Source: Jowell et al, 1988

Thus, a majority expressed the view that parents and pupils have less respect for teachers than they did 10 years ago, that teachers were less dedicated to their jobs and that the job of a teacher was more difficult than it was 10 years ago. Although responses to these questions are strongly skewed towards a belief that teachers have major problems the combination of responses means that the overall impression is not a strong criticism of teachers themselves. When each of the four questions and answers is considered it is reasonable to ask 'Why?'. Why do parents and pupils have less respect for teachers? Why is it believed that teachers are less dedicated to their jobs? Why is the job of teacher seen as more difficult now? As these BSA findings were not available before the 1988 case study interviews, I did not structure the interviews in order to answer these particular questions. However, the qualitative findings generated by the case studies provide some possible explanations.

7.3.4 Qualitative data in 1988

As the 'discipline' debate was highly topical at the time of the case studies it is not surprising that many informants mentioned discipline problems when they considered the standards debate. Some (for example, Informant No.20, quoted in 7.1) felt that standards had improved partly as a result of a more relaxed attitude amongst teachers, but several thought that standards had declined because of lack of discipline in schools. This was blamed on teachers, parents or society in general. One informant, for example, blamed teachers and reinforced the negative impression about teachers by elsewhere claiming that they were well paid for an easy job.

> They're not as strict now. They seem to get away with more nowadays. They seem to be more lenient. We used to get done for the slightest thing. Now they seem to laugh it off unless it's something big. They seem to stop off now and not bother. We used to have the school board round if we were off for two days. (Informant No.27, Q48)

When the 1988 case study informants were asked to compare current teaching standards with those during their schooldays the most common response was non-committal. Many had mixed views on the subject or just admitted that they did not know enough to make a comparison.

Table 7.8
Current teaching standards compared with those during informants' school-days, Q48 (case studies)

	n=
Lower now	11
Higher now	17
Same now	6
Mixed views	9
Don't know	9
Lower - higher	-5

When I asked informants to explain their answer 24 said that there was less discipline or respect for authority. This emphasis is an important feature in the standards debate and it has already been noted that levels of discipline cannot be measured. There was however, an overwhelming impression that, when informants were comparing their own schooldays with those of today, they perceived two different cultures and that discipline (or lack of it) was used as an important characteristic when distinguishing between the two. The headteacher at a junior school explained how he perceived the differences between the two.

> According to the figures that I've seen people are taking and getting more exams than when I was at school but standards of behaviour seem to be getting worse. Mind you I'm making a comparison with grammar schools where, apart from belting you regularly, they could expel you. (Informant No.08, Q47)

130

When asked to compare teaching standards one informant began by observing the major differences between the two school cultures, emphasised the relative lack of discipline today, but used an illustration that only suggested a similarity.

> It's different because when I was there you had a teacher teaching three or four subjects. They're more specialized now and better qualified. It's a different type of teaching. We put tables on the board and repeated it parrot fashion. Now they use computers and calculators. There was nothing like that when I was at school. You were frightened of the teachers. There was more discipline. You had a lot of respect for the teachers and they cared. They went right through the day with your dinner duty. At secondary school I once got a semi-detention (half an hour) for walking along the border of the flower bed and I was dreadfully ashamed. My daughter got one the other day and got a right telling off and was grounded. (Informant No. 41, Q48)

Most of the informants who claimed that educational standards had fallen associated the fall with lack of discipline. However, the pattern suggests that those closest to the education system (parents, teachers and people employed on the periphery) are most likely to believe that standards have risen since they were at school. Those with little experience of present conditions are most likely to believe that they have fallen.

> I've not been inside schools but the way kids come out they don't seem to have the respect for the teachers that we used to have. It would appear from the results that standards are lower but I don't know whether its just the attitudes these days. I don't think it helps that they're not allowed to reprimand these days. It's just a thing of the times these days. If I'd spoken to my boss in the past as they do now you'd be down the road. (Informant No.30, Q48)

> On the whole, and because I'm from a grammar school, I'd say the standard of teaching has improved in terms of the effort that's gone into it, but the self-image of teachers is lower than it was. Society thinks less of them. (Informant No.08, headteacher, Q48)

One parent with a son at secondary modern school complained about the low teaching standards there.

> At [son's secondary modern school] they seem to teach themselves in some of the subjects. There's not much homework. They seem to let

them go along on their own sweet way. No one tries to improve them. With [son] his marks are always about the same, always about average. They just let them drift along. (Informant No.47, Q48)

However, in answer to question 17, Informant 47 said that it seemed to be a 'good school' and his attitude to the teachers was quite deferential. He said that at the annual parents evenings parents were 'allowed' to speak to five teachers and gave no indication of other contact with the teachers. Despite his criticisms he had not tried to move his son to another school.

> Some of the lads have gone to a school in [area with comprehensive schools outside Torytown] which is supposed to be good but he decided to go to the same one as most of the lads from his junior school. (Informant No.47, Q48)

A police officer argued that the standard of education had fallen but that teaching standards had risen and was emphatic in blaming parents for their lack of discipline.

> Lower. A lot of it boils down to discipline and authority. When I was at school and did something that meant getting punished I went home, told me mum and got punished again. I wouldn't be a school teacher for £300 a week [A large wage in 1988]! A lot of it is a case of parents that think that their kids can do no wrong and won't let the teachers discipline them. It's not lack of teacher control, it's lack of parent control. You've got to back them, whether its teachers, police or what, in order to bring society into line - otherwise it becomes a case of the survival of the fittest. [His definition of standards] Basically respect for their parents, the school, the teachers, the environment. The ability to read and write - I don't think that comes into your question. It's just discipline that's falling apart. In [Torytown] at a little primary school - the language is choice there. The kids don't know half the words they're saying. Some of the words they're only copying - they must have heard them somewhere. (Informant No.28, Q47)

Another informant produced a similar argument but believed that both the standard of education in general and teaching standards had gone up.

> There's less respect for the teachers by children now. I don't know why, just that there is. The standard of teaching hasn't gone down.

> I just think that the way children are brought up now makes them treat people differently. (Informant No.44, Q48)

Some people expressed a sense of despair about society in general, including both the home and the school.

> Its the way society is now. A lot of children don't want to know and the teachers go along with it. They've no influence or control. When we were kids, even though we were boisterous and restless, if we were told by the right person we did it. Now nobody seems able to control them. (Informant No.47, Q47)

Similar comments to these were made when some informants described their knowledge of the murder of a schoolboy at Burnage High School (7.7.3). Although newspaper reports during the summer of 1988 may have heightened awareness of discipline problems as part of the standards debate, general concern about a perceived growth in public disorder was noticeable in responses to other questions. For example, questions about spending priorities elicited some concern that policing methods had not improved in line with increased spending on the police. Some informants expressed a preference for more police officers on the beat and fewer in patrol cars and some gave examples of riotous behaviour (7.7.3).

7.3.5 Summary of findings

The problems involved in identifying and defining reality are emphasised throughout this book but nowhere are they more pronounced than in the case of discipline as a sub-issue. At the time of the 1988 case studies the Elton committee was still collecting evidence from various sources and the evidence often seemed to be contradictory. 'Facts' are in any case often open to dispute but, as far as discipline was concerned, there was simply no way of assessing whether one individual's knowledge of the sub-issue was more accurate than another's.

Nevertheless, it is possible to assess attitudes towards discipline as a sub-issue. The two models presented (7.3.1) of political attitudes emphasise the polarization of egalitarian and authoritarian sympathies. In each case the blame for excessive or inadequate discipline could be directed at teachers, parents or society in general. Examples could be found for all of these explanations in the 1988 case studies. Thus, the BSA survey respondents' (7.3.3) perception of a lack of respect for teachers can be qualified by the finding that case study informants did not blame teachers entirely (7.11). The case studies revealed mixed views about teaching standards; the most common

being that they had improved. However, concern about lack of
in schools was widespread, cannot be overlooked and deserves more
_____ than has been possible in this short section.

7.4 Curriculum

Three particular curriculum-related themes are considered in this section; the
questions of who should control the curriculum, what the content of the
curriculum should be, and how children should be assessed. All three themes
were particularly topical at the time of the case study interviews because of
their inclusion within the Education Act (then still a Bill) 1988 via the
National Curriculum. The Government's proposal was to reduce local control,
standardize the contents of the curriculum and monitor pupils' progress by a
series of tests taken at the ages of 7, 11 and 14.

7.4.1 Defining the curriculum

It has been argued (5.4) that the subjects studied in schools and their
presentation are not natural but are defined and constructed by social and
political processes. The processes are reciprocal in that the curriculum is both
effected by and affects normative values. If, for example, the curriculum
successfully legitimizes authority, voters who have internalized the message
will believe that schools should teach respect for authority. The tautology
continues in other ways as the knowledge transmitted feeds attitudes towards
the knowledge transmitted. It is for this reason that politicians are particularly
interested in the determination of the curriculum; who decides what it should
be and how it is transmitted. The introduction of a National Curriculum for
state schools seems to be incompatible with the Conservative laissez faire
philosophy but is compatible with its tendency to define its own values as non-
controversial. Central government's increased control of local authority
income and expenditure (6.1) is to be paralleled by central control of the
school curriculum, although non-maintained schools are again given the
freedom to design their own curriculum.

7.4.2 Central or local control?

In the British Social Attitudes surveys respondents were asked, 'Do you think
that what is taught in schools should be up to the local education authority to
decide, or - should central government have the final say?'. In both 1985 and
1987 the majority favoured local education authority control (53 per cent and

48 per cent respectively in each year) but the balance between the two alternative had evened out by 1987.

Table 7.9
Control of the curriculum by central government or local education authority? BSA, 1984/5 and 1987/8

	LEA	Central government
	%	%
BSA 1985: (totals)	53	39
Vote		
Conservative	42	53
Alliance	49	45
Labour	61	32
Social class		
Non-manual	46	49
Manual	60	34
Income		
£12,000per annum or over	39	54
Under £12,000	57	36
School-leaving age		
17 or over	40	56
16 or under	56	35
BSA 1987: (totals)	48	47
Vote		
Conservative	34	62
Alliance	51	44
Labour	62	31

Source: Jowell et al, 1985 and 1987

The BSA found a tendency for LEA control to be favoured by Labour voters, manual workers, the relatively low paid and people who left school at 16 or under. Changing attitudes amongst Conservative voters were largely responsible for the shift towards greater support for central control.

In the 1988 case studies informants were asked two similar questions: firstly, (Q41B) should the Government 'introduce a national curriculum in schools covering 70 per cent of the subjects studied?' and secondly, (Q45) 'How much of what is taught in schools should be up to individual schools, the local education authority or central government?'. Nearly all of the informants understood Q45 straight away, although some had problems in deciding how the responsibility should be balanced between the various levels. Question 41B caused more difficulties because it was clear that several informants did not know what the word 'curriculum' meant. Although I explained to these informants that it meant 'what is taught in schools', using similar words to those in Q45, the responses to the two questions were quite different overall.

Responses to Q41B were mainly in favour of central government control over 70 per cent of the school curriculum. Frequencies for the 52 informants were as follows:

Table 7.10
Should the government introduce a national curriculum in
schools (covering 70% of the subjects studied)?
Q41B (case studies)

	n=
Should	33
Should not	13
Other	6
Should - should not	+20

When the reasons why informants favoured a National Curriculum were categorised, the standardization of provision was clearly the most popular (though obvious) reason. No particular pattern was found in the reasons why some informants were against the introduction of a National Curriculum. One informant produced an argument for standardization that seems to have excluded any political influences.

> If we had standardization across the country children could move around without too much upheaval, without it affecting their education, and more people move nowadays. (Informant No.39, Q41B)

Some people were very sceptical about political involvement in decisions about the curriculum.

> You get more of an evening out. At some schools they seem to teach what they think is right and not what the parents think is right, but then do we agree with what the government think? (Informant No.24, Q41B)

> I don't fully understand the full implications. I've heard about it on the radio. Is this government laying down what should be taught? There

should be a pattern but the government should stay out of things because they always make a mess of things. That's the other thing that comes with old age - cynicism about politics. (Informant No.18, Q41B)

Responses to Q45 were, however, quite different as the number favouring central government control of the curriculum was much smaller.

Table 7.11
How much of what is taught in schools should be up to
individual schools, the Local Education Authority,
central government? Q45 (case studies)

	n=
Central government	15
LEA	14
Schools	10
LEA and schools	5
Other	7
DK	1

Simplified into those for (15) and against (29) a national curriculum the index was -14, a majority being against the current government policy.

The type of wording used in the question therefore seems to have had a significant effect, largely because many informants did not identify a relationship between the two questions. The sub-issue was also apparently new to many people, something that they had not previously considered, or at least not formed any opinions about. In some cases (for example, informants 18 and 24 above) informants were genuinely puzzled because they could identify arguments both for and against.

7.4.3 Content of the curriculum

When the British Social Attitudes survey asked respondents about the importance of teaching particular topics to 15 year olds, some differences were again related to political identification Table 7.12.

137

Table 7.12

The importance of teaching particular topics to 15 year olds, those answering 'essential', BSA, 1985/6

	Total	Cons	Alliance	Labour
	%	%	%	%
Reading, writing & Maths	87	89	87	85
Discipline & orderliness	50	56	49	46
Respect for authority	41	48	36	39
Ability to make one's own judgements	41	40	41	43
Job training	38	33	38	44
Science & technology	32	31	35	33
Concern for minorities & the poor	23	17	22	31
Sex education	17	14	20	21
History, literature & the arts	14	13	15	16

Source: Jowell et al., 1986

Here we can see that there was very little difference between respondents in their attitudes to reading, writing and Mathematics (which 87 per cent regarded as essential), the ability to make ones own judgements, science and technology, and history, literature and the arts. The greatest difference was in attitudes to the teaching of concern for the minorities and the poor, which more Labour voters (a difference in scores of 14 per cent) than Conservative voters regarded as essential. Despite the Government's utilitarian and market orientated approach to education, more Labour voters (a difference of 11 per cent) regarded job training as essential. It is possible that Labour's greater emphasis on unemployment as a major social problem may have something to do with the different responses, although Marxists would argue that, as the Labour party supports the continuation of a capitalist system, it will share the Conservatives' utilitarian perspective. However, the general impression emerging from the 1988 case studies was that whether the function of education was seen as to provide a good start in life or to serve the needs of capital, the emphasis on preparation for a job would be the same. Parents and school leavers would be primarily concerned about securing the best job possible, whilst employers would be concerned about the provision of a workforce with useful and transferable skills. It seems that learning for its own sake or to improve the general quality of life beyond the workplace is more likely to be valued by teachers and other educationalists (see Broadfoot in 5.3).

The difference between the attitudes of Conservatives and Labour voters towards job training can be partly explained by the similar difference (10 per cent) in their attitudes to discipline and orderliness. The greater emphasis by Conservatives on discipline (7.3.1) compliments employers' greater emphasis on a pliable workforce, whilst the concern amongst Labour voters about authoritarianism is more closely related to the defence of workers' interests. People over 55 were nearly twice as likely as people under 35 to regard 'respect for authority' as essential (Jowell et al., 1986, p.119). Older people and Conservatives were also much less likely than young people and Labour and Alliance identifiers to consider 'sex education' or 'concern for minorities and the poor' as essential.

The 1987 British Social Attitudes survey asked different questions about the content of the curriculum. It listed 'a number of factors that some people think would improve education in our schools' and asked respondents which they thought was the most important for children in primary schools and for children in secondary schools. These factors included items other than the content of the curriculum.

Table 7.13
Factors that would improve education in schools, BSA, 1987/8

	Primary	Secondary
	%	%
More resources for books and equipment	20.7	13.5
Better buildings	1.9	0.7
Better pay for teachers	3.5	4.2
More involvement of parents in governing bodies	2.5	1.0
More discussion between parents and teachers	7.5	2.9
Smaller classes	28.8	9.1
More emphasis on preparation for exams	1.6	8.9
More emphasis on developing the child's skills and interests	16.3	10.3
More training and preparation for jobs	1.7	25.5
More emphasis on arts subjects	0.1	0.1
More emphasis on mathematics	1.1	2.0
More emphasis on English	2.0	1.5
Stricter discipline	10.8	18.8
None of these	0.7	0.6
Don't know	0.8	0.7

Source: Jowell et al., 1988

Responses in the 1988 local case studies followed a similar pattern to those found in the BSA 1986 survey; as can be seen by comparing Table 7.14 with Table 7.12.

Table 7.14
The importance of teaching topics to 15 year olds (case studies)

	Essential	Important	Not needed
	n=	n=	n=
Reading, writing & Maths	48	4	-
Discipline & orderliness	33	17	1
Respect for authority	26	21	1
Ability to make one's own judgements	30	17	4
Job training	27	19	6
Science & technology	21	21	-
Concern for minorities & the poor	15	25	8
Sex education	9	25	12
History, Literature & the arts	12	28	4
Social studies	6	24	15

Again it was found that sex education was regarded as essential by a small minority of mainly Labour and Alliance voters. A tenth category of social studies was added to the BSA's original list and it was found that this was regarded as the least essential.

7.4.4 Testing at 7, 11 and 14

The 1988 Education Reform Act introduced a national system for the criterion referenced testing of children at the ages of 7, 11 and 14, to start on a pilot basis in the autumn of 1989. Although the British Social Attitudes surveys have not asked a question that is directly related to such tests they have collected data about attitudes to examinations in general. The 1987 survey asked two questions about examinations (Table 7.15).

Table 7.15

Attitudes to examinations - two questions, BSA, 1987/8

	Agree %	Disagree %	Other %	DK %
a) Formal exams are the best way of judging the ability of pupils.	58.0	31.2	17.0	6.5
d) So much attention is given to exam results in Britain that a pupil's everyday classroom work counts for too little.	70.2	16.7	12.4	0.2

Source: Jowell et al, 1988

The support for examinations shown in Table 7.15 is therefore tempered by a concern about the emphasis placed on examinations. My case study informants tended to agree that examinations were a necessary part of education but many described them as a necessary evil when asked to elaborate on their opinions.

This was found when informants in the case studies were asked whether or not the Government should introduce a system of testing at 7, 11 and 14. The sort of uncertainty expressed about the National Curriculum was repeated. Although the majority of informants were in favour of testing, when asked to explain their reasons, several were very vague or contradicted their original answer.

Table 7.16

Should the government introduce a national system for the testing of children at 7, 11 and 14? (case studies)

	n=
Should	23
Should not	18
Other	11
Should - should not	+5

Although 23 originally said that such a system should be introduced (resulting in a majority of +5 in favour) 26 favoured such a system when they were asked to explain their reasons. Six people favoured testing provided that children were not tested at the age of 7 and, if these are subtracted from the number favouring the actual proposal for testing at three stages, the number of informants for or against was quite even. Some informants also expressed doubts about the purpose of the tests and said that they would favour them only if they were diagnostic and did not stigmatize the children who did badly.

> It's too many opportunities to tell someone that they've failed and I'm not sure how it would benefit the children and what they would do with the information when they'd got it. I think it's important to test the teachers and if you've got good teachers the children will achieve what they can. (Informant No.51, Q41E)

Those arguing in favour of continuous assessment tended to base their opinion on a personal dislike of examinations. Yet the informant (mentioned earlier) with literacy problems would have welcomed examinations as a way of drawing attention to his problems.

> That way you could drop them in a lower class. Then they could catch-up instead of being snowed under. If they'd done that with me I might have stood a chance instead of doing things that were way out of my field instead of the basics of reading and writing. (Informant No.48, Q41E)

7.4.5 Summary of findings

Voters attitudes are relatively consistent in their emphasis on literacy and numeracy (Tables 7.12 and 7.14) and on the importance of preparation for jobs (Tables 7.12, 7.13 and 7.14). However, when control of the curriculum was considered, many apparently contradictory responses were given. Several case study informants said that they favoured a national curriculum covering 70 per cent of the subjects studied (Q41B) and believed that either the LEA or the individual school should control most of the what is taught in schools (Q45). When asked to explain their responses to these questions and to the question about testing (7.4.4) many expressed reservations, noting some of the advantages and disadvantages of each policy decision. Conservative governments have, however, tended to simplify debate by presenting an image of the curriculum as a natural, non-political phenomenon, excluding the grey areas covered by informants' reservations. Findings in this section about the ambiguous and contentious nature of debate about the curriculum therefore tend to highlight the political nature of educational debate and, in particular, the bias already discussed in 5.4.

7.5 Gender

Although gender is a favourite topic of debate amongst social scientists it was not an obvious choice as a sub-issue at the start of this research. During the 1980s governments tended to ignore gender inequalities in general and to imply that girls were no longer disadvantaged by the education system. Thus, it could be argued that gender did not fit my criteria for the recognition of a sub-issue in terms of topicality. Nevertheless, as the research progressed it became clear that, there was a common assumption that sex discrimination had been excluded from education, although it clearly had not. In addition, debates about single sex versus coeducational schools continued, at both national and local levels.

At the start of the research the topic of single sex schools was not regarded as a major issue nationally but it was an important local issue in Torytown. As a result of falling rolls, Torytown was under increasing pressure to amalgamate its remaining single sex schools. The sub-issue also became more prominent in national debate throughout the 1980s as some parents (particularly Muslims) pressed for the introduction of more all girl schools on religious and cultural grounds. Torytown had several single sex schools and the question become a political issue locally as Conservative councillors tended to support the continued existence of such schools more enthusiastically than Labour councillors and Liberal Democrats. To a certain extent the views of Labour and Liberal Democrat councillors were divided between the need to accommodate religious and cultural differences and to avoid any unnecessary differentiation between the sexes. Gender can therefore be included as a topical sub-issue in relation to the question of single-sex schools.

Within this section the debate has also been widened to include a more general discussion about sex discrimination in education, partly because it does not seem to have been identified as a major problem by either governments or the majority of voters. The reasoning behind its inclusion appears to run contrary to the criteria for identifying a sub-issue but sex discrimination within the education system seems to beg inclusion simply because it is apparently hidden from the public.

7.5.1 Defining the problem

As sex is one of the main categories used in the publication of official statistics, differences between the sexes in terms of educational achievement are well documented. It has, for example, been well known, amongst educationalists at least, that the recent trend has been for girls to achieve more passes at GCE O'Level (now GCSE) and A'Level than boys, whilst more boys than girls move on to higher education. However, differences in achievement vary according to the subjects taken. Despite many efforts to interest more girls in science and technology, by the sixth form arts subjects are often labelled as 'girls' subjects whilst mathematics and sciences (but not biology) are habitually labelled as 'boys' subjects. This labelling of subjects may not, on its own, be regarded as a problem. A problem lies in the common perception of certain 'girls' subjects as being lower in the hierarchy of subjects within the wider curriculum.

Differences between the sexes in overall educational attainment are reversed as they progress through higher education. In 1984 about 37 per cent of all graduates obtaining ordinary degrees were women, about 41 per cent of all graduates obtaining honours degrees were women and about 27 per cent of all graduates obtaining higher degrees were women (Central Statistical Office, 1987, Table 5.17). Differentials in subject areas were again high with, for example, nearly ten times as many men as women taking engineering and technology courses and over twice as many women as men taking language, literature and area studies courses (Central Statistical Office, 1987, Table 5.16).

7.5.2 Sex discrimination

Evidence of sex discrimination in the education system is not hard to find, but the case studies suggest that it has not been internalized by many informants. One month before the 1988 interviews were carried out the Appeal Court rejected an appeal by Birmingham City Council against a finding that it had discriminated against girls. In Birmingham there were a total of 880 places available in eight grammar schools, 520 for boys in five schools and 360 for girls in three schools. As the number of girls and boys starting secondary school each year was roughly equal, a girl had to obtain higher marks at 11+ to secure a grammar school place. Although this case was possibly exceptional in terms of the obvious extent of discrimination, it could be seen as merely compounding an existing problem caused by the tendency for girls to mature earlier than boys and to consequently out perform boys overall in school assessments. A similar problem exists in Torytown (3.3) where assessment procedures have recently been revised due to criticism by the Equal Opportunities Commission.

> I only know fully what goes on in primary schools and I would say that on the whole girls do better up to eleven but the system expects less of girls at secondary age. At primary school it's easier to teach girls than boys because they're more eager to please. (Informant No.08, Primary school headteacher, Q46D)

144

As more girls than boys reach pass standard in the 11+ local education authorities have to raise the pass level for girls if equal numbers of both sexes are to be given grammar school places. Thus, it can be claimed that the system of selection at eleven discriminates against girls if their pass mark is higher than that for boys and discriminates against boys if allowances are not made for their later development. In either case decisions about future educational aptitude and attainment that are based on performance at the age of eleven (and possibly later) are flawed by differences in maturation between, and within, the sexes (3.3). Despite such findings the most common view expressed in the case studies was that the education system does not discriminate against girls.

Table 7.17
The education system treats girls less favourably than boys

		n=
Disagree		28
Agree		7
Sometimes		6
Other		1
Don't know		10
Disagree - agree	+21	

The common belief was that such discrimination had been eliminated in the education system, yet the BSA84/5 (Q87) found that a large majority of respondents (82 per cent) believed that women were likely to be discriminated against regarding promotion at work. Respondents were unlikely to have personal experience of the current school system, but had personal experience of their place of work. Just as they usually had to form their judgements about discipline inside schools by looking at how children behaved when out of school, so they could only judge the extent of sex discrimination inside schools by looking at external manifestations.

None of the case study informants cited a recent case of sex discrimination in school but several mentioned past examples of the discrimination of parents against their daughters. Thus, the findings add more to my later discussion about experiences of parental choice (7.9.5) than to claims of discrimination within the education system itself. One informant (No. 13, Q33) said of her mother, who left school at 14;

> She didn't go to grammar school because, although she passed the exams, her father wouldn't pay for her. He could afford to but didn't. She went to an ordinary school. (Informant No.13, Q33)

Another informant said about his wife's lack of qualifications at school-leaving age;

> Her father was one of the old fashioned sort. Girls didn't need them so she never sat them. (Informant No.34, Q28E)

If some parents retain discriminatory attitudes it is likely to be most noticeable in their willingness to pay fees to send sons and daughters to non-maintained schools. This seems to be the case if non-maintained schools are simply seen as responding to consumer pressure. During the 1980s about 72 per cent of the pupils attending the preparatory schools belonging to the Incorporated Association of Preparatory Schools were boys (ISIS, 1987). As the IAPS includes the majority of preparatory schools it can be assumed that either the overall majority of pupils attending preparatory schools were boys or that girls tended to go to (the few excluded) less prestigious preparatory schools. At secondary level, the numbers of boys and girls attending non-maintained schools were roughly equal. However, 85 per cent of the pupils attending the most prestigious public schools (so defined by membership of the Headmasters' Conference) were boys. These schools charge the highest fees and many of them only admit girls to their sixth form. Thus, although some non-maintained girls' schools are more prestigious than others, differentiation according to sex may either prevent girls from attending the most expensive and elite institutions or cause those schools to be classed as elite simply because the majority of their pupils are boys.

7.5.3 Different choices

As fewer girls than boys participate in higher education, despite their marginally better achievements in examinations at 16 and 18, it is reasonable to question the extent to which educational processes contribute to the partial elimination of girls at the age of 18. Arguments about this would involve a major digression but the essential point is that the belief amongst many voters that sex discrimination has been eliminated from the education system is mistaken. Some people may not have perceived discrimination because they were unaware of their own discriminatory attitudes. For example the BSA 1984/5 found that, although 96 per cent of respondents supported the opportunity for boys and girls to study the same subjects at school (Q86) gender stereotypes were commonly applied to particular jobs. The BSA self-completion schedule listed eleven jobs (Q19) and asked respondents to note whether each job was particularly suitable for men only, women only, or suitable for both men and women. Highly educated women were found to be most egalitarian in their responses.

Table 7.18
Number of jobs suitable for men and women, BSA 1984/5

	1-2 %	3-5 %	6-9 %	10-11 %
Men:finished schooling aged 18 and under	6	21	54	18
finished schooling aged 19 and over	4	14	56	26
Women:finished schooling aged 18 and under	7	17	53	21
finished schooling aged 19 and over	-	7	49	43

Note: The jobs listed were; social worker, police officer, secretary, car mechanic, nurse, computer programmer, bus driver, bank manager, family doctor, local councillor, Member of Parliament.

Source: Jowell et al, 1985

Although this suggests that the highly educated (which includes teachers) have the most egalitarian views, it also suggests that quite a large proportion of highly educated men still apply gender stereotypes.

When the BSA asked the same question in 1987 it found an increase in the number of respondents with egalitarian views, although traditional stereotypes were still common. Women with degrees were still less likely to apply stereotypes; 53 per cent of women graduates, and 42 per cent of male graduates regarding 10-11 jobs as suitable for both sexes.

In the case studies informants were asked if they thought that biological differences between the sexes were responsible for the different subject and career choices of boys and girls.

Table 7.19
Biological differences between the sexes are largely
responsible for the different subject and career choices
of boys and girls. Q46C (case studies)

	n=
Agree	14
Disagree	27
Sometimes	2
Other	3
Don't know	6
Agree - disagree	-13

Most disagreed, echoing the now well established belief that social conditioning, is mainly responsible for the different choices. However, it is interesting to note that over a quarter of informants believed that biological differences were responsible.

7.5.4 Single sex schools

Neither the British Social Attitude surveys nor the Greater Manchester Study asked questions involving a comparison between single sex and coeducational schools. However, as the topic was part of political debate in Torytown (and increasingly a part of national debate) case study informants were asked whether or not they favoured the abolition of single sex schools.

Table 7.20
Should the Government abolish single sex schools?
Q41G (case studies)

	n=
Should not	21
Should	10
Other	21
Should not - should	+11

Although only 21 of the 52 case study informants thought that single sex schools should not be abolished and very few favoured their abolition, a large number (seventeen) said that it did not matter whether single sex schools were abolished or not.

When asked to explain their answer, the most common response (from 11) was again that it does not matter. Eight favoured single sex schools because they felt that members of the opposite sex caused a distraction but an equal number favoured coeducational schools because they thought that it was healthy for the sexes to mix. Six argued that, as the world outside of school is mixed, schools should be mixed too. Four said that parents should be allowed to choose between coeducational or single sex schools. Nine had mixed views about the subject, seeing both advantages and disadvantages in each type of school.

7.5.5 Summary of findings

Gender inequalities still existed in the 1980s but few voters seemed aware of them (even if they were aware of discrimination in the workplace). It is, for example, probable that there are still some boys and girls attending secondary modern schools who would, under a selection system that did not differentiate between the sexes, have gone to a grammar school. It is also probable that many parents are still more willing to pay for their sons to have a private education than their daughters. Girls may therefore be discriminated in the education system itself as well as in the home and in the workplace.

Perceptions of the advantages and disadvantages of single sex schools were fairly evenly balanced. Few of the case study informants had strong views on the subject. In general, therefore, the tendency was for voters not to perceive gender differentiation and inequalities as particular problems, despite the evidence to the contrary.

7.6 Clause 28

The 1988 Local Government Act included an amendment (Clause 28) forbidding local authorities to 'promote teaching in any maintained school of the acceptability of homosexuality as a pretended family relationship'. This amendment was selected as a sub-issue because, not only was it related to the previous discussion about the control and nature of the curriculum (7.4), but it was also a very contentious issue in the months preceding the case study interviews. The absence of empirical data about attitudes to the subject demanded its inclusion. Since the case studies were carried out the 1988 BSA Report has also provided a large amount of useful data about attitudes to homosexuality.

7.6.1 Defining the problem

The government's perception of the family and family values has already been discussed (5.4) and in Clause 28 we can see an attempt to prevent children from being taught that homosexuality is acceptable (see Mrs. Thatcher's speech to the 1987 Conservative conference in 5.4). In effect, however, the clause has been little more than a gesture as, since the 1986 Education Act, decisions about sex education have been the responsibility of school governors and not the local authority. The error was not known when the interview schedule for 1988 was being designed and Conservative politicians expected the clause to be implemented in schools via local authorities.

The responses of 52 people cannot be generalised but the question was productive both regarding what was learned about methodology and about the attitudes of the case study sample towards homosexuality. The design of the question caused problems (2.7). My original intention was to follow the words of Clause 28 as closely as possible but I was persuaded by a colleague that many people would not understand it and that it should be simplified. In the interviews I finally asked, if the government should, 'allow teachers to present a favourable view of homosexuality?' (Q41H).

7.6.2 Responses in the 1987 BSA and the case studies

British Social Attitude Reports found that the proportion of respondents who are critical of homosexuality increased, from 62 per cent in 1983 to 74 per cent in 1987 saying that homosexual relationships were 'always' or 'mostly' wrong. Harding (in Jowell et al, 1988, p.36-7) speculated that this was due to the association between homosexuality and AIDS in the public consciousness. Women and (especially) graduates were least likely to say that homosexuality was wrong.

Table 7.21
Changing attitudes to homosexuality,
BSA, 1985/6 and 1987/8

	1985	1987
	%	%
Always/mostly wrong:	69	74
Women	67	72
Men	71	77
Graduates	39	51
Non-graduates	71	76

Source: Jowell et al, 1988, Table 5.1 and p.73

When respondents were asked whether it was acceptable for a homosexual to teach in a school or a college/university, the proportion saying that it was acceptable increased between 1983 and 1987 (after a decline in 1985).

Table 7.22

Changing % saying it is acceptable for a homosexual to teach, BSA

	1983	1985	1987
	%	%	%
Teach in school	41	36	43
Lecture in college or university	48	44	51

Source: Jowell et al., 1988

Again it was found that respondents who were graduates tended to be more tolerant of homosexuality: in 1987 69 per cent said that it was acceptable for a homosexual to teach in a school, 83 per cent in a college or university. Women were also more tolerant than men in all age groups. It has consistently been found that attitudes to lesbians are less censorious than to male homosexuals.

Case study informants were asked if the government should allow teachers to present a favourable view of homosexuality.

Table 7.23

Should the government allow teachers to present a favourable view of homosexuality? Q41H (case studies)

	%
	%
Should not	35
Should	5
Other 12	
Should not - should	+30

Most of the informants answered that it should not, and the majority of them (25) thought that it was very important that it should not. Many informants looked surprised, perhaps even shocked, that the subject should even be mentioned in the interview and, when asked to explain their answer, 16 said that they did not want to consider the subject. This is perhaps an example of the intrusion of a subject from beyond a normative framework that informants could accept as compatible with their socially constructed definitions of reality. They may have disagreed with some of the perspectives or lifestyles within that normative framework but on those occasions were prepared to consider and argue. Homosexuality was however regarded with total incomprehension and was not to be even considered. A teacher emphasised the importance of this normative framework.

> I think from a personal point of view that sex education in schools should refer to what the majority of society regard as normal behaviour. (Informant No.45, Q41H)

Five thought that teaching about homosexuality could influence children to experiment with homosexual relationships whilst one informant was sure that no naturally heterosexual child could be influenced.

> I think schools need to prepare children for life outside and life as it is and I think the line should be that there's nothing wrong with homosexuality but I'm against a strong pro-homosexuality stance. My teaching would be that there are certain people who are like this and, provided they don't harm anyone, let them get on with their lives. I doubt whether a gay teacher could inspire a pupil to be gay unless the pupil was inclined that way. (Informant No.08, headteacher, Q41H)

Some people thought that the subject was suitable for adult conversation but not for children in the classroom.

> This is clause 28. I'd never heard of them as a kiddy. I've learned about homosexuality as an adult and therefore accept it. I wouldn't want children to accept it as a norm. Learning about them when you're older, you just accept them for what they are - full stop. I don't think they should be emphasised. (Informant No.22, Q41H)

Other informants felt that the subject could be discussed in lessons but had reservations about how it should be presented by the teacher.

> I don't know the answer to that one. I think that any responsible teacher would not present a favourable view of homosexuality but I think it would be dangerous to ban the subject because, in any discussion you have with pupils about a responsible attitude to growing up, I think its the teachers job to answer those questions without bias or prejudice. I think its an educational matter. If it was found that a member of staff was actually selling homosexuality as a favourable thing then there ought to be some disciplinary action taken by the education authorities rather than the government. (Informant No.51, Q41H)

However, a strong impression was that informants still had problems in interpreting the supposedly simplified version of Clause 28 in the question.

> Because I don't understand the question. I interpret it as they would be happy to allow them to teach about homosexuality as part of teaching about general life. I wouldn't say 'No you can't talk about it or have it in discussion'. It could be just part of their normal teaching about awareness. (Informant No.25, Q41H)

> I don't understand the question. What's a favourable view? If you said that the Government should allow teachers to teach children to tolerate homosexuality I'd say 'Yes'. That's a different thing than teaching them a favourable view. I don't think it's got anything to do with the Government. (Informant No.44, Q41H)

The word 'favourable' was just as vague as the word 'promote' in the actual clause. Use of the original words in the clause would have been more productive as personal definitions and interpretations help to explain personal attitudes.

7.6.3 Summary of findings

It is clear that there was a high level of intolerance towards homosexuals, and towards male homosexuals in particular. The Government's attempt to prevent teachers from defending homosexuality may not be seen as positively encouraging intolerance, but it was certainly not designed to discourage it. Thus, a hostile attitude towards a large number of people in British society can be identified (for example, by Informant No.45) as part of the normative framework of debate.

The significance of this particular sub-issue lies in its challenge to claims that the curriculum is a natural, uncontroversial and non-political phenomenon. A dispute does exist, and some voters (notably graduates) did not exhibit an intolerant attitude towards homosexuals. This leaves many unanswered questions which, given fresh data from the British Social Attitudes surveys (and others) is worth more attention than is possible in the present context. Why, for example, were the most highly qualified respondents the most tolerant? Why did women seem to be more tolerant than men on this particular sub-issue? How would findings about this government's involvement in making intolerance acceptable compare with the activities of other governments?

7.7 Multicultural and anti-racist education

It is notoriously difficult to assess a respondent's race and no attempt was made to do this in either the Greater Manchester Study or in my case studies. Racial identity is in any case an extremely vague concept based on subjective associations rather than genetic structure. Some members of my own family, for example, look 'white' but have black ancestors, and we have no way of knowing how many people in this country have a similarly mixed heritage, dating back over centuries. Yet the labelling of people according to their colour and the racism associated with it does cause problems in education, as in society in as a whole.

The mixture of ethnic groups, cultures and languages amongst schoolchildren also places particular demands on the education system, although Britain is not isolated in facing such demands. Responses to the multicultural and multi-racial school population in Britain tend to emphasise either the accommodation of many cultural groups or the need to use the education system to combat racism in society as a whole. These two approaches are called respectively multiculturalism and anti-racism. Decisions about which approach should be taken, or on whether to adopt a mixture of both, are highly political, therefore justifying the inclusion of the debate as a sub-issue. However, it was possible that many informants knew nothing about the multicultural and anti-racist approaches to education. It was therefore necessary to include questions about something that they were more likely to be aware of. The Macdonald Inquiry's report into the murder of a Manchester schoolboy was highly topical at the time of the case studies, and was particularly relevant to the ongoing debate about multicultural or anti-racist education.

7.7.1 Defining multicultural and anti-racist approaches

Multiculturalism is often associated with a pluralist political perspective, dealing fundamentally with the pluralist dilemma of how to blend diversity with the search for consensus. Its basic answers involve teaching children about their own cultural and ethnic origins and about other people's cultures. In this way it is hoped that discrimination towards others from different cultural backgrounds will be reduced.

Anti-racists argue that multiculturalism overlooks the fundamental problem of racism by not considering the practice of labelling people according to the colour of their skin. By emphasising cultural diversity, multiculturalism does not deal with the racism that is directed at non-white people irrespective of their nationality or cultural heritage. As the Institute of Race Relations has argued,

154

Just to learn about other people's cultures...is not to learn about the racism of one's own. To learn about the racism of one's own culture, on the other hand, is to approach other cultures objectively. (Institute of Race Relations, 1980, p.82)

Critics claim that, at its worst, multiculturalism defines the black child, and not society, as the problem (Mullard, 1982, p.32-3), implying deficiencies amongst black people that can be remedied by education. Anti-racist educationalists therefore stress the importance of considering the education system within the broader social and political context of race relations. They particularly emphasise the need to tackle racism in all schools, irrespective of their cultural mix.

In the Swann Report of 1985 ('Education for all') Lord Swann reaffirmed many of the criticisms of unintentional racism in schools that had been made in the previous Rampton Report ('West Indian children in our schools', 1981). Rampton identified racism as a key factor in explaining the low educational achievements of West Indian children in particular. Swann's recommendation was a 'whole system' approach, incorporating both multiculturalism and anti-racism.

7.7.2 Political perspectives

Attitudes towards multiculturalism and anti-racism have tended to vary according to political identification. Mrs. Thatcher's cynicism about anti-racist Mathematics (5.4) was simply repeating the criticisms made by (amongst others) Baroness Cox, the Conservative spokesperson on education in the House of Lords. In 'Whose Schools?' (Hillgate Group, 1986) Cox and other writers complained of,

> . . . an increasing politicization of the curriculum, so that children, instead of learning history, geography or mathematics are indoctrinated in the fashionable causes of the radical left: 'anti-racism', 'anti-sexism', 'peace education'. . . (Hillgate group, 1986, p.4-5)

The British Social Attitudes survey of 1985/6 (Jowell et al., 1986) found that Conservative identifiers were more likely to describe themselves as prejudiced than were identifiers with other parties (40 per cent of Conservatives, 31 per cent Alliance identifiers, 32 per cent Labour identifiers). Women claimed to be less prejudiced than men (30 per cent of women compared to 39 per cent of men), a finding that compliments the finding (Table 7.21) that women were also slightly less intolerant of homosexuals.

Although individuals with racist attitudes may vote for any political party,

Conservative voters were the least likely to identify racism as a problem or to favour multicultural or anti-racist educational policies. The Conservative tendency to favour a 'neutral' approach to racial issues could, for example, be seen when in 1988 Norman Tebbit complained about the BBC's hostile attitude to apartheid, arguing that the BBC should remain neutral on the issue. To anti-racists, however, a neutral attitude towards racism and racists would be the equivalent of adopting a neutral attitude towards crime and criminals.

The different attitudes associated with party identification are indicated in the BSA survey findings in 1983 and 1987 about attitudes towards provision for cultural diversity in schools. A list of proposals associated with the multicultural perspective was provided.

Table 7.24
Provision for cultural diversity in schools,
BSA, 1983/4 and 1987/8

	1983 Total	Cons	All	Lab	White	Other colour	1987 Total
	%	%	%	%	%	%	%
Provide special English classes if required	77	77	84	78	77	80	80
Provide separate religious if requested by parents	32	27	41	36	32	41	37
Allow traditional dress if important	43	38	53	45	43	48	45
Study mother tongue in school hours	16	12	16	20	16	32	17
Teach history & culture of parents' country	40	36	46	45	40	53	40
Teach history & culture of these countries to all children	74	73	78	74	74	71	74

Source: Jowell et al., 1984, p.119 and 1988, p.27

Alliance respondents were more in favour of such provisions than were Labour and Conservative identifiers and were more in favour of some items than were non-white respondents. This is not entirely surprising as non-white respondents may be British born and as reluctant to accommodate differing cultures as respondents who are British born and white.

The 1987 BSA survey found that teachers were more liberal on such issues

156

than was the rest of the population. Nearly all teachers supported extra English language classes, 75 per cent were in favour of allowing traditional dress, 56 per cent were in favour of teaching pupils the history of their parents' counties and 41 per cent supported the teaching of pupils' mother tongue during school hours.

7.7.3 Qualitative data in the case studies

All of the case study informants were *apparently* 'white', although one informant was of West Indian origin, with an obviously mixed race background (and an Asian member of the original sample was too ill to be interviewed). The only question asked that was related to race as a sub-issue was concerned with a debate that was highly topical in the summer of 1988.

In 1986 Ahmed Ullah, a 13 year old pupil (from an Asian family) at Burnage High School in Manchester, was stabbed to death at school by another (white) pupil. An official inquiry, led by Ian MacDonald QC, completed its report on the murder in April 1988 and a media debate lasted for several weeks leading up to the interviews. The media debate was based on very little accurate information because Manchester City Council's fear of litigation meant that the full report was not made available to more than a few councillors and school governors. The council wanted the then Secretary of State, Kenneth Baker, to publish the report under parliamentary privilege so that the council could not be sued. Baker, however, wanted the council itself to publish the report, and so there was a stalemate. At first only small sections of the report were leaked but eventually media speculation led the council to publish only the eleven least sensitive chapters. Distorted reports in the tabloid press were eventually denied on 9 May when the members of the MacDonald inquiry team issued a statement declaring that it had not suggested that Burnage High School and other schools should abandon strategies for combatting racism and adopt a colour-blind approach. Mr. MacDonald stated that,

> It is because we consider the task of combatting racism to be such a critical part of the function of schooling and education that we condemn doctrinaire anti-racism. (The Guardian, 10 May 1988)

They had not urged an end to anti-racist policies.

> That, in our view, would be nonsense and it's not what we found, reported or concluded ... Racism was a factor, not anti-racism. (The Guardian, 10 May 1988)

The consultation paper published later by the council quoted the MacDonald report's criticism of those anti-racist policies that do not integrate the problems caused by other forms of social inequality,

> ... ostrich-like analysis of the complex of social relations which leaves white working class males completely in the cold. They fit nowhere. They become all-time losers. That, surely, is a recipe for division and polarisation, particularly in the area of anti-racist policies. (The Guardian, 29 June 1988)

The emphasis again was on the effective implementation of anti-racist policies.

> ...anti-racist policies do not produce racism ... Badly thought-out and implemented policies may well be counter-productive but certainly no more so than policies that pretend that race does not exist as an issue. (The Guardian, 29 June 1988)

In early June the headteacher of Burnage High School resigned, to be seconded for a year before taking up early retirement. In order to secure publication of the full report four of the MacDonald inquiry team agreed to accept personal liability in the event of litigation. However, at the end of the 1988 interviews the report had still not been published.

The 52 informants were asked about their knowledge about, and interest in, 'recent events at Burnage High School' because the debate was highly topical and involved a school in Greater Manchester. The MacDonald report was not mentioned in the question because the press had continually referred to 'Burnage' and it was thought that was how informants were most likely to recognise the subject. Both its topicality and local nature should have increased informants' interest and knowledge about the subject. However, interest and knowledge were apparently low; the word 'apparently' being used because it was suspected that, like homosexuality, racism was considered to be a sensitive subject that some informants did not want to talk about.

Fortyfour of the informants had heard about the subject, but very few were interested (Table7.25).

158

Table 7.25
Interest in discussions about recent events at
Burnage High School? (case studies)

	n=
Interested	12
No answer	16
Not interested	8
Only opinion given	5
Mixed response	1
Other	8
DK	2

When informants were asked to explain what they knew about the subject, their responses were often vague or distorted, the Chinese whispers effect (mentioned in 5.1) being most obvious.

Table 7.26
Knowledge about recent events at Burnage High School.
(case studies)

	n=
Child killed	12
Report	2
School policy	1
2 of above	14
3 of above	7
About racism	4
No answer	5
DK/vague	2
Wrong or racist answer	5

Several simply guessed that it was something to do with racism but had no more to say. Some made racist comments; for example, one said that immigrants should learn to adapt to their new country (a particularly cruel distortion of what actually happened). One informant complained that the murder had received too much attention.

About a report that was done on it and about the trouble it's caused with the Asian community. Just general things because in the end I stopped reading it. If it'd been a white boy that had been stabbed it wouldn't have lasted as long. I thought it got blown out of proportion.

It just seemed to go on and on. (Informant No.41, Q40G)

Some people had first hand knowledge of the school but, even then, impressions were rather vague and it would have been easy to reach unreliable conclusions.

> [Works near the school.] I'm interested because we see them going to school in the morning and it doesn't surprise me that they have problems because there are some very 'sweet' [being sarcastic] children going to that school and you have to count up to 10! It's not just the whites. (Informant No.47, worked near the school, Q39G)

> I don't know why they have to be like that [i.e. racist]. They're growing up together and then all of a sudden they split. Some of the kids I see going to that school are bad news. We were always in trouble but not bashing up people or bus shelters. I don't see why they can't get on together. The other week in our local park [he went bowling in Torytown] kids were running riot - yobbos. It wasn't racism as they were all white. There were 50 or 60 kids in that park. It was an absolute madhouse. They built a children's playground two weeks ago up the road and the little sods sprayed graffiti all over it. (Informant No.47, Q40G)

Another informant commented on media coverage. She had visited the school because of her job and had heard from school staff that the press had got some of their information by asking children questions in the street. The press had also, she said, used cameras with telephoto lenses, to peer into the school. She regarded that as unacceptable.

> They get some stories wrong and it makes you distrust the press. The day I went there was no feeling of racial tension and the children seemed to be mixing well. I did hear a different account to that reported in the press but that was hearsay and I don't know how true it was. (Informant No.42, Q40G)

7.7.4 Summary of findings

Supporters of multicultural education tend to argue that, if pupils become more familiar with other cultures, a multicultural society will emerge in which diversity and cohesion will form a healthy balance. Supporters of anti-racist education will tend to emphasise racism, rather than cultural diversity, as the main problem. Recent Conservative Governments have taken a more 'colour blind' approach, tending to ignore this particular debate (as it does in the case of inequalities between the sexes, 7.5) and pay scant attention to the findings of Rampton and Swann. However, a 'neutral' approach to this debate cannot be really neutral. So much data is available about the disadvantages of black (not necessarily immigrant) children in our education system that it cannot be ignored. The severity of the problems involved in dealing with cultural diversity and racist attitudes have been emphasised in this section. If anything of any substance has been discovered it is simply that ignorance amongst this small group of case study informants (largely due to the lack of reliable information and sometimes the result of prejudice) will not help to create a healthy, multicultural society.

7.8 Comprehensive versus bipartite schools

More attention has probably been paid to this sub-issue than any other. In 1969 and 1970 it was the only educational sub-issue referred to in Butler and Stokes' study of voting behaviour [1]. Ever since large-scale comprehensivization in the 1960s the debate has continued to rage and researchers have studied the effects of the changes and attitudes towards them. The Black Paper writers were particularly vociferous in their opposition to comprehensivization during the 1960s and 1970s (Cox et al, 1969 to 1975) and opposition has continued in the 1980s via the Hillgate Group in particular (1986).

Although the debate at national level has tended to subside, it remains as a contentious political issue in the few areas that have retained the bipartite system. In 1986 85.8 per cent of all secondary pupils in the United Kingdom were attending schools that were labelled 'comprehensive' by the Government Statistical Service (1987). However, as the policies of a succession of Conservative Governments take effect, it is likely that the proportion of pupils attending such schools will decline (which already seems to be the case); many moving to private schools or City Technology Colleges.

7.8.1 Defining types of schools

In the British Social Attitude surveys respondents have been asked to express a preference for either grammar schools and secondary modern schools or comprehensive schools, and their changing responses over the years have been monitored. The question was preceded by a brief reference to the differences between the three types of schools.

> Some people think it is best for secondary schoolchildren to be separated into grammar and secondary modern schools according to how well they have done when they leave primary school. Others think it is best for secondary schoolchildren not to be separated in this way, and to attend comprehensive schools. (Jowell et al, 1986, introduction to Q87)

In the case study interviews I offered no explanation of the differences and found that several informants were not sure what the differences were. With hindsight it would have been useful to have asked informants for their own definitions of the three types of school. At the time it was assumed that informants would have known the differences, but responses suggested otherwise. The differences between grammar schools and secondary modern schools were understood by most informants because most of them had been educated in a bipartite system. However, confusion about types of secondary schools in Torytown may have increased as, in the late 1980s, its secondary modern schools were renamed 'high' schools and (in one case) a 'comprehensive' school. This is discussed more fully in 3.3. In the present context it is particularly significant as, as an alternative to grammar schools (attended by those who 'pass' the 11+), comprehensive schools can be defined in Torytown as inferior.

In the case study interviews, impressions about comprehensive schools were often vague. One young informant who had attended a Labourville 'high' school did not realize that it was a comprehensive school and asked me to explain what a comprehensive school was. The title of 'high' school is therefore particularly confusing as it can be applied to several types of secondary schools. Some informants who were opposed to comprehensives also apparently thought that pupils in comprehensive schools were only taught in mixed ability groups.

> . . . because I don't think that mixed abilities can be taught in one class. I know they are to a certain extent but I think that grammar and secondary schools are much better. (Informant No.31, Q41A)

> Because I think you got a better standard of teachers in those schools as they were. My knowledge is not up to date. In comprehensives it seems to be that everybody gets thrown into a big melting pot and when you cook that way you don't get the same standard of food. (Informant No.18, Q41A)

The definition of a 'comprehensive' school was, however, problematic even for informants who were well aware of how they were organized. The primary school headteacher provided a distinction between 'real' or 'true' comprehensives and those that are comprehensive in name only. He said that 'real' comprehensive schools provided the best all-round education,

> All-round, probably a real comprehensive school. A lot of the schools in [Labourville] are really secondary moderns called comprehensives, but that's the nature of the area. The grammar school I went to in [Labourville] - lads came to it from all over the place, not just [Labourville], as there were not enough Catholic boys from [Labourville] of that ability. In [Labourville] now most comprehensives accommodate people who probably would have gone to a secondary modern. A true comprehensive would have the facilities, staff and width of the curriculum to offer a wide choice. (Informant No.08, Q42)

7.8.2 Comparing two questions and answers

Informants were asked two questions in the case study interviews in which bipartite and comprehensive schools were compared. Question 41A repeated a question asked in the Greater Manchester Surveys and question 42 repeated a question asked in the British Social Attitudes surveys. Independent variables affecting responses will be considered in detail (7.8.3, 7.8.4, 7.8.5) as the sub-issue has been highly topical in Torytown for many years.

When Edgell and Duke asked in 1980/1 and 1983/4 if the government should establish comprehensives in place of grammar and secondary modern schools throughout the country the most common response was 'should not' (61.6 per cent). This compares with 27 out of the 52 case study informants who gave the same response in 1988.

Table 7.27
Should the Government establish comprehensive schools throughout the country? (GMS and case studies)

	GMS 1980/1	GMS 1983/4	Case studies 1988
	%	%	n=
Should not	54.6	61.6	27
Doesn't matter	9.2	3.8	8
Should	30.4	27.7	17
DK/no answer	5.9	6.8	-

Source: Edgell and Duke, 1981 and 1985, adapted

In 1988 this gave an index of +10 against establishing comprehensives throughout the country. The increase between 1980/1 and 1983/4 in the proportion of respondents who were against the establishment of comprehensives could possibly be explained by the ageing of the panel and/or the salience of the debate in Torytown in particular. When case study informants were asked to explain their response the need to retain grammar schools was the most common explanation (by 14 informants). Some people contradicted their original answer when they were asked to provide an explanation and eight were so vague in their replies that it seemed possible that they did not know the difference between the two systems. One informant summed up the arguments for and against that created real difficulties for her in reaching a decision.

> I don't know. There are some very good comprehensive schools and some not. My two nieces are in a comprehensive down south and they're very pleased with it. I wouldn't want my children to be involved in a big change because things are never done properly. I don't know that one type of school suits every child. The problem with comprehensives is the size of them. (Informant No.42, Q41A)

In the British Social Attitudes surveys respondents have been asked to choose the best all-round education for secondary school children. Responses in 1984/5 and 1985/6 suggested that the balance of responses was evening out but responses were more skewed in favour of the bipartite system in 1987.

Table 7.28
Which provides the best all-round education
for secondary children? BSA

	1984/5	1985/6	1987
	%	%	%
Grammar and secondary modern schools	50	46	52
Comprehensive	40	46	41

Source: Jowell et al., 1985, 1986 and 1987

The writers of the BSA 5th Report speculate that the shift in opinion may have been due to either dissatisfaction with current secondary school standards or a change in policy preference. The shift was particularly marked amongst Conservative identifiers and amongst older respondents. Labour and Alliance identifiers changed very little. In the 1987 BSA survey a minority of teachers (48 per cent) preferred a comprehensive system.

The case study informants were predominantly in favour of grammar schools and secondary modern schools, although the frequencies were different to those given for question 41A. Some informants therefore gave answers to the two questions that could be interpreted as contradictory.

Table 7.29
Which provides the best all-round education
for secondary children? (case studies)

	n=
Grammar and secondary modern schools	24
Comprehensives	13
Other 5	
Don't know	10
Bipartite - comprehensive	+11

The apparent contradiction between the two answers may be explained by the more precise nature of question 42. To believe that the Government should not replace grammar schools and secondary modern schools with comprehensives is not necessarily the same as believing that the bipartite system is the best. It could, for example, reflect a belief in local freedom from central government control and it is therefore possible to accommodate it (although rather uncomfortably) with a belief that comprehensive schools provide the best all-round education.

7.8.3 Male and female attitudes

It is possible that women may develop a more sceptical attitude towards school systems and that this may be because of their more frequent contacts with their children's schools. For example, when male and female responses in the BSA 1985/6 were compared, both sexes tended to be fairly equally balanced in favour of both. However, slightly more women (10 per cent) than men (7 per cent) gave another answer and this pattern was repeated in the case studies, when six out of 30 women answered that it does not matter, compared to none of the 22 men. The differences related to gender were slight and not generalizable from the small case study sample. However, a tendency amongst those with most contact with the education system to have more balanced attitudes in favour of both systems could be related to the realization that in both systems some schools are better than others.

7.8.4 Educational experience and attitudes

The British Social Attitudes report of 1986 noted that comprehensive schools were favoured by a majority of younger respondents '... partly, we presume because a higher proportion of younger respondents actually attended comprehensive schools' (Jowell et al, 1986, p.117).

Table 7.30
Which provides the best all-round education
for secondary children? BSA, 1985/6

	Bipartite	Comprehensive	Other,D/K
	%	%	%
Age:			
18-34	44	50	5
35-54	48	45	8
55+	49	40	13
Age left F/T Ed:			
16 or under	45	46	9
Over 16	50	43	7
Schooling of household:			
State only	44	48	8
Private (any member)	58	33	9

Source: Jowell et al., 1986

Such age differentials could also reflect differences in life-cycle as respondents in the two younger age groups were most likely to be parents of children currently being educated in comprehensive schools. Knowledge about comprehensive schools tended to affect the level of support for them, those with the least knowledge of comprehensives being most likely to favour a bipartite system. The general pattern was that most respondents favoured the school system they were most familiar with. If school leaving age and the type of education consumed by the household is considered we can see that the group with the least knowledge of comprehensive schools, those households consuming private education, were most likely to favour the bipartite system. The BSA 1987 survey found that the shift in favour of selective education was greater among older than among younger respondents. A small minority in state educated households favoured the comprehensive system and a majority of the respondents who stayed at school after the age of 16 favoured the bipartite system. This may have resulted from experience of a grammar school education rather than a secondary modern school education. Pupils attending secondary modern schools were less likely to stay at school after school-leaving age.

When the question from the Greater Manchester Survey is considered it can be seen that former comprehensive pupils were equally divided in their responses whilst fewer of the former secondary modern school pupils (34.1 per cent) and even fewer former grammar school pupils (22.2 per cent) favoured the establishment of a universal system of comprehensive education.

Table 7.31
Should the government establish comprehensive schools
in place of grammar and secondary modern schools
throughout the country? (GMS2)

	Should	Should not
	%	%
Respondents' school:		
Comprehensive	38.5	38.5
Secondary Modern	34.1	49.9
Grammar	22.2	69.3

Source: Edgell and Duke, 1985, adapted by computer

The BSA finding that households currently consuming education were most likely to favour comprehensives was supported by the 1988 case studies, although that support was merely balanced compared to the skewed attitudes from informants whose household was not consuming education (Table 7.32). The association between the type of education consumed and attitudes to the comprehensive and bipartite systems is, however, rather weak and affected by so many individual experiences that it is difficult to summarize. For example, one informant in 1988 had children at both a grammar school and a secondary modern school and, although full of praise for the grammar school, was rather critical of the secondary modern school. Another informant observed that,

> In our locality secondary moderns have a bad reputation. The secondary modern schools are at fault. Everybody fears them like the plague. There is a comprehensive in [other area] and a lot tried to get their children into that because that comprehensive's got a good reputation - even if it means bussing. (Informant No.33, Q42)

Table 7.32
Should the Government establish comprehensive schools in place of grammar and secondary modern schools throughout the country? (case studies)

	Should n=	Should not n=	Other n=	Total n=
Consumption sector				
No education household	6	16	2	24
Some education household	11	11	6	28
Production sector				
Unemployed	4	11	1	16
Private	4	11	4	19
Public	9	5	3	17
Area				
Torytown	7	18	3	28
Labourville	10	9	5	24

Thus, attitudes towards the bipartite system were often split between respect for grammar schools and criticism of secondary modern schools. Hence the 14 informants in 1988 who gave the retention of the grammar schools as their main reason for opposing the establishment of comprehensive schools. This failure to get parity of esteem for secondary modern schools was also affirmed by, the former Education Secretary, Sir. Keith Joseph when he said that grammar schools had not been reintroduced by Conservative councils because '... they fear the reintroduction of secondary modern schools' [2].

When two informants expressed satisfaction with their childrens' secondary modern school education it was found that their children had later moved to grammar schools. Would they have been equally satisfied if they had remained in a secondary modern school?

> [Torytown] have a good arrangement that if you fail the 11 Plus you can be reviewed at 12 to go to the grammar school. You can move at any age. It was easy for my daughter to move to a grammar school from a secondary modern to do A'Levels. (Informant No. 52, Q8)

Another parent (Informant 24), whose son went to a grammar school, started to question the bipartite system after attending a public meeting about proposals to change Labourville to a comprehensive system. A grammar school headteacher spoke at the meeting about the different 11+ pass rates that were applied to various schools in the area in order to give children in socially disadvantaged areas a better chance of passing (3.3). The informant had thought that the same pass rate applied to all and, although he was concerned about socially disadvantaged children, he decided that whether or not allowances were made for differences between schools, the whole problem meant that the 11+ system was unfair. His son's school, in Labourville, became part of a comprehensive school whilst his son was still a pupil there and the family had no complaints.

7.8.5 Production sector

In view of the affects of social and economic disadvantages on a child's performance in the 11+ exam, it is not surprising that the BSA surveys found that manual workers tended to be slightly more in favour of comprehensive schools than non-manual workers. However, the BSA surveys also reported that the main shift towards favouring comprehensive schools was amongst non-manual workers.

In the case studies it was found that equal numbers of unemployed informants and private employees were for and against the establishment of comprehensive schools but the balance was reversed in the case of public employees.

7.8.6 Political identification

When responses in 1988 from the two areas were compared it was found that in Labourville they were fairly balanced whilst in Torytown they were skewed against the establishment of comprehensive schools. As the debate was prominent in Torytown, voters tended to polarize their attitudes along party lines, with stronger allegiance to their respective parties' views on the sub-issue. The association between party identification or voting behaviour and attitudes towards the two school systems holds in both the BSA and the GMS and holds over time (Table 7.33). The responses of Labour and Conservative identifiers were skewed for and against the two systems whilst the attitudes of Alliance identifiers were fairly balanced. When the attitudes reported in the GMS are considered (Table 7.34) we can see a similar relationship, although distorted percentages in 1979 and 1980 resulted from the small number of Liberal and SDP respondents.

Table 7.33
Which provides the best all-round education for secondary children? BSA, 1985/6

	Bipartite	Comprehensive	Other,D/K
	%	%	%
Party identification			
Labour	33	57	10
Alliance	46	47	8
Conservative	64	31	4
Non-aligned	40	44	15

Source: Jowell et al., 1986

Table 7.34
Should the government establish comprehensive schools in place of grammar and secondary modern schools throughout the country? Voting behaviour, GMS1 and 2

	Should		Should not	
	TT	LV	TT	LV
	%	%	%	%
1979 General Election				
Labour	54.3	47.1	35.4	36.2
Lib/SDP	16.7	0	55.6	66.6
Conservative	16.0	15.9	71.3	76.6
1980 Local Election				
Labour	54.6	47.9	32.4	32.0
Lib/SDP	28.5	0	61.9	100.0
Conservative	11.2	16.3	76.7	74.4
1983 General Election				
Labour	54.1	51.2	42.4	37.2
Lib/SDP	23.0	20.7	65.0	75.4
Conservative	7.1	10.9	84.1	80.0
1983 Local Election				
Labour	57.3	51.4	31.7	35.8
Lib/SDP	24.5	23.0	64.7	73.3
Conservative	5.9	13.0	87.3	76.1

NOTE: These figures depend on the differential turnout in different elections and are not therefore ideal for making comparisons over time.
Source: Edgell and Duke, 1981 and 1985

Conservative support for the bipartite system rose overall from 1979 to 1983 and, apart from during the 1979 General Election, it was stronger in Torytown than in Labourville. Labour voters' attitudes to the two systems were more evenly balanced but Labour support for the comprehensive system rose a little from 1979 to 1983. A larger proportion of Labour voters in Torytown favoured comprehensive schools than did the Labour voters in Labourville. This may again result from familiarity with the system. Liberal and SDP voters too tended to vary their attitudes according to the local area. Although the majority of Liberal and SDP voters were opposed to comprehensive schools, in Labourville they were more strongly opposed.

7.8.7 Summary of findings

Both quantitative and qualitative data reveal strong support for the bipartite system of secondary education. However, secondary modern schools were so lacking in public esteem (possibly explaining Torytown's decision to rename them) that this support could be more accurately described as support for grammar schools.

The strongest (but still quite weak) support for comprehensive schools came from those with the most knowledge of them; respondents aged 34 and under, those who attended comprehensive schools themselves and those in households currently consuming state education. This pattern was particularly noticeable in the case of Labour voters, who were, at a national level, more likely than other voters to support comprehensive education. Labour voters in Torytown were, however, less likely to support comprehensive schools than were Labour voters in Labourville. Lack of familiarity is therefore likely to bread contempt and many informants in the case studies knew little about educational provision. Some informants (including one in Torytown) thought that grammar and secondary modern schools no longer existed in any part of the country.

Findings also highlight the problems involved in defining comprehensive schools. Very few Labourville children attended private schools, and relatively few (when compared with Torytown) attended schools in other areas (3.3). In theory then, Labourville comprehensive schools could be described as 'true' comprehensives, but Informant No.8 (7.8.1) argued that, as the larger Labourville borough included some particularly deprived areas, some comprehensive schools lacked the social mix, ability range and facilities that he associated with a 'true' comprehensive school.

It is not, therefore, always clear what is being discussed when the relative merits of the systems of secondary education are assessed. In Torytown a comprehensive school is also a secondary modern school and (Roman Catholic) independent schools are also state schools, in that a large proportion of their funding comes from local rates. As a sub-issue, the debate about comprehensive versus bipartite education at first seemed to be relatively straightforward, but this has not proved to be the case.

7.9 Parental choice

In the 1960s and early 1970s the normative paradigm emphasised the role of the state in providing a safety net to ensure that all children had the best education possible. Comprehensive schools and the identification of educational priority areas were just two of the many attempts made to equalize educational opportunities. The normative paradigm generated by the Conservative Governments of the 1980s, however, emphasised the role of parents in determining the best education possible for their children. This has led to claims that inequality of educational opportunity gained renewed acceptance (Hall, quoted in 1.3). The problems emerging from this normative paradigm, the attitudes of voters towards it and the effect of parental choice on informants and their families are considered in this section. As Conservative Governments presented parental choice as the main theme of their education policy, the subject has already considered in some detail (notably in Chapter 1, 3.3, 4.2, 4.5, 5.4, 6.2.4, 6.3 and 7.2.3).

7.9.1 Political definitions

It has already been noted that theoretical support for the rights of parents to choose the sort of education that they want for their children belongs to no particular political party. Politicians tend to be torn between the aim of providing the maximum freedom for parents to choose and the aim of ensuring that the best education possible is provided for each child. They will differ however in the degree to which they emphasise each of the two aims. Conservatives will tend to emphasise parental choice, claiming that if parents are free to choose they will choose the best education possible for their child. Socialists will emphasise the need to provide the best education possible for every child and the probability that some children will suffer if their education is determined by parents in a society that is pervaded by unequal opportunities. The problem for policy-makers and for voters in framing their opinions is to what extent should children's education be determined by their parents and to what extent by the state, acting as an arbiter in the interests of the child.

7.9.2 The cost of private education

The cost of private education has already been considered in the context of local education authority spending (6.3). Here it is considered again in order to provide a knowledge base with which to compare voters' attitudes. This is particularly important in view of the commonly expressed belief that private education is financially independent of the state. Torytown council's policy of paying the fees for Roman Catholic pupils to attend independent grammar schools has already been discussed (3.3 and 6.3). However, many of the pupils attending private schools are financed wholly, or partly, by their parents. Some politicians have claimed that, with effort and sacrifice any family can afford the fees for a private education for its children. This is clearly not the case.

Many problems have to be considered when parents want to have their children privately educated. The fees are very high indeed; in 1988 annual fees were from £450 at the cheapest preparatory school to £7,050 for a prestigious public school (IFSF, 1988). Most people have no idea of the total average cost of keeping a child at a private school from 11 to 18. In 1988 only 10 per cent of a sample surveyed by IFSF quoted the correct figure of about £70,000 and most grossly underestimated it. If previously wealthy families fall upon hard times there is no guarantee that they will be able to obtain any help from the state in order to continue paying the fees; although some local authorities (including the ILEA until the mid 1970s) have done this in the past.

The actual cost to the government of subsidizing private education are unknown and speculation has placed it as high as £500 million per year during the 1980s. Caroline Benn criticised the practice of using public money to pay the private school fees for some privileged parents, such as senior military officers and diplomats, whilst not paying the fees for lower ranking personnel whose lifestyles causes similar disruption to their families. She listed some of the other ways that taxpayers' money has been used to subsidize private education.

> Direct taxpayer subsidy was nearly £200 million a year by the end of the 1970s. Indirect subsidies were far higher: tax concessions for fee-paying parents; tax relief for private schools classed as charities, who often pay no rates on expensive properties; money for new types of state private schools, like European Schools; money for services to the private system from the state, like educational exchange arrangements; money for holiday travel fares for private school pupils, including air fares. Including money for special education and money to educate and train the teachers who teach in private schools, the total bill is now approaching £500 million a year...... (Benn, 1983, p.119)

Her main objections were that much of this money was going to families who were already advantaged and that state schools were suffering.

And every year ratepayers and taxpayers are going to be asked to shift more public money from the majority's own public education service into the minority's private one. Objectionable enough in the best of times, it is intolerable when the public's own educational service is being cut, run down, and sold off to private bidders in search of private profits .... Under the Conservatives 'independent' schools are getting more dependent each year. It is highly doubtful if any genuinely independent secondary schools exist any more at all. (Benn, 1983, p.121)

7.9.3 Assisted Places

The 1980 Education Act set up the Assisted Places Scheme to provide government grants to less affluent parents wanting to send their (usually 'academic') children to private schools. Families are means tested, with children from poorer families having all their fees paid whilst other families make a contribution to the fees according to family income. However, a DES survey (reported in the Times Educational Supplement, 3 February 1989) found that in 1988 about 10 per cent of the Assisted Places in England and Wales were not being used and that the take up rate varied in different areas of the country. In the North-east about one third were not being used and in the South-east the figure was about one quarter. It is possible that parents in the South-east were discouraged because the higher cost of living there makes parental contributions prohibitive. However, a likely reason for the low take up of Assisted Places in England and Wales in general is the finding [3] that about 60 per cent of parents had not heard of Assisted Places.

In the case studies it was found that 39 of the 52 informants had not heard of Assisted Places. It is possible that the scheme may have been known to informants for what it is rather than by the label attached. This may account for the apparent lack of knowledge of some informants but the low take up of places and other comments made still suggest that a large proportion of voters are totally unaware of the scheme. When asked to explain what they knew about Assisted Places only two noted correctly that they were paid for by central government. Three informants (one in Torytown, two in Labourville) thought that they were financed by local government.

Table 7.35
Knowledge and interest in Assisted Places (case studies)

	n=
Heard of them:	
No	39
Yes 11	
Possibly	2
Interest:	
Not heard of them	41
Interested	2
Not interested	7
Opinion only	1
DK	1
Knowledge:	
Not heard of them	41
Fees paid (DK how)	5
Fees paid by local government	3
Fees paid by central government	2
DK	1

Many informants expressed the belief that private schools provided a superior form of education and some showed their lack of awareness about Assisted Places by expressing regret that less affluent families could not send their children to them.

> [Against abolishing private schools.] Because the quality of teaching is very good. I'm not saying these schools are perfect but the quality of education is very good. I do think though that there should be a way of ordinary or rather extraordinary children getting into them. If I had the money I would have sent my daughter to a private school. (Informant No.18, Q42F)

The deferential attitudes of many parents could be another possible reason for the low take-up of Assisted Places. Some of the informants interviewed in the case studies obviously thought that private schools were for upper-class children and that their own children were automatically excluded. One informant expressed both deference and resentment.

> You've got to have the leaders and the followers, and the private schools produce the leaders. That sounds awful because I hate them, but they're there and I think they're necessary. We're a very class-

conscious country and, even though I don't like it, it'll always be that
way. You've got the upper class, the middle class and the working
class, and the upper class become the leaders and the working class
become the workers. And I think that's why this country is falling
apart - because we're forgetting what class we're in. (Informant No.44,
Q41F)

7.9.4 Support for private schools

In the Greater Manchester Study respondents were asked one question about
private schools and in the British Social Attitudes surveys they have been
asked two. On each occasion a majority of respondents favoured their
continued existence. Each year the BSA surveys asked if there should be,
'..more private schools... about the same number as now... fewer private
schools ...or no private schools at all' (Table 7.36). They also asked, 'If there
were fewer private schools in Britain today...state schools would benefit..state
schools would suffer...it would make no difference' (Table 7.36).

Table 7.36
Should there be more, about the same,
fewer or no private schools? BSA

	1983/4	1985/6	1987
	%	%	%
More private schools	11	9	11
About the same number as now	67	59	65
Fewer	8	13	11
No private schools at all	11	16	11
Other answer	2	3	3

Source: Jowell et al., 1984, 1986, 1988

The BSA findings suggest an increase in hostility towards private education
between 1984 and 1985. In the 1985/6 report the proportion of respondents
who felt that there should be fewer or no private schools rose to 29 per cent
(from 19 per cent in the previous surveys). The number believing that state
schools would benefit from their reduction also rose. However, the 1987 BSA
survey found that the popularity of private schools had increased again. The
change was common amongst all social groups and identifiers with all parties.

Table 7.37
If there were fewer private schools in Britain today
would state schools..., BSA

	1983/4	1985/6	1987
	%	%	%
Benefit	18	24	20
Suffer	18	12	16
Or would it make no difference	59	58	60
Other answer	4	6	5

Source: Jowell et al., 1984, 1986, 1988

Table 7.38
Attitudes to private schools and party identification, BSA

	1983/4			1987/8		
	Cons	All'nce	Lab	Cons	All'nce	Lab
	%	%	%	%	%	%
Should there be more, the same, fewer or no private schools?						
more	19	7	4	19	4	5
the same	73	74	59	69	74	53
fewer	3	9	14	5	9	19
none	4	8	20	3	9	21
other answer	2	2	2	3	3	2
If there were fewer private schools would state schools...						
benefit	12	18	25	11	21	32
suffer	26	16	12	23	13	10
no difference	59	63	57	63	63	53
other answer	3	2	5	3	3	6

Jowell et al., 1984 and 1988

Although the pattern suggests that Conservatives were most in favour of private education and Labour voters least, support crossed party lines and even a slight majority of Labour voters supported the continued existence of private schools. The most common response was an acceptance of the present situation: most responding that there should be about the same number of private schools as now and that a reduction in the number of private schools would make no difference to state schools.

This finding was reflected in the case studies, when the majority again answered that it would make no difference.

Table 7.39
If there were fewer private schools would state schools . . .
(case studies)

	n=
Benefit	10
Suffer	10
No difference	31
Other	1

The most common reason given for the belief that state education would suffer was that it would increase the demands on state schools. However, other informants felt that state schools would benefit from the extra input.

> [Benefit] If all the private schools shut down, their pupils would all have to come to the state schools. The fact that their parents felt that education was high on their priorities would help them to do well. Many people send their children to private schools for social reasons, not academic, because they don't want them mixing with rif raf and to make the right connections. (Informant 08, Q43)

In the Greater Manchester Study Edgell and Duke asked if the government should '..abolish the private schools which are outside the state education system' (Table 7.40). The percentage in favour of the abolition of private schools was similar to the percentage of BSA respondents who argued in favour of a reduction or the abolition of private schools in 1983. When the same question was asked in the case studies a smaller proportion favoured the abolition of private schools but a larger proportion said that it did not matter.

Table 7.40
Should the government abolish private schools?
(GMS2 and case studies)

	GMS 1983/4	Case studies 1988
	%	n=
Should	19.6	8
Doesn't matter/mixed	7.3	8
Should not	70.4	36
Don't know	2.3	-
Should not - should	-	+28

Source: Edgell and Duke, 1985, and case studies

When case study informants were asked to explain their answer the most common response (from 12) was that people should be free to spend their money as they chose and 10 said that a choice should be available.

Table 7.41
Attitudes to private education, explained (case studies)

	n=
Free to spend as choose	12
Good to have a choice	10
If had money my kids would have gone	5
Benefits state education	4
Other for	7
Anti private education	5
Mixed views	6
No answer	3

Let them that's got the money pay and let them that's not got the money go to others. If people don't have to rely on the state let them. Then there's more for them that do. (Informant 21, Q41F)

State schools would suffer. There'd be more children in them and a higher ratio of children to teachers. (Informant No.52, Q43)

Several informants referred to the source of finance for private education,

179

apparently believing that the government contributed nothing towards it.

> They [the Government] don't pay for them. We've got to have brains
> at the top otherwise we couldn't have brains in the middle. If I had the
> money I'd have sent mine. You've got to have highly educated people.
> (Informant No.48, Q41F)

> If people want to send their children to private schools they're entitled
> to do so as long as they pay for it. They pay for it. There's nobody
> else. (Informant No.49, Q41F)

A teacher showed some knowledge of government subsidies to private
education, and had mixed views.

> Educationally I think they should be [abolished]. In terms of the rights
> of individuals they shouldn't. There should be freedom of choice so
> long as the money doesn't come out of the public purse to subsidize it,
> and that includes tax relief or Assisted Places. (Informant No.45 a
> teacher,Q41F)

The low take up of the relatively few Assisted Places provided also means
that during the 1980s there was no noticeable increase in the number of
children from less affluent families receiving a private education. Edgell and
Duke found that the consumption of private education was closely related to
social class and attitudes.

7.9.5 Experiences of parental choice

Conservative idealism about the effects of parental choice on their children's
education was not supported by the experiences of those informants
interviewed in the case studies. From this small sample emerged a large
number of illustrations of the effects of relative depravation on educational
achievement. For example, a child's school leaving age was found to be
largely determined by family income. To many of the informants education
beyond the usual school leaving age was totally out of the question because of
the family's need for an extra wage. One informant said that his mother left
school at eleven,

> . . . which was allowed in those days if you had a one parent family.
> (Informant No.26, Q33)

Another informant (No.29) spoke of his mother leaving school at 14 to look after her mother who had had a stroke. His father ran away from home at 14 because his parents wanted him to work down the local mine. A strong Conservative identifier left school at 15 because of the financial needs of the family.

> My father came out of work, so I was taken away and told to earn some pennies. (Informant No.46, Q25)

Financial constraints on the type of education children have appear to have been passed from generation to generation. For example, one informant talked about his mother's and father's education and how they tried to pay for him to have a private education.

> [Fathers' education] He went to a boys secondary modern school because they couldn't afford to let him go to the grammar school because they had to buy their own books and were so poor that they couldn't afford them at that time. [Mothers' education] She went to grammar school but left at 14. They pulled her out before the end because they couldn't afford to keep her there.
> [Informants' education] Instead of taking the 11+ I went to a boarding school because mum wanted me to. She had to pay to send me and my brother there. I went when I was 10 or 11 until I was 13. Then I went to a secondary modern school. (Informant No.40, Q21, Q32 and Q33)

Another informant said that his mother left school at 12 and that he had to leave his elementary school at 14, although he would have liked to have had a better education.

> They [his parents] were both from big families. They had to leave school to help keep the family.
> [Why informant left at 14] Because I had to. Because I had to go and get a job and start work to help keep me brothers and sisters.
> [His preferred education] I would rather have gone to an all boys school. In them days there was no such thing because you're parents couldn't afford it. Mine couldn't anyway. (Informant No.49, Q22, Q25, Q33)

Other families tried to pay for their children to be privately educated but had problems in keeping up the payments.

181

> [Mother's education] For a while she was at a girls' private boarding school. Her father died. Therefore she left and I don't know where she went. She got some further education and a Pitmans shorthand typing qualification. (Informant No.36, Q33)

> [Informant left private school at 15] It was just at the end of the war and I was off school a lot. Mother was ill and I wasn't doing well in my exams, so dad said I'd better get out and go to work. (Informant No.43, Q25)

When a family had enough money a child could stay at school after the school leaving age and despite examination failures. The following informant, for example, had an affluent, self-employed father. He stayed at his grammar school until he was 19, later graduating and becoming a teacher.

> I left school at 19 because I failed my O'Levels the first time and had to take an extra year. I was sport mad and spent more time on that than in the classroom. (Informant No.45, Q25)

This can be contrasted with one informant who was a single-parent. Her daughter was eligible for free school meals.

> She [daughter] could have had them but I wouldn't embarrass her. We made sandwiches instead. (Informant No.48, Q58)

Yet financial constraints were not the only educational disadvantages. The informant who left school with literacy problems was obviously bitter about the lack of support from both of his parents who, he claimed were both 'clever'.

> He was very clever and an excellent writer and speller but he never had the patience to teach me. (Informant No.48, Q32)

Those informants who had recently consumed private education also had problems. A self-employed Torytown builder had one child with an Assisted Place to which he contributed.

> If my income was fixed I'd be laughing. It fluctuates and therefore there's just enough to maintain the house. I'm in debt and therefore living above my means. (Informant 33, Q66)

Another informant went to a direct grant school herself but would not want her own children to have the same sort of education because of the distance she had to travel to school.

> There are a lot of benefits in being educated locally. I had to travel a long way to the direct grant school and my contemporaries at school were not otherwise known to me. (Informant No.51, Q23)

7.9.6 Social class

The problems involved in operationalizing social class are considered in detail in 4.5. I have not utilized social or occupational class categories to the full partly because of those problems, but that should not imply that respondents' social class has no affect on attitudes to private education. The following table of responses in the second Greater Manchester Survey shows a clear pattern of attitudes and experiences changing through the hierarchy from employer to worker. However, the small number of respondents in some cells (a total of only 15 employers) limits the generalizability of the data.

Table 7.42
Use of services, attitudes to public spending
and vote in 1983 General Election
by respondent social class: second interview, GMS2

	n=	Ever used private education %	Approve of cuts in general %	Voted Conservative in 1983 %
employer	15	40	53	67
petty bourgeois	45	24	44	60
controller	225	12	34	41
worker	393	11	20	27

Source: Edgell and Duke, 1985, Appendix IV B222 adapted

Despite the difficulties involved in operationalizing attitudes there is abundant evidence (dating back further than the Plowden Report of 1967) of an association between social class and educational achievement. Of particular relevance in the present context is the language used in debates about access to education. The social class system can be seen as perpetuating itself through the promotion of parental choice as a pseudonym for the inheritance of educational privilege.

Despite the many illustrations of financial constraints on their families' educational histories a majority of informants in the case studies favoured the continued opportunity for some parents to choose a privileged education for their children. When informants were asked if they were aware of social class differences in Britain (Q51A) 42 out of the 52 answered 'Yes'. Of these, 19 said that social class affected opportunities a lot, seven said that it affected job opportunities and three identified a national North/South divide rather than social class divisions. However, whilst the majority perceived the existence of social class, many deferential statements were made during the interviews. Several seemed to regard class distinctions as natural phenomena rather than social constructions.

> [About social class affecting opportunities.] It does. There's the rich, the middle class and the poor - so it does seem to have some effect. Naturally the poor can't be like the middle class and the middle class can't live up to the rich - so you've all got your own grades. (Informant No.20, Q51)

Three people believed that opportunities had improved during their lifetimes (compared to one who thought that they had worsened).

> It's not as bad as it used to be. There is and always will be. In my day, if you were born in the working class, you stayed in the working class. You hadn't a cat in hells chance of getting out. You can today. It certainly does help to come from a good home and a well to do family but the underprivileged have a better chance today. (Informant No.34, Q51)

In the case studies informants were asked if they had heard about proposals (in the Education Reform Bill) to let schools 'opt out' of local authority control. Few had heard of this (see 5.5) but one who had argued that it would worsen existing inequalities.

> If they opt out what will happen to the inner cities? You're likely to get those opting out in areas where they're more motivated and there's more finance. It concerns me that it'll become a two tier system and that the ones that are left will have concentration to lower ability, lower household financial ability as well, which means that extras can't be provided as they would be in the opted out of system. (Informant No.51, Q40E)

Despite her concern about unequal educational opportunities the above informant later said that she did not think that private schools should be abolished.

7.9.7 Summary of findings

Informants therefore seemed to find the phrase 'parental choice' appealing, even when they have experienced a parental 'handicap' in their own education or when they acknowledged that such a handicap has affected the education of others. There was very strong support for the continued existence of private schools and an assumption that they provided a superior form of education when compared with state schools. This support existed despite the general lack of awareness of Assisted Places and the common belief that a private education was beyond informants' financial means.

The apparent contradiction between experience and attitudes could be explained as the result of deference or false consciousness. It could also be claimed that social class distinctions are not now as obvious as they were in the past. Thus, informants may have been thinking in relative terms; the idea being that, although inequalities in educational opportunities remained, they were not as bad as they were in the past (7.2.4). If the definition of 'parental choice' favoured by the present Government becomes an even more influential feature of the structure of the education system the experiences described in 7.8.5 will appear in a more modern context. The idealized image of the parent as a caring, intelligent and (most of all) affluent individual may apply in some families but many case study informants have not experienced this.

7.10 Student grants or loans?

The continuing Conservative policy of cutting back on educational spending involves attempts to make further and (especially) higher education more self-sufficient. At the time of the case studies the most contentious sub-issue relating to higher education was that of the gradual phasing out of student grants, to be supplemented by loans to be repaid over a period of years after graduation. The debate was highly topical and (it was envisaged) relatively straightforward when compared with other issues.

7.10.1 Defining the problem

In June 1988 the press reported a current shortage of graduates in Britain and predictions that the shortage was going to get worse throughout the 1990s (Institute of Manpower Studies report, in the Guardian, 17 June 1988) partly because of falling rolls during the 1980s and resulting decline in the number of school leavers. At the same time the Government was considering ways of reducing its spending on further education whilst aiming to increase student numbers. The government sponsored debate centred mainly on the introduction of a system of loans to top up frozen student grants. In theory the contribution from former students would help to expand further education and promote individual responsibility, expanding the role of the consumer in a market-led educational economy.

At the time of the 1988 case study interviews the debate was not based on any firm proposals and it was not until November 1988 that the Government gave a clear indication of its plans in a White Paper on student finance. Its three main proposals were, firstly, the freezing of the student grant and parental contributions in cash terms, secondly, a low interest loan facility of about £1,200 over three years, increasing with time and thirdly, the removal of Housing Benefit, Unemployment Benefit and Income Support from students.

The freezing of the student grant would, however, be more or less a continuation of existing government policy. According to the 1987 Edition of Social Trends, parents were already expected to pay an increasing proportion of the grant, rising from an average contribution of 12.7 per cent in 1980/1 to 25.3 per cent in 1984/5. This assumed that parents would make the full payment and in many cases this has not been the case, because parents were either not willing or not able. Many students have therefore been suffering hardship for several years and most are already partially dependent on bank loans or overdrafts. The Government's proposal was to increase dependence on loans but make them more manageable by reducing the interest rate. By the end of the 1980s students were also expected to pay 20 per cent of the Community Charge.

7.10.2 Quantitative data - opposition to loans

The British Social Attitude surveys asked two questions relating to students' access to further and higher education; one a general question and the other dealing more specifically with the option of student loans. Respondents were asked, if opportunities to go to higher education should be increased and, 'Should students continue to get grants as now from a LEA or loans to be paid back?' (Table 7.43).

Table 7.43
Should opportunities to go to higher education be
increased, reduced etc.? BSA

	1983/4	1985/6	1987
	%	%	%
Increased	44	49	53
About right	49	43	42
Reduced	5	5	3

Source: Jowell et al., 1984, 1986 and 1988

The proportion saying that opportunities should be increased rose from 44 per cent in 1983/4 to 53 per cent in 1987. This rise was consistent across all political categories although the proportion of support for increased access tended to vary along party lines; Labour voters being most in support and Conservative voters least.

Table 7.44
Percentage saying that opportunities for higher education
should be increased, by party identification, BSA

	1983/4	1987/8
	%	%
Conservative	38	45
Alliance	44	56
Labour	54	61

Source: Jowell et al., 1988, p.28

The second BSA question revealed strong support for the continued payment of grants to students rather than a loans system. A majority of all the main types of political identifiers favoured grants (Table 7.45).

Table 7.45
Percentage saying that students should get grants, BSA

	1983/4	1987/8
	%	%
Conservative	51	56
Alliance	58	68
Labour	66	77
Total 57	65	

Source: Jowell et al., 1988, p.29

In the case study interviews informants were asked if the Government should replace student grants with a system of loans (to be repaid after the student qualified).

Table 7.46
Should the government replace student grants with loans?
(case studies)

	n=
Should	14
Should not	33
Other	5
Should - should not	-19

A particularly large proportion of women did not favour loans; 22 out of 30 women were opposed to them, compared to 11 out of 22 men. This complements the BSA findings in 1985 that there had been a particular increase in women's support for grants since 1983 (from 56 per cent to 62 per cent). Mens' responses were fairly balanced, with 10 of them favouring loans whilst only 4 women favoured loans. The figures for females matched those for informants whose households currently consumed education (i.e. 22 against loans and 4 in favour out of a total of 28) whilst those for males matched the responses of people whose households were not currently consuming education (i.e. 11 against and 10 in favour). This greater opposition amongst women to loans would be more surprising in a larger, random sample because men are more likely than women to have experienced the problems of surviving on a grant. In the case studies the effect was not noticeable because equal quotas of men and women with experience of further education were chosen.

7.10.3 Qualitative data - explaining opposition to loans

When informants in the case studies were asked to explain their answers the most common response (from 11) was that students might have problems in repaying the loan.

> Because at the time the student qualifies they are at a time of thinking of settling down and finding a house and a job and I think they have enough commitments without having to repay a loan. (Informant No.37, Q41I)

> I think the grant should be increased. I don't agree because there's no certainty of someone getting a job after they leave and that would be putting a chain round their necks. They might never repay it back. They can't live on their grants as it is today. (Informant No.18, Q42I)

> Not in the present situation of jobs being so difficult to get. (Informant No.52, Q41I)

Six said that students were contributing to the whole country's welfare in some way.

> I think it'd be very hard for them to pay back. They're trying to get a better education (they're our future) to get jobs so why should they have a debt round their necks. A girl that works with us as a Saturday girl gets a grant but it's not enough. (Informant No.16, Q41I)

> It's the governments responsibility to teach students and to pay for it. Students will repay the government with their work. I don't think we should pay back for our education. We'll be paying for primary schools next. (Informant No.17, Q41I)

Others also argued that further education was as much a right as a student's earlier education.

> You don't expect people to pay for their education in their early lives and you shouldn't expect them to do it later. (Informant No.44, Q41I)

Five said that the prospect of repaying a loan would discourage potential students from taking courses and two argued that the existing payment of income tax was already an effective method of repaying the state.

But should they lower the taxes? You can't say 100 per cent that they would get jobs after they've qualified. There'd be problems getting the money back. Everybody's paying taxes anyway for the grant and it benefits everybody. (Informant No.25, Q41I)

7.10.4 Summary of findings

There was strong support (even from Conservatives) for the continued payment of grants to students rather than a system of loans. Although informants tended to support parents' *right* to choose and pay for their children's education in a private school they disagreed with the idea of students being *obliged* to finance their own higher education. Access to higher education was regarded as a right rather than a privilege that should be bought.

The question of payment for education appears to be crucial to most debates about education as a political issue. Often when sociologists and politicians discuss access to higher education they use the term 'deferred gratification'. This is rather misleading as it implies that pleasure can be deferred until some future time when the student will reap his/her rewards. In reality, however, basic necessities are not pleasures that can be deferred and it is naive to assume that highly qualified individuals will secure well-paid jobs. Findings about educational experiences suggest that it is more realistic to see 'deferred gratification' as a euphemism for having the support (financial and otherwise) needed to continue in education after school leaving age (see 7.9.5). Access to higher education for working-class young people in particular is often cut off by the lack of a student grant for A level students. This, combined with the debts that are likely to be accumulated during a long course, provides a most effective way of perpetuating social class inequalities through the education system.

7.11 Attitudinal types and sub-issues

Parkin's definitions of three attitudinal types are particularly useful in this analysis of attitudes to sub-issues (5.4, Parkin, 1971). Some informants accepted the dominant value system endorsing the existing order, some accommodated their attitudes to the dominant value system and others had a radical value system which promoted an oppositional interpretation of inequality. Such categorizations are, however, over-simplifications as an individual may have attitudes that span all three; for example, a radical attitude to public spending, an accommodative attitude to private education and a dominant attitude to anti-racist education. Nevertheless, the three categories are useful tools for the analysis of attitudes to education as a political issue.

During this research several examples were found of informants internalizing the dominant value system. For example, Informant 20 (quoted in 7.9.6) spoke of people having natural grades and accepted private education as a proper reflection of those grades. Informants also tended to endorse the education system that existed during their own school days; the type of education they had being regarded as the norm. Hence a tendency to favour a bipartite system of secondary education, because that is still the system that is familiar to most adults. Similarly many people were sceptical or hostile to that which was unfamiliar to them; for example, homosexuality and anti-racist education. Such attitudes are encouraged by certain newspapers, by the traditional values remaining in British society and by the Conservative politicians who promote them (5.4).

There were also many instances of a subordinate value system encouraging accommodative responses. For example, when considering private education, Informant No.44 (quoted in 7.9.3) said that she did not like British class consciousness and even hated 'them', but thought that a division between leaders and followers was necessary to stop the country from 'falling apart'. It was in connection with private education and informants' own educational experiences that the most accommodative responses were found. Although most case study informants had no experience of private education, because they and their families could not afford to pay fees, the majority favoured the continued availability of private education for those who could afford it (most had not heard of Assisted Places). At the same time, the majority believed that there were social class inequalities in Britain. Dissonant attitudes were explained in various ways: by the belief that educational opportunities had improved during their lifetimes, that the children attending private schools were more intelligent than other children and deserved a better education or by the common belief that the existence of private schools saved the taxpayer money that could be spent on state schools. The last point can be challenged by the finding that Torytown council paid the fees for some of its local children to have a private education whilst spending less than Labourville council on each state educated pupil (unit costs).

At a national level it is also noticeable that there was a common belief that educational standards had fallen, but that reactions tended to be mainly accommodative; a general loss of respect for teachers and an increased demand for private education. Even though the vast majority of voters were opposed to cuts in public (and educational) spending, the Conservative Party obtained the largest share of votes during the 1980s. Either the criticisms that could be levelled at the policy-makers were directed elsewhere or other influences on voting behaviour were more important (see next chapter).

Although less apparent than dominant or subordinate attitudes, there are some examples of a radical value system promoting an oppositional interpretation of class inequality. The most obvious example is in attitudes to a student loans system. It was generally seen as an overt means of perpetuating inequality and was opposed by the majority of voters. However, it is possible that accommodative responses may develop as the scheme becomes established. Just as private schools have been accommodated by the rhetoric of parental choice, student loans may eventually be accommodated in terms of self-sufficiency and the incentive to get a marketable qualification.

Notes

1. Butler and Stokes asked whether respondents had 'warm' or 'cold' feelings towards comprehensive schools. They were asked to provide a temperature between 0 degrees and 100 degrees. In 1969 (Butler and Stokes, 1974) the average temperature was 61 degrees, in 1970 it was 62 degrees.
2. Article by Sir. Keith Joseph, 'Destroying the underachievers',
The Guardian, 20 April 1988.
3. ISIS opinion poll carried out in 1988 and reported in the Times Educational Supplement, 3 February 1989.

8 Votes: The political alignment of attitudes

8.1 Interest and issue motives

How are attitudes towards education as a political issue involved in the process of deciding how to vote? Although little research has been carried out regarding education as an individual issue, political scientists have for many years studied the relationship between attitudes to issues in general and voting behaviour. However, the issue model is but one model of voting behaviour. The influence of personal interest on attitudes to education has already been considered in Chapter 4 but here it will be considered with reference to voting behaviour. It will, for example, be argued (see Crewe, 1987) that, rather than making a reasoned assessment of parties' issue agendas, voters tended to consider what they perceived as their own best interests when they were deciding how to vote in the 1987 General Election more.

8.2 Assessing the issue motive

Some criteria for assessing the issue motive had to be found and, in common with many other researchers, I utilized the criteria applied by Butler and Stokes (1974) and devised an index system to simplify findings.

8.2.1 Butler and Stokes' criteria

Butler and Stokes (1974) have made one of the most thorough attempts at clarifying the issue motive. They identified three criteria by which an issue can be judged in terms of impact on voting behaviour. First, a large proportion of voters must have strong feelings on the subject. Second, the issue must be associated differently with the parties in the publics' mind, ie. the parties' stance on the issue must be recognized and seen to differ. (These first two criteria relate to both the impact of issues on individual voters and impact in general.) The third relates to electoral impact in general. It is that opinion must be skewed; i.e. it must be seen to favour one side of the argument in order to be seen as important. Butler and Stokes' three criteria can therefore be used as a model to assess the strength of education as a political issue.

Strength of feeling is obviously an important criterion for judging the impact of attitudes to education on voting behaviour. It has, for example, been shown that education was regarded as a more important political issue in Torytown, where Labour and Conservative voters had stronger attitudes towards the bipartite/comprehensive debate (see 7.8). This resulted in a sharper polarization on that sub-issue than was found between Labour and Conservative voters in Labourville. A large proportion of Torytown parents sent their children to private schools (3.2) or grammar schools and thus perceived their best interests in voting Conservative because the Labour Party was opposed to both types of schools (at least in theory, see 7.9.4). In view of the marginal nature of local politics in Torytown, votes based on this type of self-interest assumed an importance that was out of proportion to their number. If non-consumers and the parents of children attending secondary modern schools shared such views or were relatively indifferent to the sub-issues involved the Conservative Party could be assured of a secure education-related Conservative vote.

It was found (Chapter 4) that the usually instrumental nature of interest in education as a political issue meant that a large proportion of voters regarded it as unimportant simply because they were not directly involved in it as consumers or producers. As only about one third of households are consuming education at any one time strength of feeling is permanently diluted within the electorate as a whole. The National Health Service on the other hand emerged as the issue most likely to incite strong feelings primarily because it is a service that is consumed continually throughout the life-cycle. In contrast case study informants spoke of an 'educational age' (4.4) as a relatively short stage of transition. Edgell and Duke also found that 25 per cent of their respondents (see 5.5) thought that their local education system was the responsibility of the Greater Manchester Council, rather than their borough council. This suggests that many voters did not recognize education as a political issue in local elections.

The criterion that education *must be associated differently with the political parties* in the public's mind cannot easily be satisfied because educational sub-issues were perceived as relating to party policies in various ways. Conservative governments are now strongly identified with cuts in educational spending and this aspect of education as a political issue may be found to satisfy all three criteria at a national level at least (locally it may differ). The bipartite/comprehensive debate in Torytown was also closely related to competing local party policies; grammar schools and secondary modern schools being associated with the Conservative party and comprehensives with the Labour party. Yet comprehensive schools had long been established in other areas with Conservative councils and there is a paradox between central government's emphasis on parental choice and Torytown Conservatives' preference for selection at eleven plus. In addition voters' definitions of, and distinctions between the two secondary school systems were often unclear (7.8.1). This provides a weak basis for as association with different parties even though there is a clearer association with this issue than with some others. Central versus local control of the school curriculum, teachers' strikes and the closure of schools due to falling rolls are examples of sub-issues that were less clearly associated with individual party policies.

Butler and Stokes' third criterion is that *opinion on an issue must be skewed*, as an issue will have little impact on elections unless opinion strongly favours one side of the argument. As education as a political issue contains various sub-issues, the overall pattern of responses does not favour one political party, but consists of a large number of indicators that are skewed in different directions or not skewed at all. Moreover, to reduce questions about education into the dichotomies that are needed to identify skewness can mean that the policies of only two political parties are considered and that multiple responses or 'don't knows' are ignored. In this research there has been a tendency to concentrate on the Conservative and Labour parties, but this is because of confusion in the centre ground of British politics. At the time of the case study interviews in 1988 the Alliance (of the Liberal party and SDP) was being dissolved and reconstituted as a single party, the Social and Liberal Democratic party, with the remnants of the SDP remaining as a much smaller party. The Green Party emerged as a political force during the following year but lost its impetus before the 1992 General Election. The middle ground was changing rapidly and it was found that attitudes to educational sub-issues could be most clearly assessed by presenting the Government's definitions of reality and challenging them. This helped to create a dichotomy (favouring a skewed response) but the qualitative nature of the case studies meant that multiple responses could be analyzed. Thus, the use of an index of attitudes towards sub-issues has helped to provide an overall picture whilst analysis of varied responses, educational experiences and interest in, and knowledge about, sub-issues has added depth.

8.2.2 Index of case study responses

Although qualitative data has been collected in the case studies and the findings are not therefore statistically valid, the collection of simplified summaries in the form of an index helps to provide a limited, but useful sketch of the case study findings. The index figures collected in the case studies and used in Chapters 6 and 7 were given plus and minus signs according to their relationship to present government policy. In general a plus indicates support for government policy, a minus indicates opposition. This was a rather arbitrary process as government policy on some sub-issues was not always clear and responses were often too complex to be summarized in this way. For example, the index of -14 indicates a majority in favour of more spending on the YTS and other job training schemes. The government had already spent a lot of money on such schemes but the tone of responses to this question (Q14E) was often very critical of the government.

> [More spending] Definitely not. Not the way they're organized. The employers should make up what the government gives them to make it into a decent wage. Employers use them as handrags and then chuck them out rather than give them a decent wage. It's demoralizing. (Informant No.48, Q14E)

Many informants wanted better quality schemes and many claimed that more money should be spent on providing real jobs rather than training schemes. Similarly, a majority (-12) thought that educational standards and teaching standards (-5) had improved since they were at school. These figures are given a minus because, although officially the government argued that standards had risen, the tone of the normative paradigm promoted by governments since 1976 has been very critical. The normative claim is that, if standards have risen, they have not risen enough. Many Conservatives will, moreover, continue to argue that a fall in standards was inevitable with the large-scale introduction of comprehensive schools (and consequent abolition of many grammar schools). As there is no clear party differentiation between party policies towards single-sex schools, when it was noted that a majority (+11) think that single sex schools should not be abolished, the intention was not to suggest that responses supported only Conservative party policies.

The following table (8.1) of indexed responses emerging from the case study interviews is therefore intended to provide an overview of attitudes to various sub-issues and their relationship to government policy, but it cannot be fully understood without reference to the qualitative data provided in Chapters 6 and 7.

Table 8.1
Index of support for Conservative policies

	Index	Question
Supported sub-issues		
Clause 28	+30	Q41H1
Retaining private schools	+28	Q41F1
Gender opportunities now equal	+21	Q46D
Bipartite system best	+11	Q42
Retaining bipartite system	+10	Q41A1
Mixed or contradictory views		
National curriculum	+20	Q41B1
Who controls curriculum	-14	Q45
Teachers' pay	+6	Q49A
Testing at 7,11 & 14	+5	Q41E
Spending on nurseries	-1	Q14A
Spending on universities	-8	Q14B
Unsupported sub-issues		
Spending on colleges	-17	Q14c
Student loans	-19	Q41I
Extent social class differences	-26	Q51B
Spending on schools	-29	Q14B
General education spending	-32	Q11C
Aware of social class	-32	Q51A

NOTE: A plus sign represents majority support for Government policies, a minus majority disagreement.

The figures here represent immediate responses to the questions, and explanations offered later may add up to a different figure. For example, when informants were asked to explain their reasons for favouring a bipartite system of secondary education, the number supporting grammar schools and secondary modern schools fell. Similarly, when asked to explain why they favoured testing at 7, 11 and 14, some said that they did not favour testing at seven. The table also shows the contradictory views regarding control of the school curriculum, +20 supporting the Government's introduction of a National Curriculum but a majority of -14 favouring control of the curriculum by the local authority, individual schools or both. However, a clear and well supported finding was that a large majority of informants did not support the Government's spending restrictions on state education. This was moreover, combined with a belief that class distinctions still existed and with the informants' personal experience of the effects of financial constraints on their own families' education (7.9.5).

8.2.3 Index, position and valence issues

The above index (Table 8.1) only gives a very limited impression of the qualitative data collected during this research. Qualitative data has been particularly useful in recording values and beliefs that cannot be simplified in the form of support for individual, easily-identifiable policy statements. Such attitudes must be considered in view of my particular interest in the normative framework of educational debate (1.1).

In this context, the analysis of qualitative data has been enhanced by the separation of issues into two types; position issues and valence issues. Butler and Stokes used position and valence issues to identify skewed attitudes. Where parties appeal to rival bodies of opinion, position issues may be easily identified by the voter. Labour and Conservative policies on educational spending were, for example, generally identified and opposing attitudes could be associated with them (in the second Greater Manchester Survey 34 per cent of Conservative voters, 72 per cent of Labour voters and 57 per cent of Alliance voters wanted more spending on all three welfare state services, i.e. health, education and personal social services). The items listed in Table 8.1 tend to fit into that category.

Some other issues are so generally favoured that skewness is assumed. These *valence* issues consist of consensus views concerning values or goals; for example a high standard of education and teaching, efficiency, and concern about childrens' welfare. They do not generally relate to the means of achieving those goals. Thus, we can return to Wright Mills' statement that,

> ... some value cherished by publics is felt to be threatened. Often there is a debate about what that value really is and about what it is that really threatens it. (C.W. Mills, 1970, p.8, see this book 4.1).

In their attempts to claim a monopoly of traditional values (5.1) and to identify threats to such values (7.3.1) Conservatives politicians are, in effect, trying to obstruct any association that voters may otherwise make between valence issues and other parties. A positive association between the Conservative Party and valence issues (for example, educational standards and discipline) may thus overcome opposition to some of the individual policies listed in Table 8.1.

8.2.4 Survey data and issue preference

The three main criteria suggested by Butler and Stokes provide a useful model but they [1] and Campbell et al. (1960 and 1966, research in the USA) found that in practice very few issues passed all three. Campbell et al. applied the criteria to 16 issues in 1956. One third of the voters questioned had no awareness of any issues. Only between 18 per cent and 36 per cent could be classified as potential issue voters, i.e. they might switch parties on the basis of an issue. However, most of these were already firmly committed to a party and unlikely to switch. Butler and Stokes' conclusion was that long term party identification instils a habit of viewing political issues from a partisan perspective. Kavanagh observed that intense support for a party or belief meant that apparently conflicting attitudes had to be accommodated,

> The more central the belief is, the more reluctant a person is to change it, and the more likely he is to adopt various strategies to ward off information which challenges it. (Kavanagh, 1983, p.15)

Dissonance (5.5 and 8.3) is however, likely to occur whether or not a voter identifies strongly with a particular party. More recent research indicates a reduction in the level of long term party identification, with increased numbers of floating voters and changes in political alignments. According to Dunleavy and Husbands,

> The growth of sectoral cleavages cross-cutting occupational class not only makes third-party voting more likely but also implies a blurring of issue attitudes, especially those where class and sectoral interests diverge. (Dunleavy and Husbands,1985, p.25)

Class and sectoral interests diverge in the case of education (4.6) which can consequently be seen as an issue that is likely to stimulate changes in political alignment and a 'blurring' of attitudes. Kavanagh, however (1983, p.88-94), suggests that as a smaller proportion of the electorate identify with a party, issues may be seen as more important.

> Strong party identification does influence issue preferences but among weak party identifiers there is a greater tendency to vote in accord with their own issue preferences and perceptions of the parties' stand, rather than with partisanship. (Kavanagh, 1983, p.98)

Other research, however, provides strong support for the argument that issues have little impact on actual vote. Crewe's survey at the time of the 1987 general election included an open-ended question about the most important issues influencing respondents' vote. Education was the third most frequently mentioned issue and was mentioned by 13 per cent more respondents than in the 1983 general election (Table 8.2).

Table 8.2
Mentioning an issue as one of the two most important influencing their vote in the 1987 general election

	1987	Change 1983/87
	%	
Unemployment	49	-23
NHS/Hospitals	33	+22
Education	19	+13
Defence	35	-3

Source: Crewe, 1987

Amongst those who mentioned the top three issues on the list, Labour was considered to be the most capable party, and Crewe believed that education lost the Conservatives votes. The majority (including the majority of Conservative voters) felt that conditions had deteriorated regarding the top three issues. Even when the lack of support for Labour's defence policy was taken into account, Crewe found that Labour would have been 2 per cent ahead of the Conservatives if the election had been determined by voters' attitudes to the four main issues. He concluded that it was a perception of personal prosperity that led many to vote Conservative.

The last three factors shown in Table 8.3 helped to compensate for the poor image of the Conservative Party concerning the three most important issues. By a 55 per cent to 27 per cent majority respondents believed that a Conservative government was most likely to bring 'prosperity'. Thus, Crewe argued that instrumental motives were paramount and made a similar distinction to that made in 4.3 between the private and the public sphere.

> When answering a survey on the important issues respondents think of public problems; when entering the polling booth they think of the family fortunes. (Crewe, 1987)

Table 8.3
Perceptions of recent change, General Election 1987

	Got better %	Stayed the same %	Got worse %	% better -% worse
Unemployment	10	10	80	-70
NHS waiting lists	4	28	68	-64
Quality of education	10	22	68	-58
Opportunities to get ahead	46	27	27	+19
General economic situation	45	25	30	+15
Your household's financial situation	30	41	28	+2

(Source: Crewe, 1987)

Even when respondents expressed an interest in education as a political issue it could not be assumed that they would vote according to their attitudes towards education. Self-interest was likely to prevail and was encouraged by the continuing dominance of the New Right's individualist philosophy. Crewe's findings also support my previous suggestion (8.2.3) that voters may have favoured the Conservative Party because of its emphasis on valence issues rather than as a result of their support (or apparently, lack of support) for position issues. The first three items in Table 8.3 are position issues whereas the last three are vague and more easily defined as valence issues.

8.3 Assessing the interest motive

8.3.1 Social location, policy preferences and party

Throughout this book it is argued that attitudes to education are most strongly influenced by consumption or non-consumption of the service. It is moreover argued that voting behaviour is often based on instrumental motives emerging from consumption and production sectoral cleavages (see 4.6). A relationship is therefore suggested between the consumption of education, and/or employment in the public sector, and political orientation. However, the relationship may not take the form of a straightforward association.

The complexity of the relationship can be clarified by using the three models devised by David Denver (1989, pp.75-6). He postulates three possible relationships between social location (for example, consumption and production sectors), policy preferences and party. In the first model, social location determines both party choice and policy preferences, resulting in an indirect relationship between party choice and policy preference. In the second model, social location determines policy preferences which determine party choice. This results in an indirect relationship between social location and party choice. According to the third model social location determines vote and policy preferences are adjusted to accommodate party choice, resulting in an indirect relationship between social location and policy preferences.

It has not, however, been concluded that there is a clear causal path between attitudes to education, educational policy preferences and voting behaviour. Within the single issue area of education there are many sub-issues and, in order to assess the relationship between attitudes and voting behaviour, models such as those provided by Denver, would need to be provided for attitudes to each sub-issue. Even then it would be difficult to define attitudes to some sub-issues. Contradictions have been particularly apparent in responses to questions about the control of the school curriculum (7.4.2). It would also be necessary to accommodate the different levels of interest that respondents have in individual issues and sub-issues. A voter may, for example, have radical views about the National Health Service which may outweigh his/her dominant attitudes to education and result in a Labour vote. Thus, attitudes to education cannot alone predict voting behaviour. They would have to be considered together with attitudes to other (both position and valence) issues as well as any other possible influences. Nevertheless, when an aggregate of votes is considered there does seem to be relationship between social location, attitudes to education and voting behaviour. It is possible to identify which social locations are most likely to be associated with certain educational attitudes, and with party choice; either in a combination with other issues or when respondents' attach most weight to their attitudes to education.

8.3.2 Consumption sectors and social class

Consumption sectors have been found to have a particular effect on voting behaviour. This can be seen most clearly in Duke and Edgell's comparison between the effects of consumption sectors and social class on political orientation. In the following table (8.4) they considered the effects of cumulative consumption locations by dividing private from public consumption of health services, housing and transport. Findings from the British Election Survey of 1983 (Butler and Kavanagh, 1984) were used for comparison. As noted in 4.6, education was left out because the proportion of the sample

202

consuming private education was too small. However, when the consumption of education is considered in a wider sense in the next section (8.3.3) it will be shown that respondents who lived in households that were consuming education were less likely to vote Conservative than were non-consumers.

Table 8.4
Political orientation by overall consumption location
and social class, GMS and BES compared, including social class

% Conservative - % Labour

Consumption location:	BES	Controller	Worker	GMS	Controller	Worker
3 private	+61	+71	+40	+26	+27	+24
2 private 1 public	+19	+23	+10	0	+15	-15
2 public 1 private	-9	+3	-24	-8	-14	-14
3 public	-31	-44	-29	-23	-20	-28

Source: Duke and Edgell, 1984, Tables 5,6 and 7, amended

The table indicates that political orientation was more closely related to overall consumption location than to social class. Labour support was strongest amongst the least privatized workers and controllers and Conservative support was strongest amongst the most privatized workers and controllers. This provides strong support for Dunleavy's theory (4.6) concerning the relative independence of consumption sectors from social class in terms of their effect on political orientation. The middle class radicalism and working class conservatism emerging from different consumption locations help to explain the continuing class de-alignment found in the general elections of 1983 and 1987. In the 1987 General Election the largest proportion of manual workers since the war voted Conservative; 36 per cent compared to 42 per cent who voted Labour (Crewe, 1987). A majority of skilled manual workers voted Conservative; 43 per cent compared to 34 per cent who voted Labour. As governments have continued to pursue privatization policies the proportion of privatized working class Conservative voters has grown. The proportion of voters consuming private education also increased during the 1980s and will probably become a more salient feature of attitude surveys as the exodus from state education continues.

8.3.3 Production sectors and education

The effects of production sectors on voting behaviour followed a similar pattern. Workers employed in the private sector were more likely to vote Conservative than those employed in the public sector. At the 1987 General Election Crewe (1987) found that 65 per cent of private sector employees voted Conservative (a rise of one per cent since 1983) compared to the 44 per cent of public sector employees who voted Conservative (a fall of four per cent since 1983). This is at least partly explained by a decrease in the proportion of teachers and other highly educated people who voted Conservative. Many of these voters deserted the Conservative party for the Alliance which, according to Crewe, '...has become the leading party in what it might wish to call the "thinking electorate".' In 1983/4 Edgell and Duke also found that a larger proportion of voters with some further education voted Alliance (26 per cent) than those without any further education (14 per cent). Crewe found in 1987 that the Conservative Party was still, however, favoured by the less highly educated middle class.

> ...the 'self-made' middle class (ABs), who have received no form of further education, continued to vote Conservative in over-whelming numbers (74 per cent) as did the majority (57 per cent) of those with some sort of further education short of a degree. (Crewe, 1987)

The Conservative vote fell by nine per cent amongst the university educated.

Table 8.5
Vote of the university educated in the 1987 General Election

	1987 %	1983/87
Alliance	36	+4
Labour	29	+3
Conservative	34	-9

Source: Crewe, 1987, Table 4 adapted

This change was also reported in polls carried out for the Times Educational Supplement at the time of the general elections in 1983 and 1987. By amalgamating the results of the two TES polls it is possible to see a significant difference between the voting intentions of teachers and the vote of the general electorate as a whole (Table 8.6).

Table 8.6
Teachers' voting intentions, 1987 General Election

	Teachers, 1983 Eng & Wales	Teachers, 1987 Eng & Wales	Scotland	Whole electorate
	%	%	%	%
Conservative	44	24	15	43
Labour	26	28	33	31
Alliance	28	46	39	23
Scottish Nationalist	-	-	14	-

Source: MORI poll reported in Times Educational Supplement,
29 May 1987   ©Times Newspapers Ltd. 1987

The reversal of teachers' votes between 1983 and 1987 is likely to be a direct result of government education policy as, not surprisingly, 77 per cent of teachers in 1987 thought that education was the most important issue in the election. It is also clear that, although teachers were voting against Conservative policies, the Labour party was not the favoured alternative. This may be explained by the reluctance of many teachers to be 'politicized' by associating themselves with unionism and left-wing radicalism (see 9.4).

8.3.4 Manipulation of survey data

The influence of consumption and production sectors, and the pattern emerging from analysis of the Greater Manchester Study and British Social Attitude surveys, led to the design of the case study sample in 1988. In the following table (8.7) public sector employees, private sector employees and unemployed respondents were divided into those who were parents of children currently being educated (consumer) and those who were not (not consumer). These variables were crosstabulated with the party identification variables used in both of the surveys. In each case respondents were asked which party they most closely identified with. Thus, variations in the votes in national and local elections are not considered but responses are more closely related to perceptions of long-term party identification.

205

Table 8.7
Production sectors, education consumption
and party identification,
GMS (1983/4 interview) and BSA (1983/4) compared

	GMS	BSA	Conservative		Labour		Alliance	
			GMS	BSA	GMS	BSA	GMS	BSA
	n=	n=	%	%	%	%	%	%
Public:	125	294	31	43	46	33	23	24
Consumer	46	137	17	40	52	36	30	23
Not consumer	79	157	39	45	42	30	19	25
Private:	230	822	43	46	40	38	17	16
Consumer	94	351	39	48	45	37	16	15
Not consumer	136	471	45	45	37	39	18	16
Unemployed:	234	403	37	42	41	43	22	14
Consumer	46	194	28	38	54	45	17	17
Not consumer	188	207	39	46	38	41	23	12
Total consumers	186	682	31	44	49	39	20	17
Total not consumers	403	835	41	45	38	38	20	17
Totals	589	1517	38	45	42	38	20	17

Source: Edgell and Duke, GMS2 adapted by computer; BSA, 1983

Table 8.7 shows some radical differences between GMS and BSA responses. The bottom row of totals shows that more respondents in the national sample identified with the Conservative Party. One possible explanation is the so called 'North-South divide'; the tendency of more voters to support the Conservative Party in the south of England in the last two general elections. However, the areas from which the Torytown and Labourville samples were taken are predominantly middle-class and, according to research carried out in the past, likely to produce more Conservative voters than average.

Production sectors and the household consumption of education also seem to have had a greater effect on voting behaviour in the local sample than in the national sample. Although both reveal the tendency of fewer consumers of education to identify with the Conservative Party, the difference is very slight in the BSA survey and quite strong in the GMS (see 'Total consumers'). This is particularly noticeable in the comparison between those publicly employed Conservative identifiers who were consumers of education and those who were not: the BSA survey recorded a difference of five per cent, the GMS a difference of 22 per cent. However, the validity of the GMS findings on this point must be suspect because of the small number of respondents in those particular cells. Nevertheless, in 1983 the consumption of education seemed to have a greater significance in the local study than in the national study. Employment sector also seems to have had a greater effect in Torytown and Labourville than in the country as a whole. Although both surveys found the Conservative Party to be more popular amongst the privately employed than the publicly employed, the BSA found that the largest proportion of its publicly employed respondents favoured the Conservative Party, whilst the largest proportion of publicly employed respondents in the GMS supported the Labour Party.

In order to examine the differences between local and national data further, I separated Torytown and Labourville respondents and compared the results with the national data. The possible effects of different education systems could, in theory, be analyzed by comparing the responses of education consumers and non-consumers (Table 8.8).

Table 8.8
Education consumption and party identification:
Torytown, Labourville and national data compared,
GMS 1983/4 and BSA 1983/4

	n=	Conservative %	Labour %	Alliance %
Torytown:				
Consumers	84	33	40	26
Not consumers	204	45	30	25
Labourville:				
Consumers	103	29	55	16
Not consumers	200	38	47	15
BSA 1983/4:				
Consumers	682	44	39	17
Not consumers	835	45	38	17

Source:Edgell and Duke, GMS2, computer analysis; BSA, 1983

In Torytown, Labourville and (to a lesser extent) in the national data a smaller proportion of education consumers than non-consumers identified with the Conservative Party, and a larger proportion of consumers than non-consumers identified with the Labour Party. This suggests that education consumers were more likely than non-consumers to support Labour's education policies; a finding that has further support in Table 8.12. The difference between the two areas was too small to suggest a strong reaction against Torytown education policies, but it does suggest a slight negative reaction. If Torytown education policies were winning support for the Conservative Party in 1983, the support seems to have been mainly amongst those voters who did not have a vested interest in the education system at the time. It is, of course possible that an intervening variable may challenge the validity of this finding. However, further analysis (Tables 8.11 to 8.14) also suggests that consumers had more radical attitudes to education than did non-consumers. Such findings add a new dimension to the national data which, as it covers a wide range of local conditions, provides a more even distribution of responses.

Both voting behaviour and attitudes towards education tended to be more polarized in Torytown than in Labourville. From 1979 to 1983 a larger proportion of Conservatives in Torytown (than in Labourville) were opposed to comprehensives and a larger proportion of Labour voters in Torytown were in favour of comprehensives. More Alliance voters in Torytown (than in Labourville) were in favour of comprehensives and more Alliance voters in Labourville were opposed to comprehensives.

Table 8.9
Voting behaviour in Torytown and Labourville, general and local elections (GMS)

	Cons.	Labour	Liberal/ Alliance	Did not vote
	%	%	%	%
Torytown & Labourville:				
1979 General Election	41	37	5	12
1980 Local Election	27	32	3	35
1983 General Election	34	31	20	13
1983 Local Election	31	28	15	24
Torytown only:				
1979 General Election	43	33	10	11
1980 Local Election	31	31	6	31
1983 General Election	36	24	25	11
1983 Local Election	34	23	21	19
Labourville only:				
1979 General Election	41	41	1	11
1980 Local Election	26	36	0	35
1983 General Election	33	39	14	14
1983 Local Election	28	33	9	29

Source: Edgell and Duke, GMS1 and 2, computer analysis

A larger proportion of the electorate in Torytown voted for the Alliance parties and a smaller proportion of the electorate in Torytown abstained. Even amongst those who abstained it is possible to see an awareness of the position of education within political debate in Torytown.

> [Labour supporter who did not vote in local election] Because this area's Tory and I didn't think it'd make much difference.
> [What local issues?] Education because they'd been talking about going comprehensive. Ironically my indifference in not voting for them may have affected them because the overall balance was upset and they went back to being Tory. (Informant No.50, Q7 and Q8)

8.4 Cohesion, radicalism and partisanship

8.4.1 Cohesion

Attempts have been made to assess the cohesion of respondents' attitudes to a range of educational sub-issues in order to gauge the extent to which they converge or diverge. For example, if a respondent was in favour of both the continued existence of private schools and of universal comprehensive education this combination of views may be seen as divergent or dissonant (see 5.5). The fundamental principle behind comprehensive education is one of equal educational opportunities whereas private schools may be seen as promoting unequal opportunities. As the principles are logically inconsistent a respondent whose attitudes diverge in this way can be said to have dissonant educational attitudes. Furthermore, attitudes to educational sub-issues can be tested for compatibility with voting behaviour. For example, support for private education is in theory compatible with voting Conservative but incompatible with voting for the Labour party. Thus, an analysis of the coherence of attitudes to educational sub-issues, with each other and with voting behaviour, provides some information about coherence within the general framework of educational debate.

A possible lack of coherence has been suggested throughout this book. At its most extreme this is expressed in Crewe's findings (Table 8.2) that if voters had voted in 1987 according to their attitudes towards the four main issues (including education) Labour would have won the General Election. An opinion poll carried out near the time of the 1988 interviews [2] found that support for an increase in spending on public services (even if it meant higher taxes) was even stronger than it was at the last election. The majority, of Conservative voters as well as others, also believed that there was one law for the rich and one for the poor. Yet, despite attitudes to individual issues the

Conservative party was still ahead in the opinion polls. The proportion of strong Labour supporters exceeded that of strong Conservative supporters but Labour could not secure enough support from the uncommitted voters to overtake the Conservatives.

As far as education is concerned a most noticeable divergence between attitude and vote can be seen amongst the many Labour voters who favoured the bipartite system of secondary education and the continued existence of private schools. When personal motivations are studied the analysis becomes even more complex; as for example, in the case of Informant 34 (5.5) who may have favoured student loans rather than grants because his own experience of financial hardship left him feeling resentful towards successful students.

A simple method of measuring the coherence or dissonance of attitude agendas and voting behaviour involves the use of an attitude scale. These over-simplify the relationship but at least help to generalize findings to a wider population. Several scales have been commonly used in the study of political attitudes; most noticeably the F-Scale (Adorno et al., 1950) and the C-Scale (Wilson and Patterson). However, in the present context a simple scale had to be devised that utilized the available survey data and was appropriate for the specialized study of education as a political issue. As the educational radicalism scale emerged out of secondary sources and is limited by them, it is not proposed as a model for further use, but merely used as a simple way of manipulating data in the present context. Attitudes to the three sub-issues chosen (comprehensive schools, private schools and government spending on education) do not provide a thorough representation of the degree of cohesion but they do give some indication of the potential lack of cohesion.

8.4.2 Egalitarian radicalism

Edgell and Duke's manipulation of the data and the attitude scales devised by them were naturally of interest. However, some explanation of terminology is needed in view of the differences between their approach and mine. When writing about opposition to government spending cuts, and the possible increase in opposition, Edgell and Duke (1986a) used the words 'radicalism' and 'radicalisation' because of their particular interest in working-class radicalism. However, in the context of education the word radical currently has different connotations. The Thatcher governments' education policies have often been described as 'radical' in that major changes were made to the education system. The words can therefore cause confusion but I have continued to use them here, as Edgell and Duke have, to denote opposition to central government policies. As central government has the power to define its perspectives as the norm, alternative perspectives can be described as radical or extreme. The word 'radical' is used because of its usual application

210

to left-wing views in the social sciences and in the absence of a more precise alternative.

In order to assess the degree of respondents' radical or contrasting 'dominant' values and the extent to which opposition to the cuts had increased by the second interview Edgell and Duke constructed four attitude scales. They used the term 'dominant' to describe values that were compatible with the present government's values and in this sense were referring to the subject of my earlier discussion (1.3) about the normative framework of debate. Their Egalitarian Radicalism scale is interesting in the present context because it included a question about education and their findings influenced the design of the case studies. The questions used on the Egalitarian Radicalism scale were;

1. Should the government establish comprehensive schools in place of grammar and secondary modern schools throughout the country?
2. Should the government give workers more say in running the place where they work?
3. Should the government redistribute income and wealth in favour of ordinary working people?

Edgell and Duke found a strong association between attitudes on the egalitarian radicalism scale and attitudes to the public spending cuts. When attitudes to private schools were crosstabulated with the scale a similarly strong association was found, thus suggesting that it may also be useful in the study of educational attitudes.

Table 8.10
Disapproval of spending cuts in general and attitudes to private schools by Egalitarian Radicalism Scale, GMS

	Least	....	Radical	....	Most		
	-3	-2	-1	0	+1	+2	+3
	%	%	%	%	%	%	%
Disapprove of cuts:							
1980/1	23	32	41	36	70	74	84
1983/4	35	40	53	72	73	74	85
Government should abolish							
private schools:							
1983/4	3	3	5	10	24	34	54

Source: Edgell and Duke, 1985, Tables B15, B123 adapted

It was found that all categories of voters had moved towards greater disapproval of the spending cuts by the time of the second survey. Conservative voters' approval of the cuts had decreased by nine per cent (from 60 per cent to 51 per cent) whilst Labour voters' disapproval had increased by five per cent (from 81 per cent to 86 per cent). The level of Alliance voters' disapproval of the cuts lay between that of Conservative and Labour voters at 76 per cent in the second survey. A similar pattern was found in 1983 when respondents were asked about their attitudes to spending on education, health and the personal social services. Support for more spending varied from 34 per cent of Conservative voters and 57 per cent of Alliance voters to 72 per cent of Labour voters.

Edgell and Duke also found (their Radicalization Thesis) that there was a cleavage between those who supported welfare spending and those who supported law and order spending. This was related to social class in that support for more spending on welfare increased as the class hierarchy was descended, whilst support for more spending on the police and armed forces was generated amongst employers and the petty bourgeoisie. Employers also emerged as the only class to deradicalize between the two surveys on all four of the attitude scales used. It was the controllers (particularly in the public sector) rather than the workers who were most radicalized on three of the four scales.

> The public sector controllers appear as the new vanguard of radicalism and radicalization. These findings are unsurprising in view of the anti-union/pro-capital, anti-public sector/pro-private sector ideology and policies of the 'new right' since 1979. In other words, 'Thatcherism' has reinforced the dominant values adhered to by the capitalist class and has promoted public sector controllers to the forefront of the class struggle. (Edgell and Duke, 1986a, p.509)

Their emphasis on ideology tends to support my conclusion (8.2.3) that the Conservative Party won support for valence issues rather than position issues.

When I crosstabulated Edgell and Duke's egalitarian radicalism scale with production sector and education consumption a weak association was found that was slightly stronger regarding the most radical extreme than the most dominant extreme. Public employees were slightly more radical than those employed privately or unemployed and educational consumers (parents) more radical than non-consumers.

8.4.3 Educational radicalism

In order to test the compatibility of educational attitudes with party

212

identification further (see Table 8.8), I created two simple scales of educational radicalism. The GMS and BSA data sets were not directly comparable as they asked different questions about educational attitudes. Even when questions about the same subject area are asked in surveys minor differences in question wording can result in significant differences in responses (see 7.4 about responses to questions about control of the curriculum). I therefore decided to use this problem constructively to devise two scales of educational radicalism. This meant that the validity of findings about the attitudes of education consumers and non-consumers could be tested.

A question about the comprehensive/bipartite debate was not asked in the BSA survey of 1983, although it was asked in later BSA surveys. That debate was particularly salient in Torytown and a relevant question had to be used in the scale that was to be applied to GMS data. The three questions used in the educational radicalism scale were;

1. Should the government establish comprehensive schools in place of grammar and secondary modern schools throughout the country?
2. Should the government abolish the private schools which are outside the state education system?
3. The government collects taxes and rates for a variety of services. Would you like to see more or less spent on education?

It has already been noted (8.2.2) that Conservative policies were most strongly supported in the 1988 case studies regarding the bipartite/comprehensive debate (+10) and the retention of private schools (+28), and least supported regarding government spending in general (-32). Government spending cuts on various levels of education were similarly unpopular. Other findings in sections 6.4, 7.8 and 7.9 also indicated that these three sub-issues would be most appropriate for a scale of educational radicalism (Table 8.11). The scale applied to GMS data has been labelled Ed Rad I. Again radical responses are represented by a + sign.

The questions used in Ed Rad I resulted in a moderate association between current consumption of education and educational radicalism. The strength of the association could, however, have been caused by the questions used, because they had already been identified as sub-issues that would elicit skewed responses. Nevertheless, when I applied the same scale to case study informants, very few of the 52 informants produced consistently radical or non-radical answers to all three questions. Of the 16 who produced consistent responses, only four (three Labour voters and one non-voter) gave radical answers to all questions, compared to 12 (nine Conservatives, two non-voters and one Labour voter) who gave non-radical answers to all three questions.

213

Table 8.11
Educational radicalism, consumption of education and area,
Ed Rad I, GMS (1983/4 interviews)

		Least		Educ. Radicalism		.... Most	
		-3	-2	-1	0	+1	+2	+3
	n=	%	%	%	%	%	%	%
Torytown:								
Consumers	99	2.0	9.1	42.4	7.1	21.2	6.1	12.1
Not consumers	240	4.6	18.5	39.6	13.7	15.4	3.7	8.3
Labourville:								
Consumers	114	0	5.3	43.9	11.4	19.3	5.3	14.9
Not consumers	217	2.9	14.3	37.8	12.0	13.3	5.1	14.3
TT and LV:								
Consumers	213	0.9	7.0	43.2	9.4	20.2	5.6	13.6
Not consumers	467	3.8	16.3	37.9	12.6	14.1	4.3	10.9

Source: Edgell and Duke, GMS2, adapted by computer

The Labour identifier who gave non-radical answers to all three questions was strongly opposed to the Conservative Party and believed that social class affected educational opportunities. Two of her responses were fairly non-committal: on educational spending she said there should be no more but no less and, on comprehensive schools, her response was that it did not matter. However, regarding private education, she said that (despite her views about social class) people should have the freedom to spend their money as they chose. When attempts are made to measure educational radicalism, it should therefore be noted that individuals who do not measure a high score do not necessarily have extremely dominant views. In other words, if individuals are not against certain policy preferences it does not necessarily mean that they favour the alternatives presented by another party.

Three questions alone cannot represent attitudes to a whole range of sub-issues. I therefore decided to use more general questions in the design of Ed Rad II, for the analysis of BSA data. The first question in particular was a valence question which was less likely to elicit responses related to political identification. The second question was about public spending and taxation in general, rather than educational spending in particular. The third question, about attitudes to private schools, provided a closer comparison with Ed Rad I, but was still not directly comparable.

1. Should opportunities to go into higher education be increased, reduced or stay the same? BSA Q71A (see Table 7.44)

2. Choose between three options; reduce taxes and spend less on health, education and social benefits; keep taxes and spending on these services the same; increase taxes and spend more on health, education and social benefits. BSA Q54 (see Table 6.5)
3. Should there be more private schools, about the same number as now, fewer, or no private schools at all? BSA Q67A (see Table 7.37)

Table 8.12
Consumption of education, area and educational radicalism,
Ed Rad II, BSA (1983/4)

		Least	......	Educ.	Radicalism	......	Most	
		-3	-2	-1	0	+1	+2	+3
	n=	%	%	%	%	%	%	%
Consumers	785	27.0	3.1	38.3	2.4	22.7	1.0	5.5
Not consumers	975	32.3	3.7	38.0	3.1	17.5	0.8	4.5

Source: BSA, 1983/4, adapted by computer

More non-consumers than consumers favoured policies sponsored by the then government at both national and local levels and in both Torytown and Labourville. The association is moderate in the case of Ed Rad I and the GMS data, and very weak in the case of Ed Rad II and the national data. The modal answer for both consumers and non-consumers in each of the tables was -1. In Table 8.12 this is consistent with a pattern that is skewed towards dominant (Conservative) policies but in Table 8.11 (where more respondents scored +3 than -3) the pattern is very slightly skewed towards radical policies.

The use of two different scales of educational radicalism therefore helps to support the conclusion that educational consumers have more radical educational attitudes than non-consumers. Had only one scale been used to analyze either the local or the national data it is more likely that educational radicalism could have been over-estimated (Ed Rad I applied to GMS data revealed a moderate association) or underestimated (Ed Rad II applied to BSA data revealed a weak association). As an association was found using both scales and both data sets its validity is increased. The strength of that association has not, however, been determined.

Production sectors were also crosstabulated with party identification (Table 8.7), egalitarian radicalism and educational radicalism. The association between sector and both types of radicalism (egalitarian and educational) was stronger than its association with partisanship, thus suggesting that the degree of radicalism would be underestimated if judged only by vote.

8.4.3 Partisanship

A scale for political partisanship was devised by using party identification and strength of party identification; the necessary, comparable questions having been asked in both the BSA surveys and the GMS (Table 8.13). Partisanship was operationalized as the independent variable in this instance in line with claims that voters adapt their attitudes to issues to complement their political identification. However, the causal flow could also be in the reverse direction.

Table 8.13
Political partisanship and educational radicalism,
Ed Rad I, GMS (1983/4 interviews)

	n=	Least		Educ. Radicalism		...... Most		
		-3	-2	-1	0	+1	+2	+3
	n=	%	%	%	%	%	%	%
Conservative:								
strong	127	7.9	30.7	48.8	6.3	4.7	0	1.6
weak	99	4.0	25.2	45.4	12.1	9.1	1.0	3.0
Alliance:								
strong	47	4.2	10.6	46.8	17.0	12.8	4.2	4.2
weak	76	3.9	9.2	48.7	11.8	15.8	5.3	5.3
Labour:								
strong	161	0	1.2	22.4	16.2	23.6	9.9	32.9
weak	86	0	4.6	38.4	12.8	27.9	5.8	10.5

Source: Edgell and Duke, 1985, adapted by computer

Again there was a significant difference between the pattern found in analysis of the GMS data using Ed Rad I and the pattern found in the analysis of BSA data using Ed Rad II (Table 8.14). In the GMS the modal category for all categories of political identifiers was -1. The BSA survey produced no modal category.

A moderate association between political identification and educational radicalism is found in Table 8.13 but the association found in Table 8.14 was rather weak. In order to make more in-depth comparisons it would be necessary to create a directly comparable scale and to include more sub-issues. Findings in Chapters 6 and 7 suggest that a more complex scale, including more sub-issues, would result in an even weaker association between political partisanship and educational attitudes.

Table 8.14
Political partisanship and educational radicalism,
Ed Rad II, BSA (1983/4)

		Least	......	Educ.	Radicalism	....	Most	
		-3	-2	-1	0	+1	+2	+3
	n=	%	%	%	%	%	%	%
Conservative:								
strong	421	46.3	4.5	36.6	1.2	10.4	0.2	0.7
weak	255	36.9	1.5	39.2	2.0	16.9	0.8	2.7
Alliance								
strong	81	23.5	1.2	45.7	1.2	24.7	0	3.7
weak	177	28.8	2.3	42.4	1.1	22.6	1.1	1.7
Labour								
strong	306	15.7	2.0	36.6	3.3	26.8	0.6	15.0
weak	278	18.7	2.5	38.8	2.9	29.1	1.8	6.1

Source: BSA, 1983/4, adapted by computer

The different local and national patterns in Tables 8.11 to 8.14 cannot, however, be entirely explained by the differences in the scales. It can be partly explained by the greater support for the Conservatives at national level than in these two local authority areas (see Table 8.7). Indeed a large minority (15-19 per cent) of Labour identifiers at national level scored -3 on the educational radicalism scale but no Labour identifiers did so at local level. Very few Conservative identifiers at either national or local level scored +3 on the scale.

8.5 Summary of findings

The issue model of voting behaviour offered by Butler and Stokes involves the association of issues with parties and strong feelings about individual issues. This has been criticised in the past (by Butler and Stokes themselves as well as others) and, more recently, Parry and Moyser found (1986, and see next chapter) that 35 per cent of their sample had no issue agendas in mind. Nevertheless, the model has been useful in the analysis of educational attitudes and voting behaviour in Torytown and Labourville. In 1983 educational and political attitudes were more polarized in Torytown than those in Labourville.

Strength of feeling in Torytown about education as a political issue was mentioned by several interviewees, including local 'experts' (2.5). Another local contact was made early in this research via a British Sociological Association workshop. A specialist in the sociology of education who lives in Torytown provided her own views on the salience of the two areas to a study of education as a political issue. She emphasised the importance of continuity and change in political debates.

> It seems to me that Education is an 'Issue' in [Torytown] more than in [Labourville], not because of the political control, or the nature of the existing system, but because education in [Torytown] is in a state of flux. This has been true for about 10 years and will continue to be true even if the Tories regain control. They [the Conservatives] want to reorganize the schools (although not on comprehensive lines) to cope with falling rolls; nobody likes change so pressure groups form and put pressure on councillors through the ballot box (sic). It becomes *party* political because it is currently selective. In [Labourville], as far as I know, there are no major plans for re-organisation and if the opposition parties ever got in they wouldn't immediately start closing the schools - so it is not an issue. I think the question of stability and consensus versus change and disagreement is more important in creating an issue than the question of selective versus comprehensive or middle class versus working class - although historically these are all bound up. (Quoted from a letter written in 1987)

The prominence of education as a contentious local issue means that it is likely to fulfil Butler and Stokes' second criteria by being associated differently with political parties. This does not inevitably mean that, in Torytown, the third criteria will be fulfilled and attitudes towards education will be skewed. Nevertheless, skewed attitudes have been recorded (7.8) towards both educational spending and the bipartite/comprehensive debate. Both of these subjects have been regarded as contentious issues in Torytown for several years. However, education is not a singular, undivided subject, but consists of many sub-issues, and attitudes to those sub-issues often cut across party political lines. Many voters will favour one party's policies on the bipartite/comprehensive debate and another's on education spending. Similarly, attitudes to educational spending may vary according to the type of educational spending. Some Torytown residents will favour increased spending on nursery provision, because they have to pay for private nursery care; but they may not favour increased spending on Universities, because they have no contact with a university. In Labourville attitudes may be reversed, as there is generous nursery provision and a university sited in the area. Such differences in educational context can have a significant affect on attitudes.

They may also explain the level of educational radicalism in both areas. Labourville residents who are in some way connected to the university (as employees, students or their friends or relations) may display a high level of interest in education and particularly radical attitudes. Thus, although there may be little local debate about Labourville schools, education may be regarded as a highly contentious political issue in other ways (for example, regarding student loans).

The issue model also assumes a rational choice made by well-informed voters. Yet the communication of information about political issues is fraught with difficulties (5.5) and, as Butler and Stokes argued,

> Understanding of policy issues falls away very sharply indeed as we move outwards from those at the heart of political decision-making to the public at large. (Butler and Stokes, 1974, p.277)

In this research it has been found that voters who had the least contact with education were also the least radical. This was especially noticeable when perceptions of educational standards and discipline were considered in 7.2 and 7.3. It has also been found that, although a large proportion of informants in the case studies (7.9.6 and 8.2.2) were aware of social inequalities and deteriorating conditions in public services (8.2.4), a majority associated the Conservative Party with personal prosperity. Attitudes to the valence issues, associated with the normative framework of educational debate, were therefore more influential than more clearly defined position issues.

The interest motive emerged as the strongest explanation for educational attitudes and political identification but, like the issue motive, it cannot be isolated from other motives. It has not been possible to statistically define a causal path but it is hoped that the desired map (2.2) has been achieved; even though it may still be a sketch. There has been a risk of over-emphasising the importance of attitudes to education in the determination of votes (8.3.1) and it should be remembered that a large proportion of voters take little interest in education. Many will be more concerned about other issues (notably the National Health Service, see 6.4). As voters have to choose a party's whole agenda of issues when deciding how to vote it is probable that they will object to some parts of it. Some voters will vote for one party because of their antipathy towards another party. They may not therefore be voting for one set of policies, but exercising a protest vote against other policies. Some voters will be strongly influenced by the personalities of individual politicians. Some motives may be even more vague.

> [Would vote Conservative if an election tomorrow.] I've tried the other two and I might as well try a third party. (Informant No.49, Q9)

These findings suggest that there was no clear mandate for the Conservative education policies during the 1980s (or for Labour Party policies). At the time of the case study interviews the Alliance was in the process of being dissolved as a party group and voters were very confused about the identity of the 'middle ground' of British party politics. A common perception of party politics in 1988 was therefore one of confusion, which was perhaps even more pronounced than in the other years considered in this research.

When attitudes to some individual sub-issues are analyzed certain policy preferences are clear, but the combinations are not consistent or comparable with any whole party package. For example, a large majority of voters were opposed to the abolition of private education but a large majority were also opposed to a student loans system. As they supported Conservative policy on one sub-issue and opposed it on another, voters were not presenting a clear and consistent pattern of attitudes from which any party could claim a mandate. However, if Parkin's three attitudinal types are reconsidered (7.11) it is possible to identify the scope for government manipulation of educational debates. In a clash between radical values and dominant values, those who hold radical values are under pressure and are forced to either defend them or accommodate them to the dominant value system (or, as I have previously labelled it, the normative framework of debate). Furthermore, Conservative governments have presented their education policies as technical, rational and non-political (Chapter 5) and voters who had little access to and/or knowledge about the education system may have felt obliged to defer to what they regarded as the governments' greater expertise. The implications of such confusion and inconsistency on the direction of influence between government and voters are considered in the next chapter.

Notes

1. Butler and Stokes asked respondents what they thought were the most important problems faced by the Government. The proportion answering 'education' was nine per cent in 1963 and five per cent in 1970. Social welfare, housing and economic problems were considered more important both times and taxation was also considered more important in 1970.
2. Marplan, reported in The Guardian, 17 September 1988. The poll was carried out the between 9-14 September 1988. It sampled 1,279 voters in 103 constituencies.

9 Activity and influence: Participation in policy-making

9.1 Sequence: Interest, knowledge, attitudes, votes, activity and influence

It has not been possible to deal with any of the parts of the sequence used in this research (1.4) in great depth. The chapter about 'interest', although lengthy, only skimmed the surface of debates about the influence of social structure and social/sectoral locations. Much more could have been said about 'knowledge', as cultural reproduction is, on its own, a very contentious topic. Even the lengthy section (Chapters 6 and 7) about 'attitudes' involved the selection of only a few sub-issues and it could be argued that, not only were some important sub-issues missed, but that those selected were not considered in enough detail. The section ('votes') about the alignment of attitudes and votes involved particularly difficult decisions as there is a vast amount of material available about voting behaviour. Some valuable material has no doubt been missed along the way but this, rather ambitious, wide-ranging approach was deemed necessary in order to provide the clearest, and most accurate picture of the framework of educational debate during the 1980s. 'Activity and influence' provide an end to the sequence followed in this research and, in this section, findings from previous parts of the sequence will be utilised in order to assess the direction of the flow of influence between voters and the Government.

In this chapter, analysis will be less detailed than it has been in previous chapters. This is partly due to constraints on time and energy but also because this is an research area that demands more attention than can be provided within the present context. It really demands a research project of its own, in which the vast amount of material available about activity and influence (including case study data) can be used to provide a much more complete analysis of behaviour within the political context of education.

Despite such limitations I decided to follow the analysis of attitudes with a brief consideration of behaviour in order to enhance my findings about the framework of educational debate. Knowledge about attitudes tells us little about the political arena of educational debate. It raises questions about what individuals do with their attitudes, whether such attitudes provide a mandate for the Government's education policies and in what ways the Government responds to public opinion. In what direction does influence flow? Is it primarily a case of voters influencing government policy, of government policy influencing voters or an equal balance of both?

My main contention in this chapter is that, as far as educational attitudes and influence are concerned, the Conservative governments of the 1980s heard what they wanted to hear. They wanted to hear that many people were concerned about educational standards and discipline in schools, were intolerant of homosexuality, favoured grammar schools and supported the continued existence of private schools, as such attitudes supported Conservative policies. Governments did not want to hear that most people were prepared to pay higher taxes in order to increase spending on education and were opposed to a students' loans system, because such attitudes conflicted with Conservative policies.

A government also manipulates the framework of educational debate in such a way that its own values are presented as the norm (not always successfully, but nevertheless with sufficient force to dominate debate). Thus, the direction of influence was predominantly from the Government to the public rather than vice versa. For example, the Government's concept of parental choice was presented as common sense reality, and for the many who benefitted from related policies this was with good reason. However, the Conservative image of parenthood was internalized by many of the case study informants who had only experienced the negative effect of family constraints on their education. This appears to be a good example of 'false-consciousness'; concepts that conflict with personal experience being normalized via a framework of debate that is dominated by Conservative values. In the case of private education, such values have not simply been promoted by Conservative governments but have been established by centuries of tradition and class distinction.

The reverse order of influence can also be considered, as it is quite clear that voters did not always accept government sponsored values. For example, the Government failed to win the support of most voters for its education spending policies and its decision to supplement frozen student grants with student loans. Yet, despite lack of popular support, the Government continued to pursue such policies. The policies of the New Right do not involve the search for a consensus, but the determination to proceed with a programme despite public opposition. During the period of this research many examples were found of public pressure that ran contrary to government policy being ignored.

In 1988 a poll conducted by the Electoral Reform Society [1] found that 94 per cent of parents with children in school in the Inner London Education Authority area were in favour of retaining the ILEA. These findings were challenged by the Government because they did not represent the views of all ratepayers. Consequently a poll of all ratepayers was carried out by Harris on behalf of the ILEA. Again a clear majority (71 per cent) of parents were opposed to the abolition of the ILEA and, even amongst ILEA parents who were Conservative identifiers, more opposed abolition (46 per cent) than supported it (37 per cent). The majority (approximately 60 per cent) of all ratepayers also disapproved of the abolition of the ILEA. Despite the opposition of inner London rate payers, and parents in particular, the Government abolished the ILEA in April 1990. Furthermore, the Harris poll findings regarding attitudes to teaching standards lend support to my earlier conclusions about the relationship between knowledge about the education system and attitudes. Of those with children attending ILEA schools, 41 per cent said the standard of teaching was good. When non-parents were included this figure dropped to 28 per cent. This confirms my findings in 7.2.4 that those with the least knowledge of current educational provision had the lowest opinion of educational standards. Those with the least knowledge of the education system were most likely to support Conservative policies.

The failure of governments to acknowledge the opposition of parents and other voters to Conservative policies is not surprising in view of the New Right's rejection of consensus politics. However, it is more surprising to find that governments continued to pursue some policies despite the opposition (or at least lack of enthusiasm) of business interests. In the case of the introduction of City Technology Colleges and student loans the government failed to get the anticipated support of business interests and the main banks. It continued, nevertheless, to pursue its original policies by injecting a large amount of public money into City Technology Colleges, to supplement the disappointing contributions by business interests, and taking over the finance of student loans itself. This is not compatible with the New Right rhetoric of 'rolling back the state' but is compatible with its confidence in its own policies and determination to follow them through. The direction of influence is therefore more likely to be from government to voters rather than from voters to government. Even the opportunity to influence policy through the voting system is minimized by the British electoral system (9.3).

In this chapter I will consider how the government's ideology influences the framework of educational debate by again considering the importance of the language of debate. A large amount of material is available about the identity of those who are active or inactive in the field of the politics of education. This will be considered briefly, together with some of the many theories about political participation. However, a more specialized project would be needed to deal with this subject in sufficient depth.

9.2 The language and framework of participation

There are some doubts about the appropriate use of the words 'participation' and 'activity'. Most writers use the term 'participation' when discussing activity, but there is a subtle and important difference. 'Participation' implies that individuals share in or take part in the decision-making process. However, whilst an individual may be active in *trying* to influence decisions s/he may not succeed in doing so. The problem of determining who is or is not involved in making decisions has often been described as the basic problem of power (for example, Mills, 1959/1970, p.50). To assume that people who are active also participate in the decision-making process is a pluralist ideal that is not necessarily grounded on reality. Thus, my extensive use of the word 'participation' when referring to, for example, the British Participation Study should not imply that it is considered appropriate.

A rudimentary distinction between two types of activity was made during the early stages of this research in order to clarify thought. At the first level of activity voters select those representatives who may play a major part in policy formulation. Voting behaviour is here referred to as one of the many activities in the political sphere of education, but an individual who confines him/herself to voting and does not try to exert influence at the second level is regarded as relatively inactive.

At the second level, activity can be identified as attempts to influence the decision-making process directly (not simply through a representative). This level would include such activities as membership of pressure groups, governing bodies, local authorities, political parties or contact with the media. It is this level that is of particular concern in this section of the book; although the voting system will also be considered.

In the British Participation Study, Parry, Moyser and Day were careful to define what they meant by participation. However, they did not distinguish between attempts to influence policy ('activity') and involvement in the policy-making process ('participation').

> The study adopts a very broad definition of political participation as 'taking part in the process of formulation, passage and implementation of public policies'. It is concerned with action by citizens which is aimed at influencing decisions which are, in most cases, ultimately taken by public representatives and officials. This may be action which seeks to shape the attitudes of decision-makers to matters yet to be decided, or it may be action in protest against the outcome of some decision. (Parry, Moyser and Day, 1992, p.16)

This sort of input would include the activities of politicians, pressure groups (for example the Campaign for the Advancement of State Education, the Independent Schools Information Service and teachers unions), journalists, researchers etc.. The input side is nevertheless only an ideal when central or local government does not actively seek a consensus and chooses to ignore many of the representations made by pressure groups. In such circumstances input is minimal and the activities of many pressure groups could only be described as participation at a superficial level in that only some of their opinions are communicated and many are not particularly influential.

Parry and Moyser describe the 'output' side as 'citizen participation' in the implementation of policies and government administration; for example on school governing bodies, tribunals, or voluntary service. It is the output side rather than the input side to which Conservative governments refers in their promotion of active citizenship. Citizens are to be involved in the process of implementing government policy rather than determining it. Influence of this type is primarily incremental rather than formative; small changes, or no changes being made during the process of implementing policy-makers' directives. There is some room for manoeuvre in the output side and the processes involved have already been well-documented (for example Archer, 1979, Kogan, 1986, McNay and Ozga, 1985). However, in the present context it is the input side of activity and influence that is the prime concern. Is there, for example, a contradiction between government rhetoric about participation and the reality of public control of the education system?

The language and framework of educational debate were discussed in detail in Chapter 1. It was argued that the rhetoric of the time is an important indicator of definitions of reality. When participation in education is considered in the present political context the expressions 'parental choice' and 'accountability' must also be considered. To a certain extent they are synonymous with each other via the emphasis on the consumer and, ultimately on the control of education through 'consumer sovereignty' (10.2). Kogan noted that the consumerist theme involves demands that the education system,

> . . . will yield to more immediate democratic control, not as provided through the ballot box democracy of local government elections, but through the power of the laity to review, criticise, influence and/or control the service given.
> . . . it will be a matter for historians to determine whether the normative models for education accountability match what is actually happening in educational administration or whether they are folk concepts which provide the rhetoric necessary for the stimulation of debate. (Kogan, 1986, pp.22-3)

225

Kogan offered three models of educational accountability (1986, p.24). Accountability could function according to one or more than one of the models.

1. Public or state control, which entails the use of authority by elected representatives, appointed officials, and the heads and others who manage schools.
2. Professional control, that is, control by teachers and professional administrators. This is associated with self-evaluation.
3. Consumerist control or influence which might take the form of (a) participatory democracy or partnership in the public sector; or (b) market mechanisms in the private or partly privatised public sector.

The rhetoric adopted by Conservative governments during the 1980s favours 3b., although many of their actions (for example, the abolition of the ILEA and increased control over local expenditure on education) suggest that 1. is more appropriate. 'Local management of schools' places more responsibility for the management of individual schools in the hands of their headteachers (1 above) and the assessment (but not primarily self-assessment) of teachers has also been promoted.

To Kogan the major problem lies in deciding who education should be accountable to and highlights potential conflict between the many groups who want to influence educational policy. These groups will have unequal access to and knowledge about the education system. The lack of knowledge about educational provision and educational sub-issues described in this research is not particularly surprising, as institutions and processes tend to be closed to public scrutiny. Even parents, who are most likely to take an interest in education (4.2), are notoriously hesitant about approaching schools and teachers. Some teachers do not encourage communication and, even when they do try to involve parents (9.5) they may have little success.

Donald argued (1981) that the institution of a form of participatory democracy was as a cosmetic exercise in legitimation. He suggests that the appearance of participation disguises the real power-base behind educational policy-making. Thus, central government can play an increasingly directive roll whilst claiming that it is providing more scope for participation within the system. Hall claims that Conservative governments have expropriated popular left-wing ideas and converted them to justify right-wing policies.

> For a brief period in the 1960s and 1970s, the involvement of parents with the school was the left's most democratic trump card. The dismantling of this into 'parental choice' and its expropriation by the right is one of their most significant victories. They stole an idea

226

designed to increase popular power in education and transformed it into the idea of an educational super-market. (Hall, 1983, p.9)

Some theories about educational accountability emphasise its appeal in terms of industry-inspired cost-effectiveness and productivity. Economic priorities are seen to dominate both in the funding of education and in the emphasis on education as serving the needs of the economy. The economic utility and accountability of education are accepted and promoted as cures for the 'British disease' (1.3). Thus, the influence of industry and the education system's accountability to industry are emphasised in the encouragement of closer relationships between schools and industry; for example, the educational 'compacts' that guarantee jobs with certain employers to pupils who prove their worth at school, and the various 'enterprise' schemes that have now become commonplace in secondary schools. Whereas the phrase 'child-centred education' was popularized during the 1960s, the 1980s saw education becoming economy-centred or parent-centred, the economy and parents being regarded as the consumers of education rather than pupils or students. In using the word 'consumer' throughout this book I have, to a certain extent, assumed the rhetoric of the moment. From a researchers point of view the word is a useful shorthand expression, representing voters (usually parents) who have pupils or students living in their households. Alternatives may sound rather clumsy but the common description of the parent, rather than the child, as the consumer of education has all sorts of implications. These will be considered in Chapter 10.

9.3 Electoral influence

At a fundamental level, democratic principles suggest that a citizen's ability to influence government is primarily through the ballot box. The reluctance of a government to accommodate opposing views would therefore cause little concern if it had been elected by a clear majority of the electorate. However, this was not the case either in 1983 or in 1987.

We have long known that our electoral system tends to produce governments which represent only a minority of the electorate. Proportional Representation too is rarely perfect but we can see in Table 9.1 that, when compared with elections in other European countries, Britain fared badly regarding the percentage of voters who voted for the party forming the government.

227

Table 9.1
Percentage of vote for the winning party in European countries:
Position in 1987

	%		%
Switzerland	77.5	Norway	49.0
Luxembourg	68.4	Finland	48.9
Italy	57.4	Ireland	47.3
Germany	55.8	Greece	45.8
Austria	52.9	France	44.9
Netherlands	52.0	Spain	44.1
Denmark	52.0	Portugal	44.0
Belgium	50.2	U K	42.3
Sweden	50.0		

Source: The Guardian, 10 August 1987, article by F. F. Ridley

Ridley pointed out that the British Government had less electoral support than any other government in power in a European democracy. He listed several other factors distinguishing Britain from most European democracies.

1. Britain has no entrenched constitution to limit what a parliamentary majority may do.
2. A single-party government with voting discipline in parliament gives the Prime Minister a power base that few leaders have even in their own parties elsewhere in Europe.
3. Coalition government (the common pattern in Europe) limits the power of a Prime Minister and forces compromise between parties, ensuring that policies are acceptable to a wider span of voters.
4. Regular changes of Government in Britain have, in the past encouraged parties to pursue policies that were not too far apart. Three [now four] terms of office by one party have provided it with the time to implement radical changes.
5. In the past the neo-pluralist corporate model (still common in other European countries) helped to compensate for the unrepresentative character of the parliamentary majority. In the present context, the determination of education policies in Britain involved three-cornered negotiations between politicians, teachers and administrators which were gradually been phased out during the 1980s.
6. Ridley argued that,

   The Cabinet is now dominated by people who believe they know what is good for the people and are determined to impose it on them. This ideological certainty is matched by some authoritarian instincts. Far from 'rolling back the frontiers of the state', as originally promised, the government is continuously increasing its powers: the centralisation of educational policy and controls over local government are obvious examples.

7. Most of the Conservatives' electoral support was situated in the south of the country, making the Government, '. . . dramatically unrepresentative of the rest of the United Kingdom.'

The electoral system alone is not, therefore, effective enough to keep government power in check or to ensure that public opinion is effectively represented. Political and educational activity in general, beyond the first level of voting behaviour, must also be considered in order to assess public influence on the political arena of education.

9.4 Who are the activists?

The Political Participation Study, carried out by Parry, Moyser and Day (1992) has been used extensively as a secondary source for this part of the research. It comprised a national sample (1,578) survey of the population of England, Wales and Scotland (carried out in 1984/5) coupled with a survey of citizens and leaders in local communities. This, together with data from the British Social Attitudes surveys, the Greater Manchester Study and my case studies provided a substantial basis for discussion (although the mass of data available has meant that it has, for the moment, been under-utilized).

Parry, Moyser and Day categorized respondents according to level of political activity as follows (1992, p.228):

25.8 per cent were inactive (i.e. did not vote regularly or have any other involvement);
51.0 per cent were voting specialists (i.e. only voted);
8.7 per cent were group specialists (i.e. involvement only in a group context);
2.2 per cent were party campaign specialists;
7.7 per cent were contacting specialists (i.e. contacted politicians etc.);
3.1 per cent were protesting specialists (e.g. marches, demonstrations, letters);
1.5 per cent were complete activists (i.e. active across the board).

Over 75 per cent of respondents therefore did nothing more than vote in elections. Analysis of the GMS data indicates that this finding at national level disguises differential turnout at elections (see my table 8.9). In Torytown and Labourville, for example, 31 per cent and 35 per cent (respectively) did not turn out to vote in the 1980 local election compared to 11 per cent (in each area) in the 1979 General Election.

Three preliminary questions clearly needed to be considered in this analysis of the relationship between attitudes to education and political activity: first, what sort of people were active in the political sphere of education; second, what sort of people were not active in the political sphere of education; and third, what was the effect (if any) of the characteristics of the active and the inactive?

Perception of education as a political issue is a probable prerequisite for the second level of activity (beyond the basic level of voting at elections). Parry, Moyser and Day found that complete activists mentioned an average of 2.44 issues, which was about four times the average agenda of the inactives. This tendency of the most active to have the most developed issue agendas, may be related to strength of opinion and to what are commonly regarded as 'extreme' views.

> A major theme of both the academic literature and political folklore is that activists are 'extreme', or more strongly committed on issues, than voters. By contrast, the politicians, more interested in attracting voters who are not ideological and have various policy preferences, are more 'representative' of the electorate. The activists, it is suggested, are often activated by issue concerns to become active in the first place - particularly where politics does not offer material gains, mix in a more partisan environment, and are impatient with administrative and political complexities raised by the politicians. (Kavanagh, 1983, p.107)

Parry, Moyser and Day also observe that an issue must be identified as susceptible to individual influence. They list four main reasons why people take action (1992, p.9-16):

1. Instrumentally to defend or promote their own interests.
2. Communitarian i.e. for the good of the community at large.
3. Educative and developmental i.e. increasing understanding of society or politics.
4. Expressive i.e. stating ones position on a matter that may or may not affect oneself and on which one might not expect immediate return in terms of changed policy.

They note that an individual may take action for more than one of these reasons.

The importance of the instrumental motive has been supported by many other researchers (for example, Verba and Nie, 1972). Parry, Moyser and Day also found that very little action was taken on issues that were considered to be beyond their respondents' sphere of influence. More action was taken on the relatively local issues (such as housing, the environment, education and transport) that were perceived as both affecting the household directly and most amenable to influence.

Perhaps the most substantial findings about political activity in the past relate to the social location of the particularly active or inactive. Parry, Moyser and Day's findings highlight the complicated relationship between wealth and education. They note that 'Degree level education appears to be an environment where the norm of activism is encouraged.'(1992, p.219). Degree holders have particularly high participation scores (+25) and those without qualifications particularly low participation scores (-3). However, the richest five per cent of graduates had a lower participation score than their less affluent peers and the less qualified poorest five per cent had a relatively high score (Parry, Moyser and Day, 1992, p.220). As these groups make-up a small proportion of the population the writers still conclude that 'resources' form the basis of an explanation for current levels of participation.

> By and large, these resources tend to be cumulative rather than countervailing. Wealth, education and organisational affiliations go together more than they pull in opposed directions. (Parry, Moyser and Day, 1992, p.432)

The BPPS findings about low levels of activity are supported by more findings from the British Social Attitudes' 1984 survey (Jowell et al., 1985). These also allow some comparisons to be made over time. Levels of local and national assertiveness were measured and an apparent increase (compared with BSA 1983/4 findings) in national assertiveness was found. Comparisons in local assertiveness were made over time, using the 1960 study, (Almond and Verba, 1963) and a survey carried out for the Maud Committee on local government during the early months of 1965 (Redcliffe Maud, 1967). In 1959/6 Almond and Verba asked,

> Suppose a regulation were being considered by [your local council] that you considered very unjust. What do you think you would do? Anything else?

In 1965 the Maud survey asked,

If there was something you felt strongly that the [borough or district] council ought or ought not to be doing - would you do anything to get them to change to your point of view?

In 1984 the BSA survey asked a question about activity at a national level,

What action, if any [they] would take if Parliament was considering a law which [they] regarded as unjust or harmful.

The BSA survey in 1984 also asked another question about activity at local level,

Now suppose your local council was proposing a scheme which you thought was really unjust or harmful. Which, if any, of the things on this card do you think you would do? Any others?

A direct comparison between responses to these questions would be misleading as the 1965 (Maud) question is less likely to produce a positive reply. However, all three surveys provide evidence of the greater willingness of individuals to act on their own account when roused by some proposed local action. This can be seen in responses to the BSA question.

Table 9.2
Action scores in response to the two BSA 1984/5 questions

	National	Local
Personal Action Index (PAI)	0.88	1.13
Collective Action Index (CAI)	0.74	0.69

Source: Jowell et al., 1985

A maximum (activist) score for either index was 4 and a minimum -1. Local government was therefore seen as more accessible to the action of the individual than was central government. The BSA researchers also compared their own finding with those of Almond and Verba in 1960 to consider whether or not an individual would act alone or with others (Table 9.3). This indicates that willingness to act increased, although the reliability of comparisons over time must always be challenged. Theories relating to such changes will be considered later in this chapter.

Table 9.3
Local political action, Almond and Verba (1960)
and BSA (1984/5) compared

	1960	1984
	%	%
Would act alone	41	79
Would act with others	36	61
Would not act at all	22	5

Source: Jowell et al., 1985

When the BSA researchers considered household income and school-leaving age their findings added weight to the BPPS conclusion that the most affluent (measured here by income and household tenure) and most highly educated would be most likely to take action (Table 9.4).

Table 9.4
Personal action scores (PAI), BSA 1984/5

	PAI (national)	PAI(local)
Age		
18-24	0.81	1.03
25-34	0.91	1.26
35-54	1.01	1.29
55 and over	0.77	0.97
School-leaving age		
16 or under	0.81	1.04
17-18	1.05	1.47
19 or over	1.26	1.49
still in full time education	1.22	1.41
Tenure		
owner occupier	0.90	1.18
rented (public)	0.79	1.02
rented (other)	0.92	1.14
Household income		
under £5,000	0.76	1.03
£5,000 - £7,999	1.01	1.24
£8,999 -£11,999	0.93	1.24
£12,000 and over	1.07	1.34

Source: Jowell et al., 1985

In general the subgroup differences in national political assertiveness applied also to local assertiveness, with the middle-aged and the better educated exhibiting higher scores, particularly for personal action, than the young, the old and the less highly educated. As in the BPPS, it was found that income differences exerted a less marked effect than education, although the association between income/wealth and education makes it difficult to analyze one in isolation from the other.

9.5 Activity in Torytown and Labourville

When Edgell and Duke studied political activity in Torytown and Labourville their prime concern was to assess levels of action against the public spending cuts in general. Many of their findings cannot therefore be related directly to action in the educational arena, as educational activity may have specific and separate characteristics. Edgell and Duke found, for example, that action against the cuts was related to trade union membership; yet it will be shown in 9.5 that in the case of education, even many teachers who were members of trade unions were reluctant to associate themselves with radical activity.

Edgell and Duke also found (1985, p.9) that above average rates of action were exhibited by lower professional/intermediate workers (18 per cent), skilled manual workers (16 per cent), those aged under 34 (21 per cent), public sector workers (18 per cent) and Labour voters (17 per cent). The probability that these findings cannot be generalized further than activity relating to spending cuts is suggested by the BSA finding that the personal action scores of the 35 to 54 age group were higher than those of any other age group. Thus, although the younger age group may have been particularly active against public spending cuts, the older age group, which included more parents of children currently being educated, seems to have been more active when the action was not specifically related to spending cuts.

Of greater significance in the present context is the GMS finding that there was a difference between the level of activity in Torytown and Labourville. At the second interview (in 1983/4) it was found that 33 per cent of the Torytown respondents who perceived that they had been affected by the education cuts had taken some form of action compared to 28 per cent in Labourville (Duke and Edgell, 1986). Torytown's more zealous application of spending cuts apparently lead to a greater perceived impact and consequently more action.

Edgell and Duke also found that more men took action than women, but they associated this with their finding that level of economic activity (especially full-time employment and trade union membership) was a particularly salient factor influencing level of political activity. Although women were found to be just as radical as men in terms of their action against the cuts Edgell and Duke concluded that (1981, Table 4), their traditional domestic role seemed to have reduced their opportunities to take action against spending cuts. Again this cannot be directly related to action in the educational arena as, in theory, the traditional domestic role should increase women's contact with the school system. However, the political activity of women is a sensitive issue. As Bella Abzug argued, the exploitation of many women in the home means that they are prevented from taking political action and at the same time accused of political apathy.

Other possible explanations for the lower level of political activity amongst women relate to political competence and political realism. Campbell et al. (1966) found that, amongst the American women that they polled, feelings of political efficacy were expressed by 68 per cent of the college educated, 40 per cent of those educated at high school only and 14 per cent of those only educated at grade school. This was compared to 83 per cent, 47 per cent, and 32 per cent of men respectively. Thus, amongst both sexes, it was the most highly educated who expressed the greatest feelings of political efficacy; a finding that complemented the BSA and BPPS findings (9.3). Bourque and Grossholtz (1984) argued that an explanation for the differences based on societal sex roles is inadequate and that,

> One might offer the alternative hypothesis, that given the very limited number of issues that citizens can effect, the lower sense of political efficacy expressed by women is a perceptive assessment of the process. Men, on the other hand, express irrationally high rates of efficacy because of the limitations of their sex role which teaches them that they are masterful and capable of affecting the political process. In fact, few of us have any political influence in any case. (Bourque and Grossholtz, 1984, p.107)

This alternative hypothesis

> ...rests on granting women a degree of political cynicism, realism, sophistication and understanding greater than that of men. This is something that these authors are unwilling to do. (Bourque and Grossholtz, 1984, p.107)

My primary data (from case study interviews) about political activity has not yet been exploited to the full, and findings about gender differences must await a thorough trawling of related literature in order to generate comparisons. For the moment some of the claims about gender differences can only be recorded and acknowledged. However, a forceful impression emerging from the case study data is that most informants regarded political activity as a waste of time, many stating that the present government would not listen anyway,

> The government are getting further and further away from the people. The needs of ordinary people were never much considered in the government but it's even worse now. (Informant No.18, Q3)

If 'ordinary people' were classed as working class, it was clear to many that they could not influence the government.

> The present Government, no. I don't think they're the type of government for the workers, which I suppose I am. (Informant No. 50, Q3)

When asked how they could influence the Government several informants said that they would not have a chance of doing so individually but might as a member of a group.

> I think unless you've got a voice in an organisation an individual doesn't. (Informant No. 44, Q3)

> [About local issues] Its a waste of time people like myself trying to do anything. You've got to be in some sort of large group and even then they'll not do owt. (Informant No. 49, Q8)

Thus, even at a local level, where voters tended to rate their chances of influencing policy-making as relatively high, there was a noticeable element of scepticism. One Torytown informant attended a local meeting about proposed changes but regarded it rather sceptically.

> They were information meetings about the possible change from the system we have now to comprehensives, the policies for these having changed several times over the last 10 or 12 years with the changing local government. The meetings I attended weren't designed for action but they did ask for opinions regarding coeducational versus single sex, comprehensives versus selection and the introduction of a sixth form college. Nothing really useful came out of the meeting but it was an opportunity to voice opinions. (Informant No.51, Q31)

Another Torytown resident who was not a parent emphasised the total irrelevance of educational issues to her.

[Had she attended any meetings about local changes in education?] No. I wouldn't know what they were talking about. (Informant No. 8, Q31)

In keeping with my previous findings about lack of interest in education as a political issue (Chapter 4) activity in this particular arena was minimal. Of the few who expressed an interest in education, even fewer had been actively involved. This finding is supported by the experiences of several Torytown and Labourville schools when they held 'elections' in 1988 for parent governors.

9.6 The election of parent governors in Torytown and Labourville

Findings about the election of parent governors in Torytown and Labourville are particularly significant in view of the stated intention of Conservative governments to promote parental involvement schools. The probability that there is more activity at local level has also been suggested by research findings (9.3 and 9.4). During the autumn term of 1988 schools were recruiting new parent governors, in response to a new regulation aimed at increasing the representation of parents on school governing bodies. I therefore contacted primary and secondary schools in the Torytown and Labourville wards that were used for the GMS sampling frame to find out how the elections had progressed.

At a national level reports of parental recruitment were not very encouraging. For example, a survey of 61 schools carried out by the Times Educational Supplement (TES, 21 October 1988) found that in more than a third of the schools the voting turnout was less than 25 per cent and in more than 40 per cent no elections were held because of a shortage of parent candidates. The survey also found that one in eight of the candidates was a teacher.

The nine schools that responded to my inquiry seemed to fit into a pattern that was reported across the country (although the 61 schools in the TES survey can hardly be classed as a reliable sample). Of the nine schools in Torytown and Labourville, six did not have an election due to a shortage of candidates. As the subject was quite sensitive I consulted the chief education officers in each area before contacting individual head teachers. The first attempted contact was by telephone, as it was thought that some headteachers might prefer to provide the information informally, rather than in writing. This was found to be the case in seven out of the nine schools. Indeed, several headteachers spoke at length about what they regarded as wasted efforts to encourage parents to participate in the elections (either as candidates or voters) and observed that, as they were already overburdened with work, the whole exercise was particularly frustrating.

In Torytown information was provided by one infant school, two junior schools, one boys' secondary modern schools and one girls' secondary modern school. I also tried to contact the headteacher of a grammar school but the school was in the process of reorganization; a former girls' school and a former boys' school being amalgamated to form a mixed grammar school. The headteacher was commuting between two sites, could not be contacted by telephone and was too busy to respond to my written request.

Of the five Torytown schools, two (one junior, one secondary modern) had no election despite having a total of 900 pupils on their rolls. One had just enough nominees and the other did not have enough. All of the nominees in these two schools were automatically elected. The three remaining Torytown schools had elections; the junior school head being particularly pleased that twice as many nominations were made than were needed and 67 per cent of parents voted. It was described by the head as a 'family school' and 'Parents come and go in the school as they please'. It also had a very active Parent Teachers Association, which was good at fundraising. There were fewer nominations in the other schools, despite the fact that the secondary modern had over twice as many pupils as the 'family school' on its roll. No information was received about the proportion of parents who actually voted in the other two schools.

Of the four Labourville schools, one was an infants school, one a junior school and two were comprehensive schools. None of the schools had an election. Two had just enough nominees to fill the places. The other two did not have enough nominees: in one a parent attending the Annual General Meeting was persuaded to serve, and in the other a Parent Teachers Association discussion led to the recommendation of PTA members.

The nine schools that provided me with information had a total of 4,238 pupils on their rolls. All schools went through the formality of issuing information to parents and asking for nominations (following the instructions formulated by the DES). Between them they needed 34 parent governors and had just 38 nominations (including those from the Parent Teachers Association and Annual General Meeting who were 'press ganged' in Labourville). When combined with the BPPS, BSA and GMS findings about levels of political activity this suggests that what is being considered here is inactivity rather than activity. Furthermore, the characteristics of the few activists can assume an importance out of all proportion the their number. Although 24 nominees were male and only 14 were female it is not possible to generalize from such small numbers about the influence of gender. In this instance the findings do not support the proposition that women have more frequent contacts with schools because of their traditional domestic role and are therefore more likely to be active in education. They may even be prevented from being more active in education as a result of trying to maintain the dual rolls of paid employee and unpaid domestic worker (9.7).

The occupations of parent governors must also be considered. These are shown in Table 9.5.

Table 9.5
Occupations of parent governor candidates,
Torytown and Labourville, 1988

n=	n=
6 teachers/lecturers	2 unemployed
3 school ancillary workers	1 company director
3 public sector controllers	1 quantity surveyor
3 housewives	1 industrial chemist
3 engineers	1 computer program designer
2 self employed	1 assistant to company director
2 doctors	1 sales rep
2 solicitors	1 fork-lift truck driver
2 public employee workers	1 occupation unknown
2 part-time bar-maids	
	38 total

The BPPS and BSA findings that the most affluent and the most highly educated dominate political activity seem to apply in this particular instance. Although some individuals on the list may not fit those categories, the social balance does not represent a cross-section of society. However, the small size of my sample of schools means that findings cannot be generalized. More research would need to be carried out to record the types of activists involved in education. This would include the collection of data about members of PTAs and educational pressure groups. The number of teachers on the list of candidates in Torytown and Labourville and their natural interest in education as a political issue suggests that, if any group is heavily involved and influential in the politics of education it must surely be them. Teacher activity will therefore be briefly considered in the next section.

9.7 Teacher activity

It has already been noted (4.4) that, at the time of the 1987 General Election, 77 per cent of teachers regarded education as the most important political issue, that the most highly educated were the most likely to have radical attitudes (8.4.3) and that in 1987 far more teachers stood as candidates for the

Labour Party and Alliance parties than for the Conservative Party. However, during the 1980s, most teachers did not vote Labour. The Conservative Party was the most popular party amongst teachers in the 1983 general election and in 1987, after years of educational acrimony, it was replaced as the most favoured party amongst teachers, not by the Labour Party but by the Alliance. Teachers could not therefore be described as radical left-wingers simply because many (not all) of them were opposed to Conservative government policies. Indeed the general picture of teacher party identification is of heterogeneity and this is reflected in levels of political activity.

Teachers do not form a single, coherent group of educational/political activists. They are divided into several trade unions, some of which (for example, the Professional Association of Teachers) refuse to take strike action. As political conflict escalated during the 1980s, over teachers' pay and negotiating rights and their general concern about the current state of education, their response was to divide further rather than to unite. Some teachers became particularly active in their opposition to government policies, and the National Union of Teachers often provided a vehicle for their discontent. Others who were particularly reluctant to strike left the NUT to join unions that were less likely to take strike action. Even the Government's removal of teachers' negotiating rights (and the International Labour Organization's ruling in May 1988 that this did not conform to international standards of freedom and fairness) did not lead to the emergence of teachers on a united, political front.

A look at the history of the teachers' trade unions suggests that, far from being particularly active in the politics of education, many teachers have been reluctant to involve themselves in politics. Ken Jones (1983 and 1985) argued that professional ideals prevent them from being more politically active. Writing of the NUT, he observed that, even this supposedly radical union, was restrained from taking political action by its concern about the image of professionalism.

> A too-consistent pattern of militancy, political alignment and educational controversy seems from the perspective of professional unity to jeopardize the union's highest ambitions, since the conferral of self-government upon an unruly teaching force would be impossible. (Jones, 1985, p.241)

The argument rests, he said, on the

> . . . belief that the nurture of children is a task which is politically and ideologically unproblematic and must therefore be kept free from political controversy and 'interference'. (Jones, 1985, p.242)

Jones' perception of the professional ethic as a brake on teachers' political activity must, however, be balanced by a recognition that teachers have still been more active in this particular arena than have most other social groups. Teachers have been very critical of Conservative governments. Indeed the lengthy extract from the NUT pamphlet that has been included in section 6.2.3 was expressed very forcefully. Even more forceful was the motion passed at the 1988 NATFHE conference that England was,

> . . . a squalid, ugly, uncomfortable place, an intolerant, racist, homophobic, narrow-minded, authoritarian rat-hole, run by vicious, suburban-minded materialist philistines. (Based on a quote from the film-writer, Hanif Kureishi)

Thus, although Jones' writings in 1983 and 1985 emphasized the loyalty of teachers towards their pupils and their associated reluctance to take strike action, the concern, and even despair, of many teachers cannot be overlooked. Reports of large numbers of teachers leaving the profession during the 1980s suggest that many teachers were 'voting with their feet' in response to changes in education [2]. It is also possible that in the 1980s teacher radicalism became more pronounced and that teachers have become more active. A more concentrated analysis of survey data would therefore be needed to provide an up-to-date and adequate assessment of teacher activity.

9.8 Participation theories

Why are so few people active in the politics of education? Headteachers are particularly concerned about the apparent lack of interest of many parents. Many critics of Conservative policy are also concerned about what is seen as the relative indifference of the less affluent to market-orientated policies that will leave them at a particular disadvantage. Possible explanations emerging from the study of survey data (9.3 and 9.4) were formulated into the shape of three hypotheses.

Firstly, the expenses involved in activity may be prohibitive for people on low incomes. Activity may involve travelling expenses and/or unpaid leave from work. Such costs may form a large proportion of a low income but a relatively small proportion of a high income.

Secondly, there is a strong association between level of education and social class. The less affluent may have problems that suggest the need to be active, but may deterred by a lack of the necessary verbal and literary skills or a lack of confidence in their own fluency. Similarly, lack of knowledge about facts and procedures may present another barrier. Parry, Moyser and Day note that such barriers can be overcome by group action.

> The less individually advantaged might be expected to compensate for
> any political weakness by collective, solidaristic action. However, the
> evidence of the present survey suggests that some of the traditional
> working class organisations, such as unions, are no longer the
> preserve of the have-nots and that other groups in which the less well-
> off are likely to be members are politically not very active. Who will
> then mobilise the disadvantaged to participate in defence of their
> interests? It is, therefore, possible that the initial effect or rising levels
> of participation may be to amplify the already louder voice of the
> advantaged in British society - those with the higher education and
> well-integrated into group networks. And, to the extent that
> participation is effective, not only will their voice be heard, but their
> demands may be acted upon. So long as there is a consensus upon
> objectives this may not matter, but where the interests of the better and
> the less well resourced diverge, the participatory advantages of the
> socially advantages may make themselves count. (Parry, Moyser and
> Day, 1992, p.432)

We can see how the comments above can apply in education. Activists in
education would be communicating with highly educated professionals
(teachers and administrators). Activity could thus be considered to be
potentially embarrassing by those who are not highly educated themselves.
Research (for example, the Plowden Report, 1967; Douglas, 1964; Jackson
and Marsden, 1963) has shown that many working class parents feel
particularly anxious about communications with their children's schools,
teachers and other officials. This lack of confidence in the educational field
is likely to be related to reticence concerning membership of parent-teachers'
associations, becoming governors etc.. Education can be perceived as
representing a working class/middle class barrier.

Thirdly, many individuals feel unable to devote the time and energy needed
for such activity. Personal socio-economic 'troubles' (4.1) may be seen as
depriving individuals of the opportunity to be active in general (and in this
instance) to influence educational policy-making in particular. The earlier
debate (4.1) about personal troubles and public issues must be reconsidered
regarding activity as well as interest. Personal troubles may, however, either
act as a spur to action or prevent an individual from taking any action unless
it is absolutely necessary to deal with the immediate problem. Some people
may be so absorbed in striving to resolve personal troubles that they cannot try
to influence educational policy-making. They may not, in any case, perceive
educational issues as being susceptible to their influence. Thus, what many

political commentators ascribe to apathy may perhaps be more accurately described as a feeling of impotence; public issues can only assume greater importance when personal problems are reduced.

Maslow and Inglehart have provided a theoretical framework within which to consider relative poverty, a perceived lack of competence and involvement in personal 'troubles'. They have argued that increased prosperity increases the likelihood of political participation, both at an individual and a more general level. As material security increases, so does personal assurance, the individual becomes less absorbed in private 'troubles' and more involved in public issues. Inglehart also claimed that increased post war prosperity has increased the level of political activity.

According to Maslow's theory of a hierarchy of human motivations (Maslow, 1970) an individual's material needs and psychological safety need to be satisfied before more expressive needs can be satisfied. Expressive needs include such emotions as affection, esteem and self-actualization. Although there is some overlapping of the hierarchy (affection can, for example, be felt in the most dire circumstances), expressive needs are considered less important than physical and spiritual survival. Both political activity and education could be assigned to Maslow's fifth tier of needs ('self-actualization') although education could also be associated with the fourth ('self-esteem'). They may therefore come after,

1. physical (hunger, sleep, sex, etc.)
2. safety
3. affection, feelings of belonging
4. self-esteem, ego, strength

It can be considered quite reasonable for people who are materially deprived to attach a low value to activity in educational politics. Yet when survival is a prime concern it can easily be perceived by others as political apathy. The comments made by the Labourville Chief Education Officer and quoted in section 4.5 therefore apply to activity as well as to influence. Similarly, when an individual is particularly preoccupied by other personal (perhaps non-economic) 'troubles' activity of this sort will be assigned a very low priority.

It is moreover, possible that as the economy moves between boom and depression changes in activity at an aggregate level may be noticed. Inglehart and other social scientists writing in the 1960s and 1970s tended to describe that period as one of increasing affluence, during which material needs and psychological safety were more likely to be satisfied than in any previous period.

Inglehart argued that changes in the 1960s and 1970s allowed an increased proportion of people to play an active role in formulating policy and to engage in 'elite-challenging' as opposed to 'elite-directed' activities. Elite-directed participation involved the mobilization, by elites, of mass support through the establishment of organizations such as parties, unions and churches. Elite-challenging participation involved the public in increasingly important roles in the making of specific decisions and not just in the choice between two or more sets of decision-makers. A post material or post-bourgeois attitude would also be less acquisitive because material needs had been satisfied; the emphasis being instead on activity and affections.

If the affluence post materialist hypothesis is valid then the economic problems of the late 1970s and the 1980s could have led to a reduction in levels of activity. Such a trend has not been indicated by the BSA 1984/5 comparison of personal action scores during the 1960s and the 1980s (9.4). However, as standards of living have for most people improved considerably during that time the validity of the hypothesis can only be assessed by an economic analysis that is beyond the scope of this research. It is also possible that the rate at which activity has increased has not been as fast as it would have been if a large proportion of the population had not been excluded from the increasing prosperity of the majority. Inglehart himself said that, if his interpretation was correct, the 'destruction or debilitation' of the industrial society would lead to a 'Philistine generation'.

When Inglehart's hypothesis is applied to British society during the 1980s it seems that a personal concern with the satisfaction of material needs could not be easily satisfied. Luxury items, as well as essential resources could be perceived as material 'needs' and an acquisitive attitude could be associated with the already affluent as well as the relatively poor. The post-material outlook (supposedly most common amongst the affluent) stresses participation and the need for affection and belonging rather than the more acquisitive outlook of the less affluent. This would hardly be an accurate description of the 1980s, which were to many characterized by consumerism and conspicuous consumption rather than community spirit. Conservative governments have promoted acquisitive attitudes but have not promoted a genuinely participatory political culture. Thus, the pattern tends to fit Inglehart's materialist rather than post materialist culture at least in some respects.

9.9 Summary of findings

More research and analysis needs to be carried out regarding activity and influence in the arena of educational politics. Nevertheless, it is possible to conclude that in the 1980s the direction of influence in the educational debate was mainly from government to voters rather than vice versa. The

Conservative governments' unyielding education policies were not designed to incorporate conflicting views and the participation of critics was not encouraged. A common belief that the government was not amenable to influence may provide one explanation for the low level of political activity. However, there was also very little activity at a local level, where individuals were more likely to believe that they had a chance of influencing decision-making. The least affluent and less educated, who are most likely to suffer in a market-orientated, competitive society, were the least active in the political/educational field. Their traditional scope for political influence tended to be through the trade union movement and unions (even teachers unions) were not particularly active in this field. The individual is often handicapped by a lack of confidence in personal efficacy or by a prime concern with personal 'troubles' rather than public issues.

Hence it is more appropriate to talk about *activity* in education as a political issue rather than participation or influence. Governments increased their control over the education system (6.1) and defined Conservative values and policies as rational and technical rather than political (1.2 and 5.4). If Kogan's three models of educational accountability (9.2) are reconsidered it can be seen that, although government sponsored rhetoric emphasizes market mechanisms of public accountability, it is the state (in the form of the government rather than appointed officials) that dominates educational debates and it is to the government (rather than the public) that the education system is still accountable.

Notes

1. Polls reported in The Guardian, 10 April 1988 and 11 May 1988. The Electoral Reform Society sent ballot papers (each with a pre-paid envelope) to every ILEA-educated child's home. The Harris sample consisted of 4,882 inner London ratepayers.
2. In January 1990 a report published by Alan Smithers and Pamela Robinson of Manchester University noted that about 20,000 teachers left the profession in 1989 (reported in The Independent, 1990).

10 Conclusions

Findings have been summarized at various points throughout this book. They will be reconsidered in this final chapter as some of the implications are discussed with reference to the development of theories, future research, the relationship between rhetoric and practice and wider philosophical debates.

10.1 Main findings

In order to provide a structure through which findings can be reconsidered and evaluated the emphasis within this section will be on five important questions emerging from the data. The first four questions can be seen as puzzles that may only be partly resolved, but around which the mass of data can be reorganized into a manageable whole.

The first question was raised in Chapter 1 and has been considered throughout. It is - *Is education a political issue?* I have argued that education is an important political issue in that education policies do not emerge naturally, but as consequences of political debate between competing perspectives (1.2). Education policies also have far-reaching social implications in terms of individual life chances (7.9.5) as well as national economic progress (1.3). However, the Conservative governments of the 1980s tried to present educational decisions as rational and technical and played down controversial elements, their policies being legitimized as natural and/or emerging from common sense (5.4). Although many voters disagreed with government policy on individual sub-issues, a general lack of interest in (4.1) and knowledge about (5.5) education policy helped to maintain this legitimizing process.

If an area of political debate is only defined as a political issue when the majority of voters perceive it as such (8.2.1), then education is placed in a contradictory position. On the one hand, it could be defined as a political

246

issue because of the associated conflict and social consequences but, in the other hand, it is clear that a large proportion of voters did not regard it as an important issue (in the 1980s) when they were deciding how to vote.

Education was low on many voters' issue agendas and its lack of relevance can be summarized by the reference some informants made to an 'educational age' beyond which education was not considered (4.1). Thus, education may only be regarded as a political issue by those associated with it as consumers or producers, these voters having the most radical attitudes (8.5). Indeed those with least contact with the system and little knowledge about current conditions were most likely to defer to Conservative policies and, presumed, greater expertise in the management of the education system. This was noticeable when attitudes to educational standards were considered (7.2 and 7.3). Informants with the most experience of the current education system were most likely to claim that standards had improved since they were at school, whilst those with the least experience were most likely to reiterate Conservative claims that standards had declined (presumed causes often being cited as comprehensivization and lack of discipline). Thus, the claim that education is an important political issue raises contradictions that must be considered further (10.2).

To what extent did governments during the 1980s manipulate debate? Although it has been claimed that governments have manipulated debates (1.2, 1.3 and 9.1), the scope and success of this manipulation has not been determined. It has, however, been argued that governments played an important role in deciding what issues and sub-issues should reach the agenda for political debate. Thus, Conservative rhetoric was influential in raising topics within debates (for example, 'parental choice', 'relevance' and 'accountability'). Governments also downgraded certain topics by ignoring them (for example, a 'colour blind' approach to racial issues, 7.7.2) ridiculing them, or both (as in the case of anti-racist education). Conservatives could try to claim a monopoly of traditional values (5.1), identify threats to such values (7.3.1) and promote a curriculum representing their own philosophy as neutral and non-political (5.4).

People with opposing views were pressurized into adopting a defensive role, rather than a position of strength, and may have moderated their attitudes to bring them closer to those of the government (7.11). Furthermore, in claiming support for their policies, governments benefitted from the sheer diversity of public opinions, usually hearing what it suited them to hear and ignoring awkward objections (9.1). Certainly, the common belief that education standards have fallen (both in the long term and during the 1980s) operated to the benefit of the Conservative drive towards privatization. As the state education service faced more problems, demand for private education increased, Conservative definitions of reality being supported by a

247

degenerative process that had been introduced into the state education system by the government itself. There are therefore strong indications that governments dominated educational debates during the 1980s, but a clearer picture is needed of the scope and extent of government manipulation. This research has identified the problem but more work must be carried out in order to clarify the situation.

Has any pattern emerged from apparently inconsistent responses at an individual level? Variations in responses to sub-issues often lacked consistency, few individuals being classified as totally radical or totally adhering to the government-sponsored dominant ideology. When Parkin's three attitudinal types were considered (i.e. dominant, subordinate and radical, 7.11) across a sample of sub-issues, it was found that an individual could have all three (8.4.3). For example, of the 52 case study informants, only 16 had consistent responses on the Ed Rad I scale (four all radical, twelve all non-radical).

Apparently contradictory or irrational responses were often found, the most noticeable being the level of support for the continued existence of private schools from individuals who had been denied access to such schools themselves (7.9.4 and 7.9.5). Grammar schools were also highly regarded by many respondents (7.8) and a bipartite system was favoured, despite a lack of esteem for the secondary modern schools attended by the majority of pupils in a bipartite system (7.8.4). Thus, there was strong support for a system in which the majority of pupils were regarded as having an inadequate education.

Findings related to this question suggest a state of 'false consciousness' (5.5), a concept that is well known in the social sciences but rarely tested empirically. Further analysis is needed in order to clarify the processes by which individuals are 'persuaded' to favour policies that operate against their personal interests, and to ask if a pattern has emerged to make sense of apparently inconsistent responses at an individual level. These problems will be considered in section 10.2.

Has a pattern emerged from responses at an aggregate level? Not only did attitudes to sub-issues lack cohesion at an individual level but they also lacked cohesion at an aggregate level (8.4). No clear and consistent pattern of attitudes was found to provide any party with a mandate for its education policies (8.5). The Ed Rad I scale indicated only a moderate association between political identification and educational radicalism (Table 8.13) and the association resulting from the application of the Ed Rad II scale was even weaker (Table 8.14). Thus, voters' attitudes to a group of educational sub-issues rarely corresponded with the policies of the parties with which they identified. However, a clear aggregate pattern was found in attitudes towards some individual sub-issues. There was, for example, a clear rejection of government spending cuts (6.4) and student loans (7.10.2), an acceptance of private education (7.9.4) and a general state of confusion about the National

Curriculum (Tables 7.10 and 7.11). Also, a positive association of the Conservative Party with 'valence' issues (8.2.3) may have overcome opposition to other sub-issues. The problem remains of searching for a pattern to make sense of the diversity of attitudes at an aggregate, as well as an individual level (10.2).

As definitions of reality are so problematic and attitudes so diverse, would not merging theories be too loosely based? Findings about bias in educational research (5.3) suggest that caution is needed in the formulation of theories in order to avoid over-interpretation and the degradation of data. However, the grounded theory/theory construction approach (2.1) resulted in the emergence of the most highly developed theories at the end of the research process; theories emerging having been well-supported by observation, although they still require further investigation. Triangulation, involving the use of a literature search, observation and the analysis of quantitative and qualitative data, increased the reliability of the findings and reduced the likelihood of important data being missed.

10.2 From observation to theories

No simple answers are provided here but findings indicate fertile areas for further research and theoretical debate. Indeed, three middle range theoretical positions (or areas) have emerged from the data and have already been considered to a certain extent. These can be combined and tentatively expressed as factors to explain the findings. This is done with a view to testing and development in future research. The three factors are here simply defined as the pull of tradition, the pressure of personal experience, and the priority of basic needs.

In each case it is possible to see how the factor helps to summarize findings and theories that have already been considered.

1. Theories about the pull of tradition are related to previous discussions about dominant values, valence issues and Conservative claims to have a monopoly of traditional values.
2. Previous discussions about personal interest and bias are related to the pressure of personal experience.
3. The priority of personal needs is again a simplified resume of theories relating to a hierarchy of needs, materialism and post-materialism.

The three factors are used to organize the mass of research findings and to shed light on the puzzles considered in the last section (10.1). Various combinations of these three main influences (of tradition, experience and basic needs) may be identified in the attitudes of voters at both individual and aggregate levels. Use of the three areas as analytical tools also offers

249

explanations regarding the role of governments in the manipulation of debate and contradictions in the definition of education as a political issue.

A very simple representation of some of the data will be used in order to clarify the three theoretical areas. The emergence of the three theoretical areas from empirical data can be seen most clearly in Table 8.1, where an index of case study informants' attitudes to present Government policies is provided. The index does not clearly represent survey data and the comparisons made in each section of Chapters 6 and 7 must be considered before generalizations can be made. In this instance the index is being used simply as a heuristic device.

10.2.1 The pull of tradition

We can see that in Table 8.1 most support was given for the continued existence of private schools, the claim that the education system did not treat girls less favourably than boys, the government's claim that teachers should not be allowed to present a favourable view of homosexuality, and the superiority of the bipartite system over comprehensive education. Each of these attitudes demonstrates to some degree the pull of tradition; by which I mean that long-established institutions and normative value systems have an attraction that cloaks them with legitimacy.

This can be seen most clearly in attitudes to homosexuality, private schools and grammar schools, but the identification of traditional attitudes to gender inequalities is more difficult. There are a number of possible explanations. For example, claims that girls are treated unequally may be discounted by voters who are either sexist or have a deferential attitude towards educationalists and politicians. Indeed feminism may be regarded with the sort of scepticism associated with anti-racism. Both are perspectives that voters could regard as non-traditional and politically radical.

The three theoretical areas, expressed in the three factors, cannot be isolated from each other and the overlapping or conflicting influences of the pull of tradition and personal experience can be seen when knowledge of the education system is considered. Indeed, the pull of tradition is an emotive attraction and may be based almost entirely on ignorance about the education system. Lack of knowledge about the current state of the education system could, for example, result in a sort of blind faith in the absence of gender inequalities. The pull of tradition may also help to explain apparently contradictory attitudes such as the appeal of private education as an element of 'parental choice', even amongst respondents who believed that only wealthy parents could make that choice. It also helps to explain an attraction towards the bipartite system that was almost entirely based on respect for grammar schools and a disregard for the 'feared' (7.8.4) secondary modern schools. Yet the most highly educated respondents had the least traditional attitudes in general, and we can see that the pull of tradition could be challenged by greater knowledge about the education system.

The significance of the pull of tradition is further heightened by Conservative claims to hold a monopoly of traditional values (5.1 and 7.3) a finding that also relates to government manipulation of educational debates. It is difficult to evaluate the degree of success such claims had in influencing voters' attitudes, but some attempts have been made to assess the importance of (normative/dominant) valence issues in past elections (8.2.3 and 8.2.4). Therefore, in recognizing and promoting 'traditional' sub-issues and attitudes the Conservative governments of the 1980s found a fertile area for electoral support. However, it has already been suggested that the pull of tradition can only exert a powerful influence when it is not strongly challenged by knowledge or experience.

10.2.2 The pressure of experience

The least support (Table 8.1) was given to Conservative policies on educational spending and for the claim that class inequalities did not exist. Both of these attitudes demonstrate to some extent the pressure of experience; by which I mean that knowledge arising from personal experiences will inspire attitudes and action. Thus, it can be argued that a majority of respondents had experience, or personal knowledge of, inequalities of social class and were aware of the actual, or potentially deleterious effects of public spending cuts.

Again it has been indicated that those respondents with the least contact with the education system were the least radical (8.5), the pull of tradition being most powerful when not contradicted by personal experience. At the same time both the pull of tradition and personal experience reflect the importance of familiarity. For example, experience of a certain type of secondary education tended to lead respondents to favour that type of school system; hence the continuing popularity of the bipartite system amongst respondents who were educated in a selective system and the popularity of private education amongst the many Conservative politicians who have had little personal experience of state education (5.4). However, the influences of tradition and experience may clash when an individual experiences social disadvantages as a result of social 'traditions'. If, for example, a parent who originally supports the bipartite system finds that his/her child has been selected for a Torytown secondary modern school, the experience of a low status education may result in the eventual rejection of the pull of tradition.

The identification of this theoretical area is further enhanced by findings and debates concerning personal 'troubles' and public 'issues' (4.1), private and public domains (4.3) and the importance of the interest motive in general (Chapters 4, 8 and 9). Public employees, parents, and mothers in particular were found to take a greater interest in education as a political issue. Yet, despite this interest, their level of activity may have been minimized by the priority of basic needs.

When considering the three theoretical areas it is, however, difficult to extricate knowledge from experience and distinctions between the two may be misleading. Nevertheless, knowledge about sub-issues offers a fruitful area for further research and I found many examples of the relationship between knowledge (or experience) and attitudes. Those respondents with recent experience of the education system were most likely to believe that standards had risen since they were at school (7.2.4). Thus, the pressure of experience could, in this case, be seen to successfully contradict Conservative claims that standards had fallen since the introduction of comprehensive schools. However, claims about low teaching standards and poor school discipline were made by many who had little experience or knowledge on which to base their attitudes (7.3.3 and 7.3.4). This lack of knowledge apparently operated in the interests of Conservatives in particular. For example, lack of accurate knowledge about the death of a pupil at Burnage High School tended to ferment myths about anti-racist policies and thereby enhance the pull of tradition (5.5). Lack of knowledge about the process of selection at 11+ in Torytown and about public spending on private education also helped to restrict public criticism (3.3). Indeed, the maintenance of a selective system in Torytown depends upon most of the parents of 11+ 'failures' knowing little about the process of selection, the opportunities for education in comprehensive schools elsewhere or simply being unable to manage the logistics of exercising 'choice'.

The pull of tradition was therefore most powerful amongst those respondents with the least experience of the education system and weakest amongst those who had the most experience. In particular, it was found that those who had been longest in education (the most highly educated) had the most radical educational attitudes.

10.2.3 The priority of basic needs

An associated, and well-supported, theory relates to the priority of basic needs: by which I mean that educational sub-issues and activity in the area of the politics of education were regarded as less important than the satisfaction of basic human needs. Examples of findings to support this claim are numerous. The tendency of voters to reject public spending cuts and favour social need rather than market principles is indicated in Chapter 6 (dual state thesis, 6.2.2) and in the finding that most favoured student grants rather than loans (7.10.2). This tendency is also indicated by Crewe's findings that beliefs about personal prosperity outweighed attitudes towards the most salient position issues in the 1987 General Election (8.2.3). The continual predominance of the National Health Service over education in individual issue agendas (4.1) also suggests that basic human survival took priority. Thus, basic human needs cannot be defined as simply economic but as all needs relating to survival.

Perhaps the strongest support for claims of the priority of basic needs was found when activity was considered. Conservative governments have promoted acquisitive attitudes but not a genuinely participatory political culture (9.2). Although it is not the only cause of low levels of activity, preoccupation with basic human needs depresses activity in the politics of education (9.7), the most active being predominantly affluent, middle class, highly educated individuals. It is also claimed that they are predominantly male, although in this respect definitions of 'political' activity should be considered. A contradiction may be found between the greater interest in education expressed by women and their relatively low level of activity in the politics of education. If the claim that the less the welfare state does the more women are obliged to do is correct (4.3), the rolling back of state services could result in a radicalization of women as the pressure of experience exceeds the pull of tradition. Yet, at the same time, a preoccupation with basic needs could depress their activity. This could be compared with the radicalization of teachers since 1983 as the demands of their jobs increased (9.7). Teacher activity may nevertheless be constrained by the preoccupation of teachers with their basic needs (as their relative income has fallen) and heavy workload.

More research is needed into the variety of educational activities that could or could not be defined as 'political'. The only relevant primary research carried out in this instance into activity in the politics of education was a study of the election of parent governors in nine schools (9.6). It is clear that research into other areas of activity should be carried out before generalizations can be made about the effects of domestic constraints on women's activity.

It can also, of course, be claimed that education may be accepted as a means of satisfying basic human needs via the improvement of job opportunities and may thus be perceived as having a higher priority than is suggested here. However, most of the case study informants were not personally consuming education and some spoke of the period of compulsory education as an 'educational age', the implication being that after school-leaving age their 'education' was over. Basic needs such as health and wealth generally took priority over personal development through the education system.

10.2.4 Mixed or contradictory attitudes

Theories regarding tradition and experience may therefore be used to explain majority support or lack of support for Conservative policies on individual sub-issues, but what about the sub-issues on which there are the most mixed or contradictory views? Some of these sub-issues are listed on Table 8.1. Here it can be seen that when the pull of tradition and the pressure of experience were missing, attitudes towards an individual sub-issue were most likely to be mixed or contradictory. Findings about mixed or contradictory attitudes can therefore be (at least partially) explained by the three factors considered above. For example, few informants had any personal experience of nursery provision or universities (and experiences in Torytown differed from those in Labourville, 8.5). Neither one is a part of compulsory education, nurseries are not long-established institutions, and therefore lack the association with tradition, and spending on universities could be classified as a borderline supported sub-issue. Mixed or contradictory attitudes towards the other sub-issues in this category almost certainly relate to lack of knowledge.

The common and most distinguishing feature of these sub-issues is their lack of stability. They were, to a certain extent, a moving target that could not be clearly defined even by those case study informants with recent experience of the education system. Few informants could, for example, estimate what teachers' pay was and knowledge about the National Curriculum and testing at 7, 11 and 14 was minimal (7.4): the National Curriculum and associated tests had not, in any case been clearly defined at the time of the interviews. Limited knowledge about a sub-issue could therefore result in traditional attitudes when it had the attractive cloak of tradition and legitimacy but could result in confusion when the sub-issue was so new or unstable that respondents could not even associate it with traditional values.

10.2.5 Summary of findings and theories

Caution regarding the presentation of theories has resulted in the identification of three loosely defined theoretical areas, each representing a type of influence on the formulation of attitudes. The image is of an individual voter being pushed and pulled in different directions, attitudes at any moment in time depending on the force of each area of influence.

Although the pull of tradition suggests continuity, the push of changing experiences can prevent attitudes from remaining static, and the priority of basic needs can persuade many voters that education is less important than other political issues. A combination of the pull of tradition and the priority of basic needs can result in a lack of interest in education and suggest that education is not a political issue. Yet, the importance of education as a political issue was continually reaffirmed when informants' educational experiences of parental choice were analyzed (7.9.5). The implications of education policies will be considered further when some of the differences between Conservative rhetoric and policy outcomes are outlined (10.4), with particular reference to parental choice and child welfare.

10.3 From theories to observation: future research

Findings from this research have implications both for future research into education as a political issue and research into other political issues (an obvious possibility being the National Health Service). It is, for example, clear that attitudes to one political issue can only be analyzed in depth if that issue is split into several sub-issues and the coherence of attitudes to sub-issues is considered.

One theory worth investigating further (in education and other political issues) is that the strength of the issue motive is related to the coherence of attitudes to sub-issues (8.4.1). Alternatively, the strength of an individual's attitude to one sub-issue may be more influential than conflicting or contradictory attitudes to other sub-issues. A more concentrated analysis of attitudes at an individual level as well as an aggregate level is therefore needed. In this way an individual's attitudes to a large number of sub-issues could be assessed and categorized as dominant, subordinate or radical (although other, more appropriate categories could emerge from the data). Similarly, the attitudes of individuals could be analyzed with the intention of assessing the relative pull of tradition, pressure of experience and priority of basic needs. The interview schedules administered to the 52 case study informants have, in this sense, not been fully exploited.

The available longitudinal data has been relatively neglected (although the reasons for this have been explained, 2.1) and this offers opportunities for further analysis. Valuable data has been recorded for each of the fifty-two case study informants over a period of eight years during the 1980s. This means that the influence of life-cycle and educational experiences on attitudes could be explored more fully (2.1). Family educational histories could be traced to assess social mobility and the effects of changes in the education system. Data is, for example, available about the education of informants' parents (see 7.2.3).

The influence of topical national and local events on attitudes could also be examined, particularly with a view to examining changes in the relative influences of the pull of tradition, the pressure of personal experience and the priority of basic needs. Was the pull of tradition weaker during the 1960s era of 'progressive' education than during the 1980s? Lack of the necessary quantitative data from the 1960s (1.1) makes such a comparison impossible, but the mass of data collected during the 1980s means that a comparative analysis of attitudes during the 1980s and the 1990s will be possible in ten years time.

Theories about the relationship between personal 'troubles' and public issues (4.1 and 9.8 in particular) have already been explored by many social scientists but more research could be carried out within the present context. Details about the socio-economic background of informants, collected during the case study interviews, have not been analyzed in depth and could be studied as possible independent variables affecting levels of political/educational activity. This activity could also be studied further as it is important that all potential outlets for activity in the politics of education should be considered. It is possible, for example, that women are labelled as less active than men, when they are active, but in outlets that have been ignored or wrongly labelled as non-political (see Edgell and Duke, 1983).

The following debate about consumer sovereignty also demands further research. One approach would involve an investigation of how parents in different income groups and localities manage the financial expenses incurred as part of their children's schooling.

In general, it is also hoped that future research will examine the assumptions on which government education policies are based. Only a few of the most obvious research possibilities have been mentioned in this section but many more have been indicated throughout the book.

10.4 Conflict between Conservative rhetoric and policy outcomes

It has been argued that the governments of the 1980s tended to define education out of the political arena, presenting radical changes to the education system as technical, rational and non-political (Chapters 1 and 5, 10.1). The evidence that education is a contentious political issue is, however, overwhelming.

When the market-orientated principles espoused by Conservative governments are considered it is possible to see a particularly clear indication of how contentious and political their education policies are. Throughout the 1980s governments promoted an educational rhetoric that closely corresponded with monetarist economic policies. Market-orientated principles had precedence over social need (dual state thesis, 6.2.2) even though voters tended to favour social need over market principles (6.4, 7.10.2). There was, therefore, a rift between public opinion and government policy regarding educational spending; which challenges the claim that public opinion was easily 'manipulated' by the Government. However, most voters also favoured the continued existence of private education and reproduced the rhetoric of 'choice' even when the option of a private education has not been available to them personally (7.9.5).

10.4.1 Parental choice and consumer sovereignty

A lack of consistency between attitudes to parental choice and attitudes to the cuts in educational spending associated with market-orientated education policies, suggests that political policies in this area should be studied further. Both aspects of the debate can be considered if, adopting the rhetoric of monetarism and the New Right, the concept of consumer sovereignty is applied to education. This concept tends to epitomize many Conservative education policies and it rests on assumptions about the nature of the consumer that have been challenged in this research. It also indicates that education policy decisions have far-reaching social consequences.

As the government-sponsored market place analogy is now commonplace it is important that the implications of its application to education be discussed. Can the provision of education be effectively operated by a system that emphasizes economic concepts such as supply and demand and consumer sovereignty? The emphasis in the market place analogy is on consumer sovereignty and the operation of market forces. If we apply this analogy to education we can see that ideally consumers make choices between competing producers; level of demand in effect determining which schools should or should not survive. The producers (schools) compete by aiming to provide an education of a quality and price that maximize demand. Market forces should therefore operate to satisfy the consumer by increasing choice between schools and control over the type of education produced (through demand). However, three problems can be immediately identified. What are the producer's motives? Who are the consumers? How does the consumer secure redress against the purchase of faulty 'goods'?

First, in any market system, the profit motive has to override any welfare motive in order to ensure the continued existence of the producer. Businesses can only survive in the long term when revenue is in excess of costs. Producers of education may aim to secure a profit by charging low prices to increase demand or by charging high prices for what is regarded as a luxury item. Thus, low price education can be provided for a large proportion of pupils. In order to maximize profits at a lower selling price, savings must be made by, for example, providing cheap facilities and paying low wages to staff. Education sold at a higher price to a smaller number of consumers would have all the hallmarks of a luxury service, including superior facilities and well-paid staff. The government could intervene (as it does in the sale of any other item) by introducing regulations to protect the consumer and maintain a minimum standard. However, excessive intervention would conflict with the ideal of the free operation of market forces. An essential element of the market system is that standards will vary and that some

257

consumers will purchase low price goods that are inferior to their high price counterparts.

The market system also suggests that in some cases, the product will simply not be available or that some consumers will not be able to afford it. This happened during the 1980s; for example, in the London borough of Tower Hamlets, a shortage of teachers meant that many children of statutory age were not found a school place until very late in the academic year (1889-90, [1]). As cut-backs in educational spending reduced teachers' pay, teachers could not afford to live in areas where housing was particularly expensive. Many teachers in other areas also left the profession, those remaining being left to manage a growing work-load (mainly as a result of changes introduced by the 1988 Education Reform Act) and loss of status (7.3.3).

Another characteristic of the market system is the gradual concentration of ownership into the hands of relatively few producers. It is therefore possible to envisage an educational equivalent of Unilever, providing a wide range of educational products and utilizing economies of scale whilst unfettered by democratic processes.

The second immediate problem faced by the application of monetarist theories to education lies in the identity of the consumer. Within the Conservative framework of educational debate parents tend to be labelled as the consumers of education and children's needs are perceived as represented by the effective demands of their parents (5.4, Mrs Thatcher's speech 1987). Recent arguments about educational choice almost invariably centre on parental choice.

> Schools should be owned by individual trusts. Their survival should depend on their ability to satisfy their consumers. And their principal consumers are parents, who should therefore be free to place their custom where they wish, in order that educational institutions should be shaped, controlled and nourished by their demand. (The Hillgate Group, 1986, p.7)

A leading member of the Hillgate group was Baroness Cox, a former contributor to the Black Papers (1.3) and more recently Conservative education spokeswoman in the House of Lords. Although they claimed that governments had not introduced the policies they favoured quickly enough, the views of Hillgate Group members cannot be disassociated from those of Conservative governments. Despite their habitual use of market terminology, the Hillgate Group claimed that they were not in favour of a market system, and the following extract seems to directly contradict the above quotation.

258

We accept that education cannot be treated as a market, and that 'consumer sovereignty' does not necessarily guarantee that values will be preserved. (The Hillgate Group, 1986, p.8)

In the present context the significance of this pamphlet lies in their answer to the question 'Whose Schools?'. According to the writers of this 'Radical Manifesto' the answer is quite obviously the parents - not the children. In the market place analogy, parents would be the purchasers of education, and they are apparently seen as the consumers, as their purchasing power would be found represented on hypothetical demand curves. We are here faced with a problem as old as economics itself; demand represents willingness and ability to pay a certain price for an item, it does not represent need for that item.

Demand for education in a free market system would represent parents' assessments of their children's needs, and choice from the range of goods (schools) available. The real consumers (children) would be dependent upon the actions of the apparent consumers (their parents). It is therefore possible to identify three fundamental problems. First, assessment of the child's needs is unlikely to be accurate. Few parents can be objective and they can easily underrate or overrate ability, or overlook some needs entirely. Second, decisions about what price parents will pay relate to income and thus reduce or expand the range from which educational choices can be made (for example, parents without a car are most likely to choose the nearest school). Third, choice from the range of schools available can be based on limited or misleading information.

Problems relating to choice of school also emerged during analysis of the local political and educational context in Torytown and Labourville (3.2). Both authorities allocated children according to school catchment areas, priority being given to those children living nearest to a school or with a sibling at that school. This means that many parents had no choice and that, even if it was practically possible for a child to attend a school in another area (if, for example, the family could move house or the pupil could manage the extra travelling involved), the child might only get a place once the children in the new catchment area had been accommodated. Thus, the identification of catchment areas limits choice. However, if there were no catchment areas and an entirely open market for school places, children might have to travel long distances to school because the (closer) school of their choice was full.

The bipartite system of secondary education also raises a major problem. It has already been noted that the concept of consumer sovereignty would not be compatible with selection at 11+. Torytown parents cannot choose to send children who fail the 11+ to a grammar school and few would choose to send their children to a secondary modern school. The Torytown LEA decides which school most children will go to; although some parents with money or an Assisted Place will choose to send their children to a private school and a few others will send their children to comprehensive schools outside the area. Parents' knowledge about what schools are available is therefore important and my findings indicate that few have a substantial grounding on which to base such knowledge (5.5). Few case study informants had heard of the Assisted Places Scheme and many regarded private education as being a privilege bestowed on the few from which their own children were naturally excluded. Some did not know what type of school their children went to; a finding that is likely to become more common if types of schools become more varied.

Some further research into how parents choose particular schools also tends to challenge the ideal of consumer sovereignty. Differences in legislation meant that during the 1980s parents in Scotland already had greater freedom in choosing a school than did parents in England and Wales. Adler, Petch and Tweedie (1989) carried out an exhaustive study (including a survey and various other methods) of Scottish parents and the impact of legislation that was intended to promote parental 'choice'. They found that parents often chose schools on the basis of vague impressions and that it would be wrong to assume that most of them compare brochures or examination results. The study found, moreover that, especially at primary level, parents were more concerned with the school's distance from home and how 'rough' the pupils were than with class size and educational standards.

A third problem in the application of consumer sovereignty to education relates to the consumer's redress against the purchase of faulty goods. The purchase of faulty goods is often not immediately obvious but a guarantee can prove useful. No guarantee can be given on the purchase of an education, although the implications of an ineffective (faulty) education are far more significant than in the case of most goods. It is particularly difficult to assess educational standards (7.2.1) and a school could continue to provide an inadequate education for years, whilst maintaining a favourable public image. Not only would children from poor homes be likely to suffer from the application of market forces to education but parents with high incomes (which would, in theory result in more choice) might choose for their children an education that is expensive but totally unsuitable. Without emphasis on the requirements of the real consumer, the purchase of education could prove infinitely more distressing than that of on ill-fitting shoe or an unwanted gift. Assessment of 'real' needs is a long term process involving parents, teachers and other professionals but based upon a child's abilities, needs and desires. New assessment techniques continue to appear (for example, testing at 7, 11 and 14), but when parental choice, applied via market forces is given priority, the actual needs of the child can be overlooked.

The application of the concept of consumer sovereignty is therefore problematic when we consider the motives of the producer, the identity of the consumer and the possibility of a 'faulty' or inadequate education. It is also problematic when the more general nature of market forces is considered. For example, in further and higher education, consumers do not simply respond to market forces by selecting courses that will provide them with the best job prospects. Science and technology courses may be under-subscribed as a result of the 'academic drift' that leads many students to take a course out of interest (History and Sociology for example) rather than perceived vocational relevance. If education is only valued for its contribution in terms of human capital, its contribution to critical awareness is devalued and it is simply training the worker rather than developing the person.

Accountability in the form of consumer sovereignty is therefore accountability to the few who have the knowledge and ability to manage the system to their children's benefit. It is not a particularly new or original idea, but one that, like many of the present government's economic ideals, dates back at least as far as the nineteenth century. Kogan noted this when he referred to the nineteenth century system of payment by results and quoted Bishop's description of Lingen, who was the Department of Education's Permanent Secretary in 1862:

> . . . he did not regard the education of the poorer classes as a challenge, a noble cause or a moral imperative. He thought of it more in terms of the correctly-balanced ledger, the neatly-filled form and inerrant rule-book. He reduced it to a mere commercial undertaking, conducted in accordance with closely-prescribed legalist formulae. (Kogan, 1986, p.19)

The application of consumer sovereignty (or parental choice as defined by the present government) to education is thus inextricably bound up with the welfare of the many who will not profit by the related policies. Many children will suffer if parents are labelled as consumers, because a child's needs cannot be defined in terms of supply and demand.

10.4.2 The self-sufficient family and child welfare

The reduced emphasis on children's needs (rather than parents' wishes) is shown again in the available statistics on child welfare. Several reports reveal that the general welfare of children was not regarded as a priority during the 1980s. They also indicate that it is naive to presume that all parents can secure for their children the best possible start in life; whether in education or regarding general social welfare (7.9.5). Discovered cases of neglect, physical and mental cruelty and the sexual abuse by parents of their children make it clear that many parents are not willing or able to raise their children in a healthy and wholesome environment. Statistics regarding levels of poverty in Britain indicate that many devoted parents are (despite their own efforts) unable to provide for their children anything more than a very basic existence; thus books, school trips and other peripheral educational expenses are beyond their reach.

Conservative 'cut-backs' on educational spending during the 1980s (6.1, including restrictions on LEA spending and the removal of the LEAs' obligation to provide free school meals and milk), when combined with the introduction of the Assisted Places Scheme and efforts to obtain funding from private sources (e.g. for City Technology Colleges), reflect a policy of withdrawing from previous governments' commitments to a state education system (10.4.3). In order to pursue this course it has to assume that all parents will be able to carry out the functions that the state previously performed. It is hoped that families will assume more of the functions previously performed by the state, but research indicates that many families are unable to do this.

Several reports, published during the 1980s, highlighted the deprivation experienced within many households with children. In 1987, for example, reports published by the National Childrens Bureau, the British Medical Association and the Child Poverty Action Group all described the poverty experienced by many children.

The NCB report (1987) looked at developments since the publication of the Court Committee report ten years previously. It concluded that children's needs had not been given the priority over the last ten years that they had previously. Although it noted improvements in the health of many children, it also noted a large number of negative trends and administrative problems. The proportion of children living in poverty had increased, many more lived in families that were classified as homeless, more had unemployed parents and more were likely to experience the divorce or separation of parents. HMI and parents also recorded the physical deterioration of schools and there was a prolonged disruption of school activities as a result of action by teachers' unions. Finally, the Court Committee's main recommendation was not implemented. This was for integrated services to facilitate the capacities of parents to care for their children, with prevention as the main thrust and close links between the preventative and curative elements.

The BMA report (1987) produced a mass of evidence showing how deprivation generated by unemployment and low pay caused sickness and premature death. Wives of unemployed men were found to have higher death rates than those married to wage earners, their babies also suffered higher death rates, their children were shorter and young unemployed people were more likely to use drugs. Its findings were, moreover, directly related to education as it noted that:

> Young people are held back from achieving their future physical and mental potential by the debilitating effects of unhealthy environment, lack of emotional support or intellectual stimulation. (BMA, 1987)

The experiences described by informants (7.9.5) cannot, therefore, be simply dismissed as irrelevant because they were in the past.

The CPAG report (1987) also showed that, during the period 1979 to 1985, the top 20 per cent of wage-earners saw their real salaries increase by 22 per cent. Families with real incomes in the bottom ten per cent suffered a cut of nearly ten per cent and families with children experienced an even greater cut of between 15 per cent and 27 per cent. The number of children taking free school meals rose from 12 per cent to 18 per cent during that time and, as local authorities were freed from their obligation to provide free school meals or milk (6.1), many more schoolchildren were likely to suffer.

During the 1980s, the Central Statistical Office's 'Social Trends' provided yearly reports that consistently highlighted the increasing problem of homelessness and the relative deprivation of a growing number of single-parent families. Furthermore, the 'freezing' of Child Benefit provided a further indication of the Government's policy of leaving child welfare to the vagaries of a market system in which families compete on unequal terms. Alan Walker, the CPAG report's (1987) editor, concluded that:

> The government views inequality as being helpful to incentives at both ends of the income distribution and does not regard gross inequalities in income and wealth as a problem. (CPAG, 1987)

These gross inequalities are a problem in any case, but they are of particular significance regarding the application of 'market forces' to education. If Conservatives assume that no children will be at a disadvantage as a result of their increasing dependence on family support, they are obviously wrong. Yet such families are in many cases prevented from taking political action in response to their situation by the priority of basic needs and the sheer weight of their 'troubles' (9.8).

10.4.3 Rolling the state backwards or forwards?

The gradual withdrawal of recent governments from a commitment to the provision of welfare services suggests that they have been pursuing the policy, advocated by the New Right, of 'rolling back the state'; but the evidence regarding education does not support a simple move in that direction. Central government has actually strengthened its control of the state education system by, for example, increasing its control over educational spending, introducing the National Curriculum and removing teachers' negotiating rights. Educational accountability is, moreover, largely assigned to the government by a mixture of such direct controls, its tendency to influence rather than be influenced (9.2) and the frailty of parental choice.

Rather than reducing a large educational bureaucracy, governments have tended to increase their commitments. The National Curriculum has increased the administrative workload in schools and in the DES. City Technology Colleges and student loans, which were originally intended to be relatively independent of central government control, have now become major spending commitments. Assisted Places too are administered by a large bureaucracy.

Thus, the most noticeable effect of government policies during the 1980s has been a rolling back of the local state rather than a rolling back of central government control. The effect of Conservative policies on both local and central levels has been to make the administration of education more complex rather than more streamlined. If educational provision in Torytown and Labourville are compared it is noticeable that more demands are placed on the management apparatus in Torytown as a result of selection at 11+. The effect of Conservative education policies is therefore a rolling forward of the state in terms of educational management but a rolling back of the state in terms of its rejection of responsibility for the welfare of pupils and students.

10.5 The framework of educational debate

At the beginning of this book I asked if it was possible to explain how the framework of educational debate is defined and has changed over time. I also asked if the framework was defined by the voters, politicians or both. A simple answer cannot be given in either case, but I have argued that governments dominate debate by trying to define reality according to their own value systems and associated policies. During the 1980s they did this with some success; so much so that many informants accepted government-sponsored definitions of reality even when they contradict their personal experiences and interests. However, education as a singular issue has been shown to consist of a wide range of sub-issues and voters' attitudes to those sub-issues may not follow a cohesive pattern in which they can either be seen to accept or reject government education policies. It is that very lack of cohesion and consensus that can be manipulated, or even created in the first place, by the government of the day.

This leaves an inevitable question regarding the extent to which the existing framework of debate can be challenged and either adapted or replaced. That question is considered next.

10.5.1 Changing the dominant framework of debate

Cultural reproduction has been analyzed by many writers, including Bourdieu, Bowles and Gintis, Young and Althusser. It seems to be almost inevitable that governments will try to retain and entrench their power base by defining reality and trying to reproduce such definitions through the education system. However, such a tendency is not peculiar to governments in capitalist states. The tendency of governments to impose their own ideology via the education system is no less pronounced in communist countries. A Marxist critique, based on economic determinism also has obvious limitations in states where the main feature of power relationships and the dominant ideology is religion or race. Cultural reproduction is therefore a concept that can have relevance, not just in Britain, but in states throughout the world. It does not, however, operate smoothly.

Some individuals or groups will challenge the dominant ideology even when the state apparently has a firm power base and the chances of success are minimal. The British electoral system has defects (9.3) but it does provide an opportunity for a peaceful change of government that is not shared by many other states. Nevertheless, the framework of educational debate can be retained, relatively unchanged or in an adapted form, by successive governments, as in the case of the retention of the economic utility model introduced by the Callaghan Government (1.3). The Conservative governments of the 1980s introduced many radical changes in education that were not supported by the Labour Party, but have retained a basic economic theme that was established during the 1970s.

It has also been shown that the most highly educated respondents were most likely to be educational radicals (8.4); the education system that reproduces the dominant culture also producing some of its strongest critics. In many states the intelligentsia form the most voluble group of political radicals. Sometimes reaction against wider social conditions may be dominated by other groups (such as trade unionists) but reaction against the dominant framework of educational debate tends to come from its main consumers, those who have been in education the longest. The government may therefore believe that its own interests are best served if it labels students and teachers as subversive, even if the majority are relatively inactive (9.4 and 9.7).

10.5.2 Scientific culture and educational enlightenment

Why are the most highly educated likely to pose the greatest challenge to any normative educational paradigm whilst the less well educated tend to accept education as a natural, non-political phenomenon? Contact with education has already been shown to influence educational radicalism, not only amongst the highly educated but also in those households where education is currently being consumed. It may not therefore simply be a matter of academic achievement but of instrumental motives (Chapter 4). Activity in the educational arena is also related to educational experience, feelings of political competence, and the lack of personal 'troubles' that might otherwise hamper activity (9.8 and 10.2.3). Some 'troubles' may, however, in the case of education consumers (pupils, students, parents and households) be directly related to education and thus more likely to foster a critical awareness of social injustice.

> Education has also been seen as a means to social emancipation. It is through education that socialists and feminists, for instance, have come to know their everyday unhappinesses aren't the fault of personal inadequacies but are common experiences, shared by others, and produced by particular social arrangements. (Johnson, 1983, p.20)

Hence the long and tortuous path towards the extension of access to education for underprivileged groups. Access to education tends to heighten awareness not only of the contentious nature of educational policies but also of wider issues.

Thus, when Broadfoot wrote about '...this scientific culture that we seek to teach our students...' (5.3) she was not only describing a conflict between the methods of the social scientist and the 'commercial culture', but was also referring to a problem that the physical sciences encountered and tackled centuries ago. Attempts to liberate the scientific culture from the restrictions imposed by powerful individuals and groups have, for centuries, been met by the opposition of those vested interests. Parallels can be drawn between the physical sciences and the social sciences, as we can see that, at the time of the European Enlightenment, powerful elites defended the Aristotelian paradigm because it supported the status quo. Scientific discoveries (including the astronomy of Copernicus, Kepler and Galileo) were regarded as a threat to the established order and were in some cases put down by force. The establishment of the physical sciences as (what is now commonly perceived to be) a disinterested attempt to advance both knowledge and the quality of life, was therefore a major achievement. Although some contentious issues (such as embryology) exist in the physical sciences they have acquired the sort of public respect that social scientists still strive for. The scientific culture of the social sciences is still regarded as a threat by those who have a vested interest in maintaining the established order. Hence, governments try to control public access to critical knowledge, preferring to emphasize instead the scientific and technical knowledge that was in the past regarded as subversive.

In Britain, the (traditional, 10.2.1) framework of educational debate provides a defensive barrier to support extremes of social inequality by presenting them as natural phenomena, and therefore inevitable. Self-interest and a competitive value system, in which many of the participants are socially handicapped, are defined as rational by those who are not similarly handicapped. Thus, although social scientists have for many years studied, described and clarified the social problems that generate differential educational opportunities, little progress can be made when such findings are dismissed by policy-makers.

Notes

1. The Times Educational Supplement has provided regular reports about the lack of school places during the 1989/90 academic year. A TES report on the 12 January 1990 cited ILEA figures as stating that 346 children of statutory age and 87 rising fives (normally admitted by the authority) still had no school place. The same issue of the TES also reported that two court cases were being processed on behalf of parents who were claiming that the ILEA was in breach of its statutory duties under the 1944 Education Act.

Appendix
Interview schedule

(NOTE: Some spaces for answers have been deleted.)

Area of interview; Labourville 1
                    Torytown 2

Respondent number;

Theoretical type; Public/ Private/ Not emp
                    Parent/ Non-parent
                    Had FE/ No FE Male / Female

Number of calls;

Date of interview;

Length of interview;

Interview circumstances/general comments;

INTRODUCTORY COMMENTS-

This is a new piece of research based at Salford University.
If applicable - You are one of many people who took part in the earlier study who have again been chosen at random for this new study. Again your answers will be treated confidentially.
Although many questions relate to education, information regarding a large range of subjects is needed. Some questions can be answered briefly. Some will require more time. I would be grateful if you would make your answers as full as possible.

FIRST A FEW GENERAL QUESTIONS AND QUESTIONS ABOUT POLITICS

Q1   a) Have you always lived in this area of [Labourville/ Torytown]?
G   IF NOT-

    b) (PI,Q1) How long have you lived in this part of Labourville
Torytown?

    c) Why did you come to live in this particular area?

Q2   (PI, Q33)
ACT   a) Are you a member of any organizations or clubs?

    IF YES-
    b) What are they?

Q3   (PI,Q24)
ACT   a) Do you think that people like yourself can influence what the
government does?

    IF YES-
    b) How?

    IF NO/MIXED/DK-
    c) Why/Explain

Q4   (PII, Q31 adapted)
ACT   a) Have you taken part in any activity in response to local or central
government policy?
                            Local
                            Central
    IF YES-
    b) What did you do?

    c) What effect (if any) did your action have?

Q5 (PI, Q35c)
ACT a)Have you ever been active on behalf of any political group?

IF YES-
b) Which group?

c) What sort of things did you do?

d) Are you still active on behalf of that group?

Q6 (PI,Q34b @ 79 election/PII,Q36a @ 83 election)
P a) Did you happen to vote in the general election last year?

IF YES-
b) Which party?

IF YES Or NO-
c) Why did you vote for that particular party/not vote?

d) Which was/were the most important reason/s?

LIST IN ORDER

Q7 (PI,Q34c @ May 80 election/PII,36b @ May 83 election)
P a) Did you vote in the local election in May?

IF YES-
b) Which party?

IF YES or NO-
c) Why did you vote for that particular party/not vote?

d) Which was/were the most important reason/s?

LIST IN ORDER

Q8 a) Did any issue or issues seem to be more important
P   than others in the recent local election?

IF YES-
b) What was it/ were they?

c) Why do you think they were more important?

Q9 (PI,Q34d)
P   a) How would you vote if there were a general election tomorrow?

b) Why?

Q10 (PII, Q36e)
P   Now I want to ask you about some parties you don't support. Would
    you say you are very strongly against, somewhat against or not really
    against . . .

	very strongly against	some- what against	not really against	DK
a) the Conservative Party	1	2	3	9
b) the Labour Party	1	2	3	9
c) the Social and Liberal Democratic Party (D.Steele)	1	2	3	9
d) the Social Democratic Party (D.Owen)	1	2	3	9

Q11 (PI, Q15 adapted)
AT The government collects taxes to pay for a variety of services. Would
    you like to see more or less spent on the following?
    SHOW CARD A

a) Defence
b) Health
c) Education (Ed Rad Scale)
d) Help for industry
e) Social benefits
f) The police force
g) Housing

Q12   (BSA84 Q50 adapted & 85)
AT   Which should have the highest priority for government spending, and
        which next?

SHOW CARD A

a) Defence
b) Health
c) Education
d) Help for industry
e) Social benefits
f) The police force
g) Housing

Q13   a)How much interest do you have in discussions about the
AT   following subjects?

SHOW CARD B

a) Housing
b) The police force
c) Social benefits
d) Unemployment
e) Help for industry
f) Education
g) Income tax
h) Defence
i) The rates/poll tax
j) Health

b)Which are you most interested in, which next, and so on?

1   2

3   4

5   6

7   8

9   10

Q14   (PII, Q24a & b - see also BSA85, Q84 for these questions)
EAT   Would you be prepared to pay more in taxes or rates so as to increase
        government spending on the following?

        a) nursery facilities

        b) schools

        c) colleges

        d) universities

        e) youth employment/job training schemes

Q15   (BSA84, Q68/BSA85, Q72)
EAT   Which of these three types of families do you think get the best value
        from their taxes out of government spending on education?

        High income
        Middle income
        Low income

NOW SOME QUESTIONS ABOUT YOUR EXPERIENCES
REGARDING EDUCATION

Q16   (PI, Q9a)
E   a) Do you or does your household have any children of pre-school age?

        IF YES-

        b) how many & what age(s)?

        c) do they attend play group/nursery?

        IF NO- go to g)

        IF YES-
        d) Is it provided by the local authority or a private person or
        organization?

e) How many hours (per week) do they attend?

f) How satisfied are you (and your child/ren) with that play group/nursery?

g) Would you like your child/ren to attend a playgroup/nursery?

Q17   (PI, Q7a/ PII,Q7)
E   Do you or does your household have any children at school?

IF YES
a) how many & what age(s)?

b) at what kind of school?

PROBE for type (eg.   private/state/infant/junior/sec   mod/ grammar/comp/single sex)

PROBE for experience (eg. took-didn't take 11+/moves through & types of streams)

PROBE for extra-curricula activities (eg. music, holidays, swimming)

c) Did you have a choice of schools?

IF YES
Was this your first choice etc.?

d) How satisfied are you and your children with that school?

e) How much contact do you have with the school?

PROBE for type of contact & frequency.

f) How would you describe your relationship with the teachers?

Q18   (PI, Q8a)

E   a) Do you or does your household have any children at college or
university?

   IF YES
   b) how many?

   c) at what kind of coll/univ?

   d) what course?

   e) how satisfied does he/she/they seem to be with coll/univ?

Q19   (PII, Q7)

E   a) How likely is it that your household will send any children to a
private school (ie. outside the state system)?

very likely	1
quite likely	2
not likely	3
definately not	4
already do	5
DK	9

   b) Why is that?

NOW SOME QUESTIONS ABOUT YOUR OWN EDUCATION

Q20   (PI, Q30A)
       NEW RESPONDENTS ONLY
G   In what year were you born?

Q21   (PI, Q29b)
E   What kind of school/s did you go to?

Q22   a) Would you rather have gone to a different type of E school?

IF YES-
b) What type?

Q23   a) Would you like your own children to have the same sort
E   of education and teachers that you had?

IF NO-
b) Why not?

Q24   (PI, Q29a)
E   At what age did you leave school?

Q25   Why did you leave at that particular age?

Q26   What qualifications did you leave with?

Q27   (PI, Q29c)
E   a) Have you had any further education since leaving school?

IF YES
b) what was that?

Q28   (PI, Q30b)
G   a) What is your marital status?
IF MARRIED/COHABITING- NOTE IN QUESTION 56

E   b) What sort of education did your spouse/partner have?

PROBE for
c) type of school

d) school leaving age

e) qualifications at SLA

f) further education

Q29   (PII, Q7)
E   a) Is any adult in the household at present taking any full-time or part-time educational course?

IF YES-
b) What?

Q30   a) Have you or anyone in your family/household been
E   affected by government/local authority spending cuts in education?

b) Who?

c) How?

Q31   (PII, Q31 adapted)
ACT   a) Have you taken part in any activity or group or attended any meetings as a result of changes or proposed changes in local education?

IF YES-
b) What did you do?

c)What effect (if any) did your action have?

Q32   What sort of education did your father have?

PROBE for
a) type of school (PI, Q29f)

b) school leaving age

c) qualifications at SLA

d) further education (PI, Q29g)

Q33   What sort of education did your mother have?
E

PROBE for
a) type of school
b) school leaving age

c) qualifications at SLA

d)further education

Q34   (PI, Q27a,b)
EC   What was/is your fathers job?

PROBE for
a) title of job

b) did he supervise or manage anyone else?

c) self employed

d) private or public sector?
(by public sector I mean - for central government, a local authority or a nationalized industry)

Q35   What was/is your mothers job?
EC

PROBE for
a) title of job

b) did she supervise or manage anyone else?

c) self employed

d) private or public sector?
(by public sector I mean - for central government, a local authority or a nationalized industry)

Q36   (PI, Q35b father only)
P   Can you remember which party/ies your parents voted for when you were young?

Q37 Do you think they were strong/moderate or weak
P   supporters?

NOW SOME QUESTIONS ABOUT CURRENT DEBATES THAT
YOU MAY OR MAY NOT HAVE HEARD OF

Q38 (PII, Q1 adapted)
K   Have you heard anything recently about any of these subjects?

ANSWER Q39 AND Q40 FOR EACH IF HEARD

a) Changes or proposed changes in the provision of education in
Labourville/Torytown

b) The Assisted Places Scheme

c) City Technology College

d) The Education Reform Bill (currently passing through Pariament)

EXCLUDE e) and f) IF ANSWERED HERE IN FULL

e) Proposals to let schools opt out of Local Education Authority
control.

f)The proposed abolition of the Inner London Education Authority.

g) Recent events at Burnage High School, in Manchester.

Q39 ANSWER FOR EACH ONE HEARD OF
K   How much interest do you have in discussions about these subjects?

a)

b)

c)

d)

e)

f)

g)

Q40   ANSWER FOR EACH ONE HEARD OF
K   Can you tell me briefly what you know about these subjects?
PROBE for opinions

a)

b)

c)

d)

e)

f)

g)

Q41   (PI, Q16 & PII,Q18 adapted)
AT   I am going to read out a list of things that some people believe a
government should do. For each one say whether you feel it is

SHOW CARD C AND READ OUT

very important the govt should do it	1
fairly important the govt should do it	2
doesn't matter either way	3
fairly important the govt should not do it	4
very important the govt should not do it	5
	D/K

RING ONE CODE FOR EACH

EAT   a) establish comprehensive schools in place of grammar and secondary modern schools throughout the country (Egal Rad Scale and Ed Rad Scale)

1 2 3 4 5 6

Why?

EAT   b) introduce a national curriculum in schools (covering 70% of the subjects studied).

1 2 3 4 5 6 9

Why?

If not 70%, what percentage?

Interviewer explanations;

AT   c) redistribute income and wealth in favour of ordinary working people. (Egal Rad Scale)

1 2 3 4 5 6 9

Why?

AT   d) give workers more say in the running of the place where they work. (Egal Rad Scale)

1 2 3 4 5 6 9

Why?

EAT   e) introduce a national system for the testing of children at 7, 11 and 14.

1 2 3 4 5 6 9

Why?

Interviewer explanations;

EAT   f) abolish the private schools which are outside the state education system? (Ed Rad Scale)

1 2 3 4 5 6 9

Why?

EAT   g) abolish single-sex schools.

1 2 3 4 5 6 9

Why?

h) allow teachers to present a favourable view of homosexuality.

1 2 3 4 5 6 9

Why?

Interviewer explanations;

i) replace student grants with a system of loans (to be repaid after the student qualifies).

1 2 3 4 5 6 9

Why?

Interviewer explanations;

Q42   (BSA85 Q70 & 86 Q87)
EAT   Which provides the best all-round education for secondary school children;

Grammar and secondary modern schools
or
Comprehensive schools

Q43   (BSA84 Q67b/BSA85 Q71b/BSA86 QQ89b)
EAT   If there were fewer private or independent schools, would state schools benefit, suffer or would it make no difference?

Q44   (BSA86 Q215 adapted)
EAT   Concerning the importance of teaching particular topics to 15 year olds.

What subjects do you think are most important?

Which of the following do you think are essential/ which are fairly important/ and which (if any) do you think need not be taught?

SHOW CARD D
a) Reading,writing and maths
b) Sex education
c) Respect for authority
d) History, literature and the arts
e) Ability to make one's own judgements
f) Job training
g) Politics, sociology and other social studies
h) Science & technology
i) Concern for minorities and the poor
j) Discipline and orderliness
k) Any other subjects?

Q45   (BSA85 Q69/BSA86 Q86 adapted)
EAT   How much of what is taught in schools should be up to

individual schools
the Local Education Authority
central government?

Q46   Do you agree, disagree or have no views on the following statements?

SHOW CARD E

		agree	disagree	DK
AT	a) Benefits for the unemployed are too low and cause hardship. (BSA83/BSA85)	1	2	9
AT	b) The welfare state makes people nowadays less willing to look after themselves. (BSA83/BSA85)	1	2	9
EAT	c) Biological differences between the sexes are largely responsible for the different subject and career choices of boys and girls.	1	2	9
EAT	d) The educational system treats girls less favourably than boys.	1	2	9

Q47   (BSA84 Q69 /BSA85 Q69)
EAT   a) How do you think the overall standards of education in schools today compares with the standards when you were at school?

PROBE for
b) higher/lower/about the same.

c) what respondent means by standards.

Q48   a) How do you think the standard of teaching in schools
EAT   compares today with the teaching during your school days?

PROBE for
b)higher/lower/about the same.

c)why respondent thinks so.

Q49 a) Generally speaking, do you think that teachers are
EAT underpaid/overpaid/ or is their pay about right?

b) Why?

Q50 Which do you think is the most important influence on
EAT how well we do at school - abilities that we are born
with or our experiences since birth?

Q51 (BSA84, Q76a & b adapted)
AT   a) Are you aware of social class differences in Britain?

IF YES
b) To what extent does social class affect opportunities?

Q52 (PII, Q5 adapted)
K   Where do you get most of your information about our present system
of education?

Q53 What newspaper/s do you read (national and/or local)?

NOW SOME MORE GENERAL QUESTIONS

Q54 a) Do you have a religion?

IF YES-
b) What is your religion?

Q55 (PI, Q25 & PII, Q37)
EC   a) Do you currently have a job?

IF YES go to b)
IF NO ascertain whether
Retired, housewife, student, unemployed, disabled, etc.

ASK ABOUT PREVIOUS OCCUPATION IF RELEVANT

b) What is/was the name of your job?

c) Please describe exactly what it is that you do/did.

d) Do/did you supervise or manage anyone else at work?

e) Are/were you self-employed?

f) Do/did you work for the private sector or the public sector?
(by public sector I mean - for central government, a local authority or a nationalized industry)

IF PRIVATE.
Have you ever worked in the public sector?

IF PUBLIC. Have you ever worked outside the public sector?

g) Are/were there opportunities for promotion in your line of work?

NAME FIRST OTHER (HERE AND Q64)

Q56   (PI, Q26b & PII,Q37)
EC   a) Does your spouse/partner/the head/joint head of the household have a job?

IF YES go to (b)
IF NO acertain whether
Retired, housewife, student, unemployed etc.

ASK ABOUT PREVIOUS OCCUPATION IF RELEVANT

b) What is/was the name of the first other's job?

c) Please describe exactly what it is/was that the first other does/did.

d) Does/did the first other supervise or manage anyone else at work?

e) Is/was the first other self-employed?

Q57   (PI, Q28 & PII,Q37)
EC   a) Have you or any member of your household been unemployed in the last 4 years or since the last interview?

IF YES-
b) How long were you unemployed?

Q58   (PII, Q14)
EC   Have you or anyone in the household recieved any of the following state benefits in the last 4 years?

SHOW CARD F

a) child benefit (family allowance)
b) one-parent benefit
c) family income supplement
d) state retirement or widow's pension
e) supplementary pension
f) sickness or injury benefit
g) unemployment benefit
h) supplementary benefit
i) income support
j) rate or rent rebate or allowance
k) student grant
l) school uniform/clothing allowance
m) free school meals
n) any other benefit?

Q59   (PI, Q13 & PII,Q15 is similar)
EC   a) Do you or does anyone in your household contribute to a private pension scheme?

IF YES-
b) What scheme?

Q60   (PI, Q10 & PII,Q9 adapted)
EC   a) Are you or anyone else in your household a member of any private
       health scheme, in other words outside the national health service?

       IF YES-
       b) What scheme?

Q61   (PI,Q11) EC
       a) How do you (or first other) travel to work?

       b) Do you or any member of your household own a car (or other
       vehicle)?

       c) Do you or any member of your household have the use of a
       company vehicle?

Q62   (PI, Q3) EC
       a) Do you own this house/flat or is it rented?

       IF RENTED
       b) Is it rented from the council, a housing association, private
       landlord or someone else?

Q63   (PI, Q40a)
EC   Would you indicate which income band you fall into?

       SHOW CARD G

       no answer
       a b c d e f

Q64   (PI, Q40b)
EC   Would you indicate which income band the first other falls into?

       SHOW CARD G

       no answer
       a b c d e f DK

Q65   (PI, Q40c) EC
        Do you have any other sources of income?

        IF YES PROBE

Q66   (BSA84,Q27)
EC   How well would you say you are managing on your income these days;

        very well
        quite well
        not very well
        or not at all well?

Q67   (PII,Q7 & BSA84,Q27)
EC   Compared with 4 years ago would you say you are now;

        better off financially
        about the same
        or worse off financially?

Q68   (BSQ 84,Q27)
EC   Among which group would you place yourself;

        high income
        middle income
        or low income?

        THANKYOU VERY MUCH

        ARE THERE ANY COMMENTS YOU WOULD LIKE TO MAKE
        ON THE SUBJECTS WE'VE BEEN DISCUSSING WHICH YOU
        FEEL YOU HAVEN'T HAD THE CHANCE TO SAY ALREADY?

        WOULD YOU BE PREPARED TO BE INTERVIEWED ON THE
        SAME SUBJECTS AGAIN AT A LATER DATE?

Bibliography

Adler, M., Petch, A. and Tweedie, J. (1989), *Parental Choice and Educational Policy*, Edinburgh University Press

Adorno, T.W., Frenkel-Brunswick, E., Levinson, D.J. and Sanford, R.N. (1950), *The Authoritarian Personality*, New York: Harper and Row

Almond, G. and Verba, S. (1965), *The Civic Culture*, Little, Brown, Boston

Archer, M.S. (1979), *The social origins of educational systems*, London, Sage

Ashford, D. (1974), 'The effects of central finance on the British local government system', *British Journal of Political Science*, 4, 305-22

Bailey, C. (1984), *Beyond the present and the particular: a theory of liberal education*, London, Routledge and Kegan Paul

Ball, S.J. (1990), *Politics and Policy Making in Education*, Routledge.

Bechhoffer, F. (1969), 'Occupations', in Stacey, M. (ed.), *Comparability in Social Research*, London, Heinemann

Beck, J. (1983), 'Accountability, industry and education reflections on some aspects of the educational and industrial policies of the Labour administration of 1974-79', in Ahier,J and Flude, M (eds), *Contemporary Education Policy*, London, Croom Helm

Benn, C. (1983), 'Independence and accountability for all', in Wolpe, A.M. and Donald, J. (eds.), *Is there anyone here from education?*, Pluto Press

Bourdieu, P. (1967), 'Systems of education and systems of thought', in Young, M.F.D, 1971, *Knowledge and Control*, London,: Cassell and Collier

Bourdieu, P. (1971), 'The thinkable and the unthinkable', *The Times Literary Supplement*, 15 October 1971

Bourdieu, P. (1973), 'Cultural reproduction and social reproduction' in Brown, R., Knowledge, *Education and Cultural Change*, London, Tavistock

Bourdieu, P. (1974), 'The school as a conservative force: scholastic and cultural inequalities', in Dale, R., Esland, G. and MacDonald, M., *Schooling and Capitalism*, London: Routledge and Kegan Paul·

Bourdieu, P. and Passeron, J.C. (1977), *Reproduction in Education, Society and Culture*, London: Sage

Bourque, S. and Grossholtz, J. (1984), 'Politics an unnatural practice: political science looks at female participation', Siltanen, J. and Stanworth, M. (eds.), *Women and the Public Sphere: a Critique of Sociology and Politics*, Hutchinson and Co.

Bowles, S. and Gintis, H. (1976), *Schooling in Capitalist Society*, London: Routledge and Kegan Paul

British Medical Association (1987), *Deprivation and Ill Health*, BMA

British Social Attitudes Survey (1983), Social and Commumity Planning Research, London, SPSSx file, Study No.1935, access via the ESRC Data Archive

Broadfoot, P. (1985), 'Changing patterns of educational accountability in England and France', *Comparative Education*, vol 21, no 3.

Broadfoot, P. (1988), 'Educational research: two cultures and three estates', in the *British Educational Research Journal*, vol 14, no 1

Butler, D. and Kavanagh, D. (1984), *The British General Election of 1983*, Macmillan

Butler, D. and Kavanagh, D. (1988), *The British General Election of 1987*, Macmillan

Butler, D. and Stokes, D. (1974), second edition, *Political Change in Britain: the evolution of electoral choice*, Macmillan Press

Campbell, A., Converse, P.E., Miller, W.E. and Stokes, D.E. (1960), *The Changing American Voter*, New York

Campbell, A., Converse, P.E., Miller, W.E. and Stokes, D.E. (1966), *Elections and the Political Order*, New York

Castells, M. (1977), The *Urban Question,* London, Edward Arnold

Central Statistical Office (1987), *Annual Abstract of Statistics, No.123*, London, HMSO

Centre for Contemporary Cultural Studies, (CCCS) (1981), *Unpopular Education: Schooling and Social Democracy in England since 1944*, Hutchinson, London

CPAG, Walker, A. and Walker C.A. (1987), *The Growing Divide: A Social Audit 1979-1987*, Child Poverty Action Group, London

Clegg, T. (1982), 'Social consumption, social investment and the Dual State: the case of transport policy and the Paris region', paper presented to the annual conference of the Political Studies Association, University of Kent, April 1982

Conquest, R. (1969), 'Undotheboys Hall', Cox, C B and Dyson, A E, *Fight for Education: A Black Paper*, op cit p20

Conservative Research Department (1985), *Education, Politics Today,* no 14

Cox, C. B. and Boyson, R. (1975), *Black Paper 1975, the fight for education,* J M Dent and Sons Ltd.

Cox, C. B. and Dyson, A E. (1969), 'Fight for Education: A Black Paper', *The Critical Survey,* 1968-70, The Critical Quarterly Society

Cox, C. B. and Dyson, A E. (1970), 'Black Paper Two: The Crisis in Education', *The Critical Survey,* 1968-70, The Critical Quarterly Society

Cox, C. B. and Dyson A E. (1971), 'Black Paper Three: Goodbye Mr Short', *The Critical Survey,* 1971-73, The Critical Quarterly Society

Crewe, I. (1987), 'A new class of politics', 15 June 1987, 'Tories prosper from a paradox', 16 June 1987, articles in the Guardian, (based on a BBC Gallup poll carried out on 10-11 June, with a sample of 4,035 in England and Wales, 851 in Scotland)

Crispin, A. and Marslen-Wilson, F. (1985), *Changes in Educational Provision 1980-1985,* London, Association of Metropolitan Authorities

Dale, R. (1983), 'You aint seen nothing yet: the prospects for education' in Wolpe, A.M. and Donald, J., Eds., *Is there anyone here from education?,* Pluto Press

Dennison, W. F. (1985), 'Education and the economy: changing circumstances' in McNay, I and Ozga, J, *Policy-making in Education: the Breakdown of Consensus,* Pergamon Press

Denver, D. (1989), *Elections and voting behaviour in Britain,* Philip Allan

Department of Education and Science (1982), *17+: a new qualification,* HMSO, London

Department of Education and Science (1987), *Statistical Bulletin 14/87: Education Expenditure 1981-2 to 1985-6,* London, Department of Education and Science

Donald, J. (1981), 'Green Paper: noise of crisis' in Dale, R., Esland, g., Ferguson, R and MacDonald, M. (eds.), *Education and the State: schooling and the national interest,* Lewes, Falmer Press

Donald, J. and Grealy, J. (1983), 'The unpleasant fact of inequality: standards, literacy and culture', in Wolpe, A.M. and Donald, J., (eds.) *Is there anyone here from education?,* Pluto Press

Douglas, J.W.B. (1964), *The Home and the School,* Macgibbon and Kee Ltd.

Duke, V and Edgell, S. (1984), 'Public expenditure cuts in Britain and consumption sectoral cleavages', *International Journal of Urban and Regional Research*, 8, pp177-201

Duke, V. and Edgell, S. (1986), 'Local Authority Spending Cuts and Local Political Control', *British Journal of Political Science*, 16, 253-268, April

Duke, V. and Edgell, S. (1987), 'The operationalisation of class in British sociology: theoretical and empirical considerations', *British Journal of Sociology*, 38, pp 445-463

Dunleavy, P. (1980), *Urban Political Analysis*, London, Macmillan

Dunleavy, P. and Husbands, C. (1985), *British Democracy at the Crossroads: Voting and Party Competition in the 1980's*, Allen and Unwin

Eatwell, J. (1982), *Whatever happened to Britain? The economics of decline*, London, BBC and Duckworth

Edgell, S. and Duke, V. (1981), *The Social and Political Effects of the Public Expenditure Cuts*, SSRC Report HR7415

Edgell, S. and Duke, V. (1983), 'Gender and Social Policy: the impact of the public expenditure cuts and reactions to them', *Journal of Social Policy*, vol 12, pp 357-78

Edgell, S. and Duke, V. (1985), *Changes in the Social and Political Effects of the Public Expenditure Cuts*, ESRC Report G0023107

Edgell, S. and Duke, V. (1986a), 'Radicalism, radicalization and recession', *British Journal of Sociology*, vol 37, no 4, pp 479-512

Edgell, S. and Duke, V. (1986b), 'The perceived impact of the spending cuts in Britain 1980/1 to 1983/4: social class, life cycle and sectoral location influences', paper presented at an International seminar on Production, Welfare and Mass Behaviour in Urban Politics, University of Copenhagen, May 1985

Edgell, S. and Duke, V. (1991), *A Measure of Thatcherism*, Harper Collins.

Elsthain, J.B., 1981, *Public Man, Private Women: women in social and political thought*, Princeton, U.P.

Foucault, M. (1980), in Gordon, C. (ed.), *Power/knowledge: selected interviews and other writings, 1972-1977*, Harvester

Erikson, R. (1984), 'Social class men, women and families', *Sociology*, 18, 500-514

Festinger, L. (1957), *A Theory of Cognitive Dissonance*, Evanston, Row

Fowler, G. (1979), 'The politics of education', in Bernbaum, G. (ed.), *Schooling in Decline*, Basingstoke, Macmillan

Government Statistical Service, 1987, *Educational Statistics for the United Kingdom 1987*, London, HMSO

Habermas, J. (1972), *Knowledge and Human Interests*, London Heineman

Habermas, J. (1976), *Legitimation Crisis*, London Heineman

Hall, S. (1983), 'The politics of Education', in *Is There Anyone Here From Education?*, Wolpe, A. M. and Donald, J. (eds), Pluto Press

Hillgate Group, (1986), *Whose Schools? A Radical Manifesto*, London

Independent Schools Information Service (ISIS), (1987), *Annual Census 1987*, London, Independent Schools   Information Service

Inglehart, R. (1977), *The Silent Revolution: Changing Values and Political Styles among Western Publics*, Princeton University Press, Princeton, N.J.

Institute of Race Relations, (1980), 'Anti-racist not multicultural education', *Race and Class*, 22(1), pp. 81-36

Invest for School Fees (IFSF) An organization which helps parents to cope with the cost of fees, Findings from their survey published on 2nd. September 1988 and reported in the Guardian the following day.

Jackson, B. and Marsden, D. (1963), *Education and the Working Class,* London: Routledge and Kegan Paul

Johnson, R. (1983), 'Educational politics: the old and the new', in Wolpe, A. M. and Donald, J. (eds.), *Is there anyone here from education?*, Pluto Press

Jones, K. (1985), 'The National Union of Teachers', in McNay, I. and Ozga, J, *Policy-making in Education: the breakdown of consensus*, Pergamon Press

Jones, K. (1983), 'Teachers and their organizations', in Wolpe, A. M. and Donald, J. (eds.), *Is there anyone here from education?*, Pluto Press

Jowell, R. and Airey, C. (eds) (1984), *British Social Attitudes: the 1984 report*, SCPR, Gower

Jowell, R. and Witherspoon, S. (eds.) (1985), *British Social Attitudes: the 1985 report*, SCPR, Gower

Jowell, R, Witherspoon, S. and Brook, L. (eds.) (1986), *British Social Attitudes: the 1986 report*, SCPR, Gower

Jowell, R, Witherspoon, S. and Brook, L. (eds.) (1988), *British Social Attitudes: the 5th. report*, SCPR, Gower

Kavanagh, D. (1983), *Political Science and Political Behaviour*, London, Allen and Unwin

Kelly, G. (1955), *Psychology of personal constructs*, New York, W.W.Norton

Kogan, M. (1986), *Education Accountability. An Analytic Overview*, London, Hutchinson

Lane, R. (1959, pbk 1964), *Political Life*

Leys, C. (1985), 'Thatcherism and British manufacturing: a question of hegemony', *New Left Review,* p.151

Lynn, R. (1970), 'Comprehensives and Quality. The Quest for the unattainable', in Cox, C.B. and Dyson, A.E., 1970, Black Paper Two: The Crisis in Education, *The Critical Survey*, 1968-70, The Critical Quarterly Society

Mann, M. (1970), 'The social cohesion of liberal democracy', in Potter, D. (ed.) (1981), *Society and the Social Sciences*, Routledge and Kegan Paul

Marsland, D. (1988), *Seeds of Bankruptcy: sociological bias against business and freedom*, London, Claridge Press

Marsland, D. (1987), 'Controversy' in *Network*, No.40, October 1987

Martlew, C. (1983), 'The state and local government finance', *Public Administration*, 61, 127-47

Maslow, A.H. (1970), *Motivation and personality*, second edition, New York, Harper and Row

McKenzie, J. (1986), 'Attitudes to Education: a study of government policies and parents' views', unpublished M.Sc. in Advanced Educational and Social Research Methods, Open University

McNay, I. and Ozga, J. (eds.), (1985), *Policy-making in education*, Pergamon Press

Mills, C. W. (1970), *The Sociological Imagination*, Harmondsworth, Penguin Books, original 1959, rights now with Oxford University Press.

Mullard, C. (1982), 'Multiracial education in Britain: from assimilation to cultural pluralism', in Arnot, M. (ed.), (1985) *Race and Gender: Equal Opportunities Policies in Education*, Pergamon Press

(NCB) National Childrens Bureau, (1987), *Investing in the Future: Child Health Ten Years After the Court Report,* a report of the Policy and Review Group, London

National Union of Teachers, (1985), *Education: investment or impoverishment?*, London

Neill, A.S., several books between 1915 and 1972; best known work, (1962), *Summerhill,* Pelican Books

O'Connor, J. (1973), *The Fiscal Crisis of the State*, London, St. James

Parkin, F. (1971), *Class, Inequality and Political Order*, London, McGibbon and Kee

Parry, G. and Moyser, G. (1984), 'Participation and Democracy - British Style', paper no 6, *British Political Participation Research Series*, University of Manchester

Parry, G. and Moyser, G. (1987), 'Class, Sector and Political Participation in Britain', *Manchester (University) Papers in Politics*

Parry, G., Moyser, G. and Day, N. (1986), ' Political Participation in Britain: National and Local Patterns', paper no 21, *British Political Participation research Series*, University of Manchester

Parry, G., Moyser, G. and Day, N. (1992), *Political Participation and Democracy in Britain*, Cambridge University Press

Plowden Report, (1967), *Children and their Primary Schools*, DES, London HMSO

Ranson, S. (1985), 'Changing relations between centre and locality in education', in McNay, I and Ozga, J, *Policy-making in Education: the Breakdown of Consensus*, Pergamon Press

Redcliffe Maud, (1969) *The Report of the Royal Commission on Local Government in England, 1966-69*, London, HMSO, cmnd 4040

Ridley, F.F., 10 August 1987, in *The Guardian*.

Rowntree, S. (1902), *Poverty: A study of town life*, London, Longman

Saunders, P. (1981), *Social Theory and the Urban Question*, Hutchinson

Schultz, T. W. (1963), *The economic value of education*, Columbia University Press

Siltanen, J. and Stanworth, M. (eds.), (1984), *Women and the Public Sphere: a Critique of Sociology and Politics*, Hutchinson and Co

Statham, J., Mackinnon, P. and Cathcart, H. (1989), *The Education Fact File: a handbook of education information in the UK*, Hodder and Stoughton

Stillman, A. (1986) 'Preference or choice? Parents, LEAs and the Education Act 1988', *Educational Research*, vol.1, No.1, February 1986

Verba, S. and Nie, N.H. (1972), *Participation in America: Political Democracy and Social Equality*, New York, Harper and Row

Verba, S., Nie, N.H. and Petrocik, J.R. (1976), *The Changing American Voter*, Cambridge, Mass., Harvard U.P.

White Paper, (1988), *The Government's Expenditure Plans 1988/9 to 1990/1*, Vol.1

Weiner, M. J. (1981), *English Culture and the Decline of the Industrial Spirit 1850-1980*

Wilson, G.D. and Patterson, J.R, (1968) 'A new measure of conservatism', *British Journal of Social and Clinical Psychology*, 7, 264-269

Wolpe, A.M. and Donald, J. (1983), *Is there anyone here from education?*, Pluto Press

Wright, E.O. (1980), 'Class and occupation', *Theory and Society*, vol 9, pp.177-214

Young, M.F.D. (1971), *Knowledge and Control*, London, Cassell and Collier

Index